ASSESSING SERVICE QUALITY

Satisfying the Expectations of Library Customers
Second Edition

PETER HERNON + ELLEN ALTMAN

AMERICAN LIBRARY ASSOCIATION
CHICAGO   2010

Peter Hernon is a professor at the Graduate School of Library and Information Science, Simmons College in Boston; he previously taught at the University of Arizona and Victoria University of Wellington (New Zealand). He is the coeditor of *Library & Information Science Research*, founding editor of *Government Information Quarterly*, and past editor in chief of the *Journal of Academic Librarianship*. Hernon is the author of more than 285 publications and has received a number of awards for his research and professional contributions, including the 2008 Association of College and Research Libraries' award for Academic/Research Librarian of the Year. The first edition of this book, *Assessing Service Quality*, was the 1998 winner of the Highsmith award for outstanding contribution to the literature of library and information science.

Ellen Altman, now retired, was visiting professor in the Department of Library and Information Studies, Victoria University of Wellington (New Zealand) until July 1997. She has been a faculty member at the Universities of Kentucky and Toronto and at Indiana University, professor and director of the Graduate Library School at the University of Arizona, and feature editor of *Public Libraries*, the official publication of the Public Library Association. Altman was coeditor of "The JAL Guide to the Professional Literature" in the *Journal of Academic Librarianship*, a member of *Library Quarterly*'s editorial board, and a coauthor of *Performance Measures for Public Libraries*. She received the Distinguished Alumni Award from Rutgers School of Communication, Information and Library Studies in 1983.

The paper used in this publication meets the minimum requirements of American National Standard for Information Sciences—Permanence of Paper for Printed Library Materials, ANSI Z39.48-1992. ∞

Library of Congress Cataloging-in-Publication Data
Hernon, Peter.
    Assessing service quality : satisfying the expectations of library customers / Peter Hernon and Ellen Altman. — 2nd ed.
      p.   cm.
    Includes bibliographical references and index.
    ISBN 978-0-8389-1021-4 (alk. paper)
    1. Public services (Libraries)—Evaluation. 2. Public services (Libraries)—United States—Evaluation. I. Altman, Ellen. II. Title.
    Z711.H45 2010
    025.5—dc22

2009040332

ISBN-13: 978-0-8389-1021-4

Printed in the United States of America
14 13 12 11 10   5 4 3 2 1

Contents

Figures

Preface

At this time librarians are redefining their roles; seeing an expansion of the knowledge, abilities, skills, and habits of mind required for them to fill those roles; and engaging in profound change within their organizations as they cope with new methods of learning, information-seeking, source preferences, and forms of competition, as well as an ever-changing electronic information environment and changing expectations on the part of those they serve. As Duane E. Webster writes,

> In today's rapidly changing information landscape, libraries face opportunity and challenge. The only constant in this landscape is uncertainty. . . . More than in any preceding era, we know that libraries must change, but we do not know how to make this transition . . . to organizations that can thrive in dramatically different conditions.[1]

Clearly, libraries are now engaged in much more than the preservation and transition of the cultural history and having a nebulous role in meeting the needs of society and the institutions they serve.

In such a time of transition, why should librarians and students in schools of library and information science be interested in yet another book about the evaluation and assessment of library services? Perhaps the better question is, why should they be interested in a revised edition of a 1998 volume? We will address this question by reinforcing our approach. Instead of presenting a cookbook of measures to apply to various services, we identify some touchstones critical to the well-being of libraries: customers, service quality, satisfaction, loyalty, and reputation. The concepts of loyalty and reputation are relatively new in the professional literature. Although a number of librarians dispute the notion that library users are customers, this book endorses the use of that word. Furthermore, we distinguish between satisfaction and service quality; much of the literature confuses or ignores the distinction between the two.

Many in the profession strongly believe that only they, the professionals, have the expertise to assess the quality of library service. Such a belief may have validity in the abstract, but it fails to acknowledge reality. Every customer evaluates the quality of service received and decides when (and if) she will seek further interactions with the library. Behaviors and attitudes toward the library over time influence both customer perceptions about the library and the views of stakeholders who make decisions affecting the library's funding.

Service quality, as presented here, views the service provided by an organization from the perspective of the customer. It encourages the organization to meet specific customer expectations and to increase the number of customers who are loyal and delighted with the services provided.

The purposes of this book, both first and revised editions, are to

- suggest new ways to think about library services
- explain service quality and further the development of its theoretical base
- clarify the distinction between service quality and customer satisfaction
- identify strategies for developing a customer service plan that meets the library's customer-focused mission, vision, and goals
- identify procedures for measuring service quality and satisfaction
- challenge conventional thinking about the utility of input, output, and performance measures, as well as public library role adoption or service response
- suggest possible customer-related indicators that provide insights useful for library planning and decision making
- encourage libraries to take action—action leading to improved service and accountability

Although the book focuses on academic and public libraries, the basic principles, strategies, and assessment procedures presented apply in other settings.

Traditionally, the amount of resources and productivity counts have been (and still are) used to evaluate the quality of libraries. Performance and output measures were developed as better indicators of service delivery, but they have been more discussed than used, as is confirmed by the small number of public libraries reporting them. Although performance and output measures serve an important purpose, the current cross-disciplinary evaluation literature lacks a standard nomenclature for such terms as performance measures and outputs. Given that different people use the same terms but with widely varying meanings, it is time to replace such terms with new ones, and to explore other ways of evaluating and benchmarking library services. In effect, it is time to develop new ways to look at service. As the book notes, it is also time to move beyond outputs to outcomes and address the perspectives of the stakeholders interested in libraries and their institutional context.

Because technology offers new methods of information delivery, traditional counts of productivity underestimate the actual volume of business performed. New issues, such as those related to distance education, use of library websites, and partnership and consortium arrangements for gaining access to electronic collections, make it clear that volumes of business are deceptive measures—ones becoming more complex to gauge. The library community needs to shift its focus from measures reporting volume of business, such as for circulation, to more meaningful indicators of customer loyalty, expectations, preferences, and satisfaction. The new indicators should report information about present and potential customers, their needs, expectations, and preferences, as well as the problems they encounter and how library staff handles those problems. Such information is useful for promoting customer loyalty, enhancing the service reputation of libraries, and planning and decision making.

Customers are more than a source for data collection; they are the reason for libraries' existence. It is important (if not essential) to listen to, and learn from, customers and to use the insights gained to improve services. A number of libraries have ignored customers because they perceive customers as a captive audience. This book dispels that notion as it enumerates the many competitors poised to challenge the library's perceived monopoly.

As the twenty-first century unfolds, librarians need new ways of thinking and alternatives for applying a customer-centered model of service quality. We regard this work as one in progress, because it provides a base upon which others can build. The approach presented here recognizes that holistic evaluation involves the use of both quantitative and qualitative data, as each type complements the other. The approach presented here is too large and too complex for any library to undertake at one time. Rather, our intention has been to present some new ways to think about service, along with some methods for evaluating and improving service. Libraries can select, from among the methods discussed, those most appropriate to their particular situation, and implement them at a pace that suits their needs. After all, libraries have become service organizations that function in a competitive environment, and librarians must create and perfect services that better match the information needs, information-seeking behaviors, and expectations of those they intend to serve.

If libraries do not try to be truly service-centered, what are they willing to commit to? What is the source of their service inspiration? What service reputation do they generate? The answers to such questions have a definite impact on the extent to which customers are loyal to the library, and on the number of customers who are delighted or completely satisfied—not merely appeased.

Most people who become librarians do so from a desire to connect people with information—a concept that is the cornerstone of service quality. But, somehow, along the way, the profession has gotten caught up in bean counting: how many of this and how much of that, as though the items counted exist in a universe totally unto themselves. It is our hope that the ideas presented here will encourage librarians to remember the ideals that attracted them to the profession and to abandon such misperceptions as "customers cannot judge quality," "customers do not know what they want," and "professional hegemony will be undermined by kowtowing to customers."

A critical question that many readers will ask is, how does this edition differ from the previous one? We kept the same framework but differentiate between evaluation and assessment, address new developments within and outside the profession, and continue to raise issues. Revisiting the content of the first edition, we find that assessment has assumed a new meaning as discussed in chapter 4. Perhaps *Addressing Service Quality* is now a more appropriate title, but we decided to keep the original title. Since we wrote the first edition, we see that libraries have tended to back away from explicit service promises and that there is still a definite preference for conducting surveys. We encourage librarians to pursue other choices when relevant and to gain a good understanding of the concepts they are addressing. As we continue to remind readers, satisfaction and service quality differ. It is important to focus on the customers of individual libraries and realize that comparisons to other libraries (and use of mostly generic data-collection instruments) assume that customer expectations have little variation.

Note

1. Duane E. Webster, "Foreword," in *Beyond Survival: Managing Academic Libraries in Transition,* by Elizabeth J. Wood, Rush Miller, and Amy Knapp (Westport, CT: Libraries Unlimited, 2007), xvii.

Acknowledgments

We wish to thank the American Library Association for permission to reprint material from Darlene E. Weingand, *Customer Service Excellence: A Guide for Librarians* (1997); Jeannette Woodward, *Creating the Customer-Driven Academic Library* (2009); Charles R. McClure and Paul T. Jaeger, *Public Libraries and Internet Service Roles: Measuring and Maximizing Internet Services* (2009); Thomas A. Childers and Nancy Van House, *What's Good? Describing Your Public Library's Effectiveness* (1993); and Sandra Nelson, *The New Planning for Results: A Streamlined Approach* (2001) and *Strategic Planning for Results* (2008).

We also thank the Association of College and Research Libraries, American Library Association, for permission to include part of James L. Mullins, Frank R. Allen, and Jon R. Hufford, "Top Ten Assumptions for the Future of Academic Libraries and Librarians: A Report from the ACRL Research Committee," *College & Research Libraries News* 68, no. 4 (April 2007).

Chapter One

Understanding Ends and Means

Public library administrators should be concerned about the level of customer service provided by the staff ahead of any other issue.[1]

Historically, the quality of a library has been measured by the size of its collection. The acquisition of the millionth volume was cause for celebration, and press releases flooded local and national news media. The millionth volume or a million-dollar "book" budget gave bragging rights to the library's director. For decades, library directors, upon retirement, wanted to be known for the number of titles added during their tenure.

As collections grew, space became a problem, so library directors pressed for bigger buildings to house the increased number of volumes. Bigger collections meant the need for more staff and furnishings, especially shelving. Several other factors influenced collection building, especially after World War II. The expansion of colleges and universities in response to the GI Bill meant more faculty had to be hired, and they were expected to "publish or perish" to receive tenure. Of course, each author wanted the library to purchase his published works. Several publishing companies were started to translate and reprint works held by major European university libraries that had been damaged during the war.

By the 1970s, many university administrators regarded academic libraries as bottomless pits because of constant entreaties for more money to keep up with the publishing output. In the 1980s and 1990s, the pleas for more money centered on the large annual increases in the prices of scholarly and professional journal subscriptions and the need for electronically delivered resources and their requisite infrastructure.

More recently, libraries have expanded their involvement with consortia and partnerships as they seek more electronic resources while focusing on their customers' information needs and the affordability of those resources. The cost for colleges and universities has increased for nearly everything, including faculty and staff benefits (e.g., health care) and debt services on borrowed money. Issues related to debt services, the size of endowments, and cutbacks on staffing and operating costs became more pronounced during the economic recession of 2008 and 2009. Some estimate that it will take academic institutions at least four years to recover; this is especially true of those institutions that are heavily funded by tuition dollars and are in the process of major construction projects.

Some critics note the fallacy of equating collection size with quality—not all libraries count items in the same way, while others keep outdated and unwanted books to boost their volume count. Obviously, the sheer number of volumes does not necessarily mean that the library collection matches readers' interests, and many titles go unused—they do not even circulate. In the age of widespread access to digital resources, volume and title counts become less important, unless the institution is threatened by accreditation standards that set expectations for collection size. Academic libraries experience broad and extensive use of digital resources even by the faculty, who now access materials in collections miles away.

SERVICE QUALITY

Because of the previous focus on collection building, library quality has been synonymous with collection size—an assessment of what the library *has*—rather than with what the library *does*. Yet *library* quality and *service* quality are very different measures. A parallel can be drawn with the observations made by Raymond F. Zammuto and others, who studied student services offices in universities: "The idea of service quality as opposed to educational quality has not received much attention in higher education."[2] That situation is changing as most academic institutions now strive to attract and retain students. Service quality has become a topic of considerable interest for many service units on campus.

In the past several decades, as budgets for the purchase of materials have shrunk, the phrase "access not ownership" has become common. The means to achieve that access—interlibrary loan—did not change radically until recently, when the Internet became widely available to educational institutions. The result has been a major shift in resources, attention, and interest from the library "collection" to the Internet. How to use it, which websites are good, and a myriad of associated topics fill the pages of the professional literature and now seem the prime preoccupation of the library community. In all likelihood, access to Internet and associated resources will equal, if not surpass, physical volumes in the collection as the new standard of library quality. Yet such a focus still says nothing about the quality of service provided and received.

For a library, service quality encompasses the interactive relationship between the library and the people whom it is supposed to serve. A library that adheres to all the professionally approved rules and procedures for acquiring, organizing, managing, and preserving material but has no customers cannot claim quality because a major element is missing: satisfying people's needs, requests, and desires for information. Maurice B. Line defined librarianship as "managing information resources for people."[3] How the library sees and interacts with those people—customers—clearly affects the quality and nature of the service rendered. As Françoise Hébert notes, "When library and customer measures of quality are not congruent, the library may be meeting its internal standards of performance but may not be performing well in the eyes of its customers."[4]

PATRONS, USERS, CLIENTS, OR CUSTOMERS?

Organizations refer to the people they serve by many different terms: *clients, patients, students, readers, passengers, visitors, guests.* Such terms make these individuals seem something other than customers. Librarians often prefer the terms *patron* or *user*, perhaps to avoid the implication of an exchange occurring between the library and the people using the service. Yet, both words have rather negative connotations, as Darlene E. Weingand points out:

> The word *patron* is associated with the act of giving support and protection, such as occurred in the Renaissance between royalty and artists. The impression here is one of unequal status, of the powerful protecting the less powerful. This is not the type of relationship that puts libraries on an equal level of partnership with their communities. Further, while *user* accurately describes someone who uses the library, the term is quite unspecific and is widely associated with the drug culture.[5]

Special librarians and subject specialists in university libraries probably come closest to treating their users as clients. In the case of subject specialists, faculty and doctoral students who are repeat users become clients. These librarians know their clientele personally and have insights into their research and related interests. Yet, being a client does not preclude one from being treated like a customer.

Public libraries have different types of customers with different types of interests. These range from the preschooler who comes to a story hour, to the homeless man who wants to read the newspaper, to the businesswoman who needs tax regulation guidelines. All have different interests, but most want materials, information, or a place to sit and use library resources. A customer is the recipient of any product or service provided by the organization. That recipient might be either internal, such as a coworker in the same or another unit, or external—someone in the community wanting materials or information.

Weingand notes that:

> the word *customer*, which implies payment for a product or service, is a better reflection of what actually transpires between the library and people in the community. With this term the mythology of the "free" library is dispelled, and a more accurate metaphor for service is substituted.[6]

In support, Jeannette Woodward argues that it may be time to replace the word *user* with *customer*; the word *customer* "reminds us of . . . [the] new emphasis on running higher education as a business enterprise." She continues,

> Many of us find this idea repugnant. However, to survive and prosper in the twenty-first century, librarians will probably have to put aside any affection they may feel for the ivory tower library of the past. We know that customers make demands, but we rarely think of patrons demanding anything. Instead, the term brings to mind individuals who give rather than receive. You might think of patrons of the arts, for example. Their role is to support the arts, not make demands of them. Customers on the other hand, demand high-quality facilities, resources, and services. They want a library that is focused on their needs, and they have no intention of going out of their way to meet the library's needs or expectations.[7]

Some academic librarians argue that students cannot and should not be regarded as customers. Yet students surely are potential customers when they select a school to attend. During high school, they are bombarded with advertising from colleges eager to enroll them. They are customers in the bookstore and food courts on campus, and when they purchase tickets to college sporting and entertainment events.

Another interesting notion, now widely accepted, is that organizations have *internal* as well as *external* customers. Internal customers depend on or receive work from another unit of the library. Such work can include information or reports, or processes and activities to be performed. Outsourcing may be one way to meet the needs of internal customers in a timelier manner. Public service staff members are customers of the various units that acquire, catalog, process, and shelve materials.

Whatever the term used to describe the individuals that libraries serve, the people who interact with any library service are the *reason* for the organization's existence. Therefore, their needs and desires should *drive* the service. Although the total quality management (TQM) movement has focused attention on customer service, the idea is not new.

As Arnold Hirshon notes, "Customer service was not a concept invented by total quality management experts."[8] The concept dates to the nineteenth and early twentieth centuries and to practices found in retail trade and hotel management. Other chapters in this book offer further evidence of why the concepts of *customer* and *customer service* are applicable to library and information science.

Some librarians dislike library service being equated with "customer and commodity." They perceive libraries and their activities to be on a higher plane than their retail or commercial counterparts, and decry the evaluation of rather basic processes, functions, and services as pedestrian and unsuitable. Indeed, one library educator has criticized suggestions for measures that reflect the percentage of students and faculty who check out library materials or the number of courses requiring use of library resources as having "no direct connection to learning, research or intellectual activities in general. Rather they deal with the handling of things."[9] What that author fails to understand is that the library's contributions to facilitating education, promoting a love of learning, and aiding research very much depend on how well the library "handles things." None of these higher-order conditions can occur unless the library handles things in such a way that individuals find and are able to use the materials and information they seek.

We also want to nip in the bud the idea that higher-order conditions occur by some sort of intellectual osmosis. The truth is that *unless customers and the collection come together in a way both interesting and meaningful to customers, the library is nothing more than an expensive warehouse.* Hard work, much of it "pedestrian," must be performed before this coming together can occur—even in the Magic Kingdom. "As Walt Disney once said, 'there is no magic to magic. It's in the details.'"[10]

It should be clear by now that the library as a vast collection, a warehouse filled with books and other printed materials, can no longer be justified as either a concept or a reality. The economic pressures on higher education and local government are causing both academic administrators and elected officials to question long-standing assumptions about many of their units. These units are now being scrutinized for their actual value to the sponsoring organization. The severe recession of 2008 and 2009 has resulted in massive cuts to local governments and state-sponsored universities. As a result, among other things, there have been a curtailing of hours of library operations, unpaid furloughs, job losses, and reductions in spending on library materials. At the same time students' tuition costs are soaring, while public libraries are experiencing a significant increase in the number of people coming to the library asking for service.

Obviously, adding value, service quality, and customer satisfaction are pressing concepts, as they are vital to the continued well-being of libraries. After all, "the consequences of un-quality are customers who leave disappointed, who tell others about how they feel, and who may never return to the library."[11]

It is not our intention here to delve into the reasons for these pressures to improve service quality, but rather to concentrate on *how* libraries can evaluate and improve customer satisfaction, enhance service quality, and add value in ways meaningful to their sponsoring organizations. The first principle is to focus on the purpose of librarianship—"managing information resources in ways that will serve people."[12] This purpose incorporates Ranganathan's five laws[13] and allows people who seek material or information to receive it—that is, to obtain certain types of materials within certain parameters.

THE LIBRARY CUSTOMER IS STILL THE CUSTOMER

Some librarians resist the notions of *customer* and *service quality* because they equate them with the principle that "the customer is always right." Customers are *not* always right, but they do have a right to express their opinions and to learn about the library's service parameters.

Most customers have *expectations* about service, though sometimes those expectations are unrealistic. Nor are we referring here to problem patrons who engage in irrational, prohibited, and, in some cases, illegal behaviors. Customers, as defined here, are individuals who want some assistance or materials that the library might or might not hold. They might not know, however, what is unrealistic until the library tells them. This requires some thinking on the part of library administrators to distinguish between core and peripheral services and to identify those that will not be offered. This also requires notifying the community about those decisions and perhaps even gaining support for them.

The library service responses (see figure 3.1) developed for the Public Library Association lists eighteen roles or missions that a public library might assume. Obviously, it is neither practical nor realistic for any one library to undertake all of them. Therefore, it is important to choose those responses that a library believes important to its community and concentrate on doing those well. However, it is equally important that the library indicate which of the responses it is not prepared to assume so that customers will understand that every desire cannot be satisfied. For example, many libraries offer federal and state income tax forms and explanation bulletins during the first quarter of the calendar year. However, no library offers tax preparation advice to its customers. Some customers expect to find out-of-state tax forms and are annoyed that these are not available. As a result, some libraries have stopped carrying any tax forms or bulletins.

CUSTOMER SATISFACTION AND SERVICE QUALITY

Many library surveys ask about customer satisfaction, sometimes in a general context and sometimes in relation to specific services. Usually the questions about satisfaction allow for scaled responses (e.g., ranging from *not satisfied at all* through *partially satisfied* to *satisfied* and *completely satisfied*). Too often, satisfaction surveys are really intended as library report cards. In fact, some surveys actually ask participants to assign the library a grade from A to F. There is usually no intent to take any remedial action based on replies to these questions, but rather to use the responses in negotiations with administrators in the sponsoring institution.

There is increased interest in satisfaction with libraries and their services, but the concept is not well linked to customers. The terms *satisfaction* and *service quality* are frequently used interchangeably; this mistake has led to more confusion. As discussed in chapters 7 and 10, the library survey LibQUAL+ is sometimes called a service quality survey and at other times a satisfaction survey. Adding to the confusion, those applying that instrument may view it as addressing outcomes. (See chapter 4.)

Satisfaction is an emotional reaction—the degree of contentment or discontentment—with a specific transaction or service encounter. Satisfaction may or may not be directly related to the performance of the library on a specific occasion. A customer can receive an answer to a query but be unsatisfied because of an upsetting or angry encounter. Conversely, although the query might remain unanswered, another customer might feel satisfied because the encounter was pleasant and the helper interested and polite.

Service quality, on the other hand, is a global judgment relating to the superiority of a service as viewed in the context of specific statements that the library is willing to act on if customers find them of great value. The inference is that the satisfaction levels from a number of transactions or encounters that an individual experiences with a particular organization fuse to form an *impression* of service quality for that person. The *collective* experiences of many persons create an organization's reputation for service quality.

SERVICE QUALITY—PERCEPTION IS REALITY

Every organization's service has a quality dimension—ranging from wonderful to awful. Service and quality cannot be disconnected. Quality is the manner in which the service is delivered, or, in some cases, not delivered.

Service quality is multidimensional. Two critical dimensions are content and context. *Content* refers to obtaining what prompted the visit—particular materials or information, study space, or an acceptable substitute. *Context* covers the experience itself: interactions with staff, ease or difficulty in navigating the system, and the comfort of the physical environment.

Customers who come into the library as well as those who "visit" through an electronic highway experience both the content and context of the service. From these interactions, customers form opinions and attitudes about the library. Customer expectations can influence satisfaction with both content and context. These expectations may or may not match what the library thinks appropriate, but nevertheless *they represent reality for the customer.*

Expectations change according to what customers want and how urgently they want it. Sometimes they are seeking a quiet place to read, sometimes just a book for enjoyment, and sometimes a vital bit of information. Importance and urgency, though seldom considered, are likely to have a strong influence on customers' satisfaction with a service. The prevailing custom has been to treat all searches or inquiries with equal priority, except those from persons of special importance to the library, such as an administrator in the sponsoring organization. The concept of equal treatment should be reconsidered because of its impact on consequences to the customer. If the level of service for all is high, exceptions become detrimental, costly, distractive, and unnecessary.

Service quality is a complex concept: It has several dimensions beyond the content/context and the performance/performance-expectations gap. Service quality is both personal to individuals and collective among many customers. In a number of instances, impressions of service quality can be changed; perceptions move up with positive experiences and down as a result of negative ones. Chapters 6, 7, 8, and 10 present some techniques for assessing service quality and satisfaction so that libraries can review their mission and vision statements, and evaluate their service reputation and image, while adapting goals and objectives to cope better with customer expectations.

WHY INVESTIGATE QUALITY?

Libraries have gathered and reported statistics about their collections, funds, and staffs for decades. These statistics have, however, concentrated primarily on finances, the resources purchased with those finances, and workloads. Nevertheless, an information gap remains. These traditional statistics lack relevance. Most of the traditional statistics do not measure the library's performance in terms of elements important to customers. They do not really describe performance or indicate whether service quality is good, indifferent, or bad. Even worse, they do not indicate any action that the administration or any team can or should take to improve performance.

Libraries need measures to evaluate service quality on a much broader scale than resources held, resources acquired, and activities completed. The current statistics for both academic and public libraries emphasize expenditures. Focusing on money can be dangerous, because it emphasizes the cost of the library to the sponsoring organization at a time when top administrators are looking closely at costs and how to contain them. Even businesses that have relied on financial data as the ultimate indicator of performance now recognize the need for broader measures.

THE BALANCED SCORECARD

Many businesses have adopted the concept of the balanced scorecard as a method of management. The balanced scorecard is a "matrix of measures that can show the performance of the organization from the perspective of each of its stakeholders."[14] The scorecard examines different perspectives:

> *The learning and growth perspective* includes employee training and corporate cultural attitudes related to both individual and corporate self-improvement. This perspective involves more than training; it includes the availability of mentors and tutors within the organization, the ease of communication among workers when they need assistance, and the availability of technological tools.

> *The business process perspective* refers to internal business processes and how well the business operates, and whether its products and services conform to customer requirements.

> *The customer perspective* focuses on meeting or exceeding customer expectations, namely service quality and satisfaction.

Undue focus on the business perspective leads to an unbalanced situation with regard to other perspectives. In fact, the customer perspective should be the central perspective with other ones revolving around it. As a consequence, it is important to know the answers to the following questions:

- How do customers see us?
- How do we look to decision makers and the community? (business perspective)
- What must we excel at? (This question looks to the internal working of the organization.)
- Can we continue to improve and create value?[15]

The balanced scorecard is essentially a tool for strategic management. Implementing the balanced scorecard necessitates that the administration answer the four preceding questions in terms of the present situation and desired outcomes for the future. The next step is to define the factors critical for success and then to identify measures that indicate success.

Measures relating to customers might indicate, for instance, the percentage of repeat customers, the percentage of customer complaints, and the number of new registered borrowers. Internal measures might focus on cycle times and employee productivity and skills. At the end of the specified time period, all the measures are combined to produce an overall score. Although we are not advocating adoption of the balanced scorecard, its principles have merit in that they encompass a wider variety of factors than do the traditional counts reported by both public and academic libraries in their annual reports and in national compilations of library statistics.[16]

The University of Virginia uses the balanced scorecard and has developed a series of annual metrics for each perspective. Those metrics are viewed in the context of goals, targets, and methods of gathering appropriate evidence.[17] The Orange County Library System in Orlando, Florida, which also relies on the balanced scorecard, annually makes a report on its accomplishments within the context of five perspectives: internal operations, library resources, library finances, customer satisfaction, and library staff. For customer satisfaction in the report for 2008/2009, the library asks, "How well are library customers served according to the library mission? What does this mean to you?"

> We want to be sure that we are meeting your needs. We have set some standards to measure customer satisfaction. These include the following:
>
> - Availability: days and hours the library is open and the website is available.
> - Customer feedback: We look at customer surveys and have a secret shopper program to find out your opinions on how we are doing.
> - Usage: We measure how many people have library cards and how many people are visiting the library.
> - Programs and classes: We count how many people attend library events.

Also meriting mention is the library staff perspective: "Are staff available, trained, and ready to achieve the library mission? What does this mean to you?"

We use a variety of measurement tools, such as employee surveys, turnover rate, and a customer service shopper program to help us measure whether or not the library provides staff who are trained and ready to provide the best possible services.[18]

OTHER DIMENSIONS OF SERVICE QUALITY

Marketing consultant George E. Kroon offers four other ways to look at service quality: conformance, expectation, market perception, and strategic.[19] (Because the last of these measures applies only to commercial establishments, we will not consider it here.)

Conformance requires that standards for quality be set for many processes and functions. The intent is to reduce mistakes (shelving errors), streamline workflow (cut backlogs), and establish required behaviors on the part of staff (ask if the customer got what was desired). Setting standards for service quality, as opposed to targets for work productivity in technical services or restrictions on the time allowed to answer reference questions, is rather a novel idea for libraries, but one whose time has come. The library has considerable control over quality as conformance to standards that it can use to improve service in many areas.

The idea of conformance standards leads to consideration of three kinds of situations that might negatively affect service quality: predictable, foreseeable, and unpredictable. *Predictable* situations are those over which the library has considerable control, and thus can take action to prevent or at least minimize. *Foreseeable* situations are those that are likely to happen, but for which the time frame between occurrences is longer and incidences are fewer than for the predictable ones. To some extent, it is possible to plan for even *unpredictable* and unlikely situations. For example, staff trained to respond to certain disasters or crises, such as fire, bomb threats, and tornadoes, can greatly ameliorate the situation. Following are examples of each type of library situation.

predictable situations
    equipment failures (paper jams, burnt-out
        lightbulbs)
    network crashes
    no paper in photocopiers and printers
    staff absences
    patron ignorance

foreseeable situations
    power failures
    weather problems
    budget cuts and recisions

unpredictable situations
    natural disasters
    fire
    psychopaths

The downside of concentrating solely on conformance quality is that the focus is internal and may not match customer expectations or preferences. Kroon cites the Swiss watch industry as an example; it set high standards for mechanical timepieces while customer preferences had moved on to digital watches. Although conformance standards are desirable, they should not be used in isolation.

The second dimension is customer *expectations*. Expectations are influenced by factors outside the control of management, such as customers' prior experience, word of mouth, and competitor behavior. Performance that repeatedly, or in some particular way, fails to meet customers' expectations is a clear signal to management that improvement is needed. Such improvement can be facilitated by training, technology, or conformance standards. Sometimes, however, customers have erroneous or unrealistic ideas about the service. In these cases, customers should be told *why* their expectations cannot be met.

The third dimension of service quality is *market perception*—evaluation against competitors. Libraries have not really thought about competitors; usually they look at the market in terms of peer institutions. Nevertheless, competition from super bookstores, online suppliers of journal articles, the Internet, and nontraditional colleges and universities, including the virtual university, may become more serious in the future. (See chapter 12.) Even other libraries can be competitors if customers have the option of using them. Figure 1.1, adapted from one presented by Kroon, depicts the differences in quality dimensions.

THE PAYOFF FOR THE LIBRARY

With all the techniques for better management (e.g., TQM, reengineering, and empowerment) and the new technologies that have been adopted, many organizations, including libraries, suffer from what Tony Hope and Jeremy Hope characterize as "improvement fatigue."[20] These techniques hold out the promise of increased profits for business, but what can they offer to nonprofit organizations such as libraries?

Most librarians are not consciously aware of the two things that are basic to the success of their libraries—the attention they get from individual customers and their reputation. People have many choices about how to spend their unstructured time—they can watch TV or a movie, surf the Web, attend a ball game, or shop at the mall. In addition, as Ralph Norman describes it,

For a wide and complicated series of reasons, we are producing a much greater volume of text than anybody is reading or able to read. The intellec-

tual sensorium is clogged, glutted, surfeited, full, overstuffed, bloated, teeming, overabundant, [and] overflowing.[21]

Everybody is bombarded with messages and stimuli. Therefore, *attention* and *time* are two of the most valuable assets that individuals have. Those who choose to spend these assets in the library or using library resources should be regarded as precious customers.

Supermarkets began issuing loyalty cards several years ago. Showing this card to the cashier entitles the shopper to receive a discount on specific items. Airlines have long offered "frequent flyer" cards: fly the requisite number of miles and get a free trip. So many passengers became frequent flyers that it is now difficult to book a free trip at the time one chooses

---

FIGURE 1.1

DIFFERENCES IN QUALITY DIMENSIONS

	DIMENSION		
	Conformance	**Expectation**	**Market**
Viewpoint	Internal	External	Peers and competitors
Key terms	Service quality	Expectations Performance gap	Peer performance
Focus of effort	Processes Functions Services	Service Customer	Peer comparisons
What to assess	Transactions Performance Context	Customer expectations vs. performance and vs. importance	Rankings/ratios with peer data
Superior quality results in	Stakeholder satisfaction	Performance exceeding expectations Loyalty	Good reputation
Inferior quality results in	Errors Higher costs Delays Lost customers	Bad word-of-mouth Dissatisfaction	Unfavorable reputation compared to peers

Source: Adapted from George E. Kroon, "Improving Quality in Service Marketing," *Journal of Customer Service in Marketing and Management* 1, no. 2 (1995): 13–28. Reproduced with permission.

to travel. Recognizing the value of *repeat customers* is important for the success of most organizations. Repeat customers, especially the more frequent ones, tend to be loyal. The library's repeat customers already have demonstrated their interest in reading and seeking information. Loyalty means that the customers return repeatedly; they recommend the library to their friends and colleagues, and may be more forgiving when the system makes a mistake. Some of them will actively campaign for library bond issues or protest library budget cuts.

Libraries need to create more loyal customers, yet many public librarians seem to talk more about attracting nonusers than keeping present customers happy or finding out why previous customers no longer return. Academic librarians may take the short-term view—it is four to six years and gone for the largest number of students. Such an attitude fails to consider the ripple effect as former students tell friends and family about their experiences with higher education. Moreover, as these alumni prosper, the college or university will approach them as potential donors or contributors, but may encounter resentment for their past treatment. Research indicates that only completely satisfied customers can be reasonably classified as loyal. (See chapters 9 and 10.) This is a major reason why paying close attention to library service quality is critical.

The collective experience of customers creates a reputation for the library. That reputation will become known to the administrators who fund the library and to the library community—students, faculty, the public, and taxpayers. What kind of reputation does a library have? How well does that reputation match the one that library staff desires? If the library wants a better reputation, what is it doing to improve it? These questions need serious consideration. Librarians need to consider how to describe the benefits of their service better to the administrators who fund them.

Complementary to reputation is brand image. As Elizabeth J. Wood, Rush Miller, and Amy Knapp explain,

> All market sectors dealing mainly in commodities— coal, sugar, soap, and similar offerings whose essential product characteristics are not easily differentiated or distinguished one from another—have difficulty attracting the customer's attention and retaining the customer's loyalty. To compete more effectively in such environments, marketers put a premium on building and maintaining a strong brand image, one that somehow sets them apart and above competitors.[22]

For libraries, the brand is typically books. People equate libraries with book collections rather than a service culture. A number of people are surprised to learn that libraries are prepared to answer factual questions, help find information, and offer DVDs and audiobooks. They are even more surprised to learn that they can reserve meeting space, or request specific titles, even from other libraries. That these services are a surprise to many people indicates a failure of libraries to publicize their services. If libraries want community support, they need to tell the community about the various services that are available and to do so in a way in which the public will listen.

NATIONAL AWARDS

Each year the Malcolm Baldrige National Quality Award recognizes outstanding American companies. The award covers seven categories: leadership; strategic planning; customer focus; measurement, analysis, and knowledge management; workforce focus; process management; and results. The first three categories represent the leadership triad; "these categories are placed together to emphasize the importance of a leadership focus on strategy and customers."[23] Totaling eighty-five points,

> The Customer *Focus* Category examines how your organization engages its customers for long-term marketplace success. This engagement strategy includes how your organization builds a customer-focused culture. Also examined is how your organization listens to the voice of its customers and uses this information to improve and identify opportunities for innovation.[24]

Further, "'customer engagement' refers to your customers' investment in your brand and product offerings."[25]

Companies that have won this award, given since 1987, have enjoyed considerable success. Baldrige winners have included a wide variety of organizations. Recent winners have been manufacturers, health care agencies, schools, small businesses, and local government. Steve George, who has written four books about the Baldrige Award and has worked with some of the winners, lists several characteristics common among them. These include

- a genuine concern for all people using or working in the organization or its community

- a strong desire to improve in every way
- a commitment to learning from other organizations and individuals
- use of data to measure and improve an alignment of strategies, processes, and activities with the mission of the organization[26]

Within academic librarianship, beginning in 2000, Blackwell's Book Services has provided the Association of College and Research Libraries, American Library Association, with funding for an annual Excellence in Academic Libraries Award to be given to a community college, college, or university library for outstanding accomplishments. Recipients, as reflected in the applications, have demonstrated some leadership but the applications do not tightly focus on the Baldrige Award's triad.[27]

The Public Library Association does not have an award similar to the one for academic libraries. The EBSCO Excellence in Small and/or Rural Public Library Service Award honors a library serving a community of ten thousand or fewer that demonstrates excellent service to its community. The Polaris Innovation in Technology John Iliff Award recognizes a library worker or library that has used technology and innovative thinking to improve services.[28]

A FINAL WORD

The time has come to stop confusing means—process and functions related to the collection or to technol-ogy—with ends (i.e., purpose), or managing information resources for people. People are the reason for having a library; without them there is no need for any library. Service is basic to the customers' satisfaction or delight with the library:

> A service can be an idea, entertainment, . . . information, knowledge, . . . social innovation, circumstance, convenience, food, security, or any number of other things. Service may also be defined as a deed, a performance, a social event or an effort and output that is consumed where it is produced.[29]

Service quality, a complex phenomenon, is composed of the content of the service itself and the context in which the service is rendered. It is also affected by the quality of the information supplied and used, and the expectations that customers have for the service. All managers should want to avoid situations in which library performance is poor and expectations are low, but customers appear indifferent or satisfied. Service quality is both individual and collective; the collective determination of service quality and satisfaction creates the library's reputation in the community and for the administrators who fund the library.

Traditional library performance measures do not reflect service quality. Their focus is primarily on expenditures for resources rather than on delivery of service. For these and other reasons, library managers must look for better ways to measure and describe the quality of their services, and, in effect, demonstrate that the organization deserves the type of recognition bestowed on Baldrige Award winners.

Great libraries provide measurably superior service.[30]

Notes

1. Mary W. Jordan, "What Is Your Library's Friendliness Factor?" *Public Library Quarterly* 24, no. 4 (2005): 81.

2. Raymond F. Zammuto, Susan M. Keaveney, and Edward J. O'Connor, "Rethinking Student Services: Assessing and Improving Service Quality," *Journal of Marketing for Higher Education* 7, no. 1 (1996): 46.

3. Maurice B. Line, "What Do People Need of Libraries, and How Can We Find Out?" *Australian Academic & Research Libraries* 27, no. 2 (June 1996): 77.

4. Françoise Hébert, "Service Quality: An Unobtrusive Investigation of Interlibrary Loan in Large Public Libraries in Canada," *Library & Information Science Research* 16, no. 1 (1994): 20.

5. Darlene E. Weingand, *Customer Service Excellence: A Guide for Librarians* (Chicago: American Library Association, 1997), 2.

6. Ibid., 2. Another prominent use of library users as customers appears in Carla J. Stoffle, Barbara Allen, David Morden, and Krisellen Maloney, "Continuing to Build the Future: Academic Libraries and Their Challenges," *portal: Libraries and the Academy* 3, no. 3 (July 2003): 363–380.

7. Jeannette Woodward, *Creating the Customer-Driven Academic Library* (Chicago: American Library Association, 2009), 178.

8. Arnold Hirshon, "Running with the Red Queen: Breaking New Habits to Survive in the Virtual World," in *Advances in Librarianship*, vol. 20, ed. Irene Godden (San Diego, CA: Academic Press, 1996), 5–6.

9. John M. Budd, "A Critique of Customer and Commodity," *College & Research Libraries* 58, no. 4 (July 1997): 317.

10. Laura A. Liswood, *Serving Them Right: Innovation and Powerful Customer Retention Strategies* (New York: Harper Business, 1990), 17.

11. Hébert, "Service Quality," 20.

12. Maurice B. Line, "Line's Five Laws of Librarianship . . . and One All-Embracing Law," *Library Association Record* 98, no. 3 (March 1996): 144.

13. S. R. Ranganathan's Five Laws of Library Science are (1) books are for use; (2) every book its reader; (3) every reader his [or her] book; (4) save the time of the reader; and (5) a library is a growing organism. See also Maurice B. Line, "Use of Library Materials" [book review], *College & Research Libraries* 40, no. 6 (November 1979): 557–558.

14. Tony Hope and Jeremy Hope, *Transforming the Bottom Line: Managing Performance with the Real Numbers* (Boston: Harvard Business School Press, 1996), 96.

15. Robert S. Kaplan and David P. Norton, "The Balanced Scorecard—Measures That Drive Performance," *Harvard Business Review* 70, no. 1 (January/February 1992): 72.

16. See Joseph R. Matthews, *Scorecards for Results: A Guide to Developing a Library Balanced Scorecard* (Westport, CT: Libraries Unlimited, 2008); Stratton Lloyd, "Building Library Success Using the Balanced Scorecard," *Library Quarterly* 76, no. 3 (July 2006): 352–361; Roswitha Poll, "Performance, Processes, and Costs: Managing Service Quality with the Balanced Scorecard," *Library Trends* 49, no. 4 (Spring 2001): 709–717.

17. University of Virginia Library, "Balanced Scorecard: 2007–08 Balanced Scorecard Metrics," www2.lib .virginia.edu/bsc/metrics/all0708.html; Alfred Willis, "Using the Balanced Scorecard at the University of Virginia Library: An Interview with Jim Self and Lynda White," *Library Administration & Management* 18, no. 2 (Spring 2004): 64–67.

18. Orange County Library System, "Performance Scorecard for Annual 2007/2008," www.ocls.info/about/balancedscorecard/default.asp?bhcp=1.

19. George E. Kroon, "Improving Quality in Service Marketing," *Journal of Customer Service in Marketing and Management* 1, no. 2 (1995): 13–28.

20. Hope and Hope, *Transforming the Bottom Line*, 2.

21. Ralph Norman, "The Scholarly Journal and the Intellectual Sensorium," in *The Politics and Processes of Scholarship*, ed. Joseph M. Moxley and Lagretta T. Lenker (Westport, CT: Greenwood Press, 1995), 80.

22. Elizabeth J. Wood, Rush Miller, and Amy Knapp, *Beyond Survival: Managing Academic Libraries in Transition* (Westport, CT: Libraries Unlimited, 2007), 22.

23. Department of Commerce, National Institute of Standards and Technology, The *2009–2010 Criteria for Performance Excellence* [Baldrige National Quality Program] (Gaithersburg, MD: NIST, 2009), 1, www.quality.nist.gov/PDF_files/2009_2010_Business_Nonprofit_Criteria.pdf.

24. Ibid., 13.

25. Ibid.

26. Steve George, "Baldrige.com," www.baldrige.com.

27. Peter Hernon, "Traces of Academic Library Leadership," in *Academic Librarians as Emotionally Intelligent Leaders*, ed. Peter Hernon, Joan Giesecke, and Camila A. Alire (Westport, CT: Libraries Unlimited, 2008), 57–73.

28. See "Polaris Innovation in Technology John Iliff Award," www.ala.org/ala//pla/plaawards/John_Iliff_Award.cfm; Public Library Association, "ALA/PLA Awards and Grants," http://pla.org/ala/mgrps/divs/pla/plaawards/index.cfm.

29. David A. Collier, "Measuring and Managing Service Quality," in *Service Management Effectiveness,* ed. David E. Bowen, Richard B. Chase, Thomas G. Cummings, and Associates (San Francisco: Jossey-Bass, 1990), 237.

30. Glen E. Holt, "What Makes a Great Library?" *Public Library Quarterly* 24, no. 2 (2005): 84.

A Look in the Library Mirror

A goal must be to empower our users and make customer self-sufficiency a priority; that is, make our libraries and services as transparent as possible and provide a suite of integrated tools that allow user-centered retrieval and management of information and knowledge resources without our mediation.[1]

In the 1991 film *The Doctor*, John McKee (played by William Hurt) gets to experience the hospital where he is an esteemed heart surgeon from the perspective of a patient when he is diagnosed with throat cancer.[2] His long waits to see doctors, canceled appointments, and indifferent and sometimes rude treatment from both staff and physicians first anger him and then awaken him to the fact that all patients, including his own, are more than just sick bodies. The situations depicted in the film are familiar to many people who have interacted with medical facilities in recent years. Beyond hospitals, customer problems with banks, stores, airlines, and many other service organizations stem from one source—failure to view policies and procedures from the perspective of the customers.

The main reason for this failure is that the senior managers setting those policies and procedures are insulated from dealing with customers. Because many of these decisions are made in a vacuum, managers have little or no understanding of how these decisions impact customers and frontline staff. On the other hand, some organizations make a determined effort to inculcate senior staff in the reality of customer service. For example, Enterprise Rent-A-Car has a "work your way up" and a "promote from within" policy. All supervisors have had direct experience working with the customers of the company.[3]

Managers at both Disney theme parks do not hesitate to pick up trash or do whatever it takes to ensure that customers have a magical experience. Even big-name chief executive officers get involved in frontline service. Fred Smith, founder of FedEx, does not hesitate to ride with a courier, while Bill Marriott Jr., head of the hotel chain, sometimes works the registration desks.[4]

SELF-SUFFICIENCY

Because of stagnant or declining budget allocations, many libraries have made conscious attempts to foster customers' self-sufficiency. Sometimes this self-sufficiency is euphemistically called *empowering* customers. Whatever term is used, the result is that customers are expected to do more for themselves. Now, there is nothing inherently wrong in trying to promote customer self-sufficiency; most people are used to fending for themselves in supermarkets and gas stations. In fact, many customers like to be able to peruse the merchandise without sales personnel hovering in the background or actively trying to induce purchases. At some supermarkets and other businesses, customers can register their purchases with portable optical scanners and then make payment.

Libraries also permit self-checkout and the electronic filing of interlibrary loan requests; provide self-help guides (print and digital); and create other ways to permit customers to be self-sufficient. However, they should review their practices and policies to ensure that, when possible, visits do not become frustrating. *How the library helps or hinders navigating and deciphering the system alters customers' perceptions of the quality of service provided and their attitudes about librarians and libraries generally.* This does not mean that libraries—their arrangement, staff, policies, diverse collections and services, and equipment—are responsible for any and all instances of confusion and frustration.

Despite efforts to stamp out the popular stereotype of the librarian, it remains strong because people *can identify that image with their own experiences.* Many people find the library an arcane and frightening place.[5] Indeed, a number of articles in professional journals have described the condition called "library anxiety." Many customers are confused about how to locate what they want. It may be difficult to find a particular book in a library. Call numbers and online public access catalogs (OPACs), with the diverse resources available through them, are not easily understood by the uninitiated. In addition, customers may be unsure of the appropriateness of asking for help, especially when staff seems preoccupied with other tasks. And reports of unpleasant experiences by those who do ask are not uncommon.[6]

In the OCLC report *College Students' Perceptions of Libraries and Information Resources,* which surveyed 396 participants, it was found that their use of the Internet has dramatically increased and their use of libraries, newspapers, television, and radio has decreased. However, when they do visit a public or academic library, which is still frequently, they prefer to use the Internet, search engines, and electronic resources. They view the library as a place to study and do homework, and they prefer self-sufficiency. "When asked to give advice, many student respondents suggested increasing libraries' open hours, improving the lighting and furniture, hiring friendlier staff and allowing food and drink in libraries."[7] Furthermore, they "trust information they get from libraries, and they trust the information they get from search engines. The survey revealed that they trust them almost equally, which suggests that libraries have no monopoly on the provision of information."[8]

"Self-service," as Thomas Childers and Nancy Van House note, "limits both the library's ability to serve and its ability to assess and represent its service."[9] All this underscores the importance of customer contact with library staff and the role this contact plays in service quality.

To promote self-sufficiency or "coproduction," where customers participate in the service delivery process, it is first necessary to make the organization welcoming and easy to navigate, not hindering customers in their pursuit of materials or information.[10]

Following are ten practices that hinder customer coproduction and perhaps induce frustration:

1. Having unclear signage, which customers may ignore[11]

2. Not trying to simplify the layout of the library

3. Permitting long delays in reshelving items (i.e., books, periodicals, and videos)

4. Requiring customers to bring in items for renewal

5. Failing to monitor or restrict use of the OPAC and other workstations for receiving and sending e-mail messages, thus making queuing a problem as customers wait to use the computers

6. Having multiple interfaces for using online resources and electronic texts, thereby confusing customers

7. Providing poor quality printers for computer workstations

8. Not posting directions for obtaining a photocopy card on or near the copiers

9. Filling paper trays for copiers and printers only once a day, no matter how much the machines are used

10. Failing to post instructions on the photocopier indicating how to position the item to be copied. Sometimes the paper tray is in the portrait position, other times it is in the landscape position. Customers must guess, and half the time they guess wrong, and waste their first copy.

To summarize:

Library operations don't occur in a vacuum. They take place within an institutional culture and physical environment. This institutional milieu creates the service atmosphere and significantly influences the approach that staff members take when performing routine tasks. In libraries where a commitment to service is present but at a minimum level, the institutional culture may be task-oriented; administrative and staff concerns are directed toward the successful, efficient completion of routine duties.

At the opposite end of the continuum the library culture regards customer satisfaction as the primary goal, and both administrators and staff direct their energies and activities toward that goal.[12]

To enable customers to become more self-sufficient, libraries might, among other things, initiate online payment for fee-based services (assuming there is institutional support for this), and permit customer self-checkout and check-in. Most libraries are already providing numerous resources in digital form for customers to access remotely and on-site, as well as converting microfilm into digitized resources that customers can e-mail to themselves or others. It is important to remember that, on the whole, Generation Y (born between 1977 and 1994) does not prefer to learn by reading.[13]

SIGNAGE

There are many instances of signs that are unclear, confusing, or assume knowledge on the part of the customer. Flickr captures some examples; a search of that site in April 2009 reveals 211 results matching *library* and *sign* and *funny*. The intelligent placement of well-designed signs ought to reduce customer frustration and enhance customer self-sufficiency. When signage is poor or limited, the library becomes a maze for many of its customers. It is not uncommon for libraries to shift collections but fail to update the signage.[14]

Signs posted flat at the ends of stacks that indicate classification numbers are an annoyance. In some libraries, these signs have been removed or need updating, as reprinting them each time that books are moved from range to range is considered too much trouble. Some public libraries have abandoned this practice, instead opting for the bookstore model and using words like *cookbooks, business,* or *biography.* In large, multistoried libraries, a map on each floor showing layout empowers customers and answers many of their questions about location.

To lessen the need for so many signs and cope with the fact that customers may not understand library terminology, Hillman Library at the University of Pittsburgh added bright new signs to help direct patrons:

Located mainly on the ground level and first floor, signs stenciled on walls and wrapped around structural pillars in bold red, orange, green and blue have replaced an understated color scheme. Furthermore, the change also reflects simplified language University Library System has adopted in other areas, such as on its website. Some color-coding is at work: collection-related signage is blue; action-related signs are red. . . . The reference desk is located near a red "ask" sign; lending has become "checkout" and interlibrary loan "requests from other libraries." In the stairwells, patrons can more easily orient themselves with signs listing main areas and services as well as an indication of where the user is in relation to them.[15]

Public libraries, especially those housed in storefronts, need to make sure that the hours of operation are prominently posted along with the library's phone number so that passersby can make note of them.

STAFF

Because of financial stringency, students and support staff (many of whom are part-time workers) are now assigned to do work formerly handled by librarians or paraprofessionals. The proportion of students and part-time support staff working at public service desks is especially high on weekends. Some of the newer staff members do a good job. It is, however, disconcerting to encounter staff at public service desks too engrossed in checking collection order slips, chatting with friends, or playing games on computer terminals to answer customer questions. Clearly, expectations for proper service have not been made explicit, and proper training has not been provided to these employees. They need to be instructed so that they can be knowledgeable about both the library and how to access information to meet customer inquiries. The training of support staff and new librarians is a major undertaking that needs to be assigned to a specific staff member so that information important to their jobs does not fall through the cracks.

A common practice in many public service departments was for the staff to make a tick mark for each question asked by a customer. At the end of the day, the number of such marks was tallied and added to the total for the monthly, quarterly, and annual reports. The library proudly announced that it handles *x* number of reference inquiries over the year. No distinctions were made between directional (e.g., Where is the bathroom?) questions and informational questions. No effort was made to check or to ensure that the questions were answered accurately or that the customers felt that the questions were answered completely. It was assumed that a question asked was a question answered.

Fortunately, now that attitude seems to be changing. A number of libraries use LibQUAL+ to review *affect of service*, the personal service provided at the service desks. (See chapter 7.) Based on the results, a library might conclude that staff

- gives users individual attention
- deals with users in a caring fashion
- understands the needs of their users
- is viewed as willing to help users

Furthermore, as discussed in chapter 10, companies, in partnership with public libraries, are creating management information systems and capturing survey responses which are analyzed and graphically presented. For instance, with the customer satisfaction data and the library data management system provided by Counting Opinions, it is possible to create an array of performance measures and gain insights into a library's customers and how that library compares with other libraries.

REDUCING "DUMB" QUESTIONS

Many customers have never asked a question at reference desks or via e-mail and chat services. It has been speculated that the reasons are as follows:

- They do not want to ask a "dumb question" or appear incapable of doing the research themselves.
- Libraries and research make them anxious.

- They do not know they need help.
- They are overconfident.
- They really do not need our help.
- They forget that reference services exist.
- They do not know that reference services exist.
- They had a bad reference experience elsewhere that turned them off the service.[16]

Despite the fact that many customers do not ask questions, the issue of *dumb questions* persists, at least in the minds of some public service staff. A question commonly perceived as dumb is "Where is . . . ?" Considering that libraries range in size from hundreds to thousands of square feet, it is not surprising that customers cannot find their way. "Where is . . . ?" is probably a commonly asked question in airports, supermarkets, restaurants, and museums. Lots of good signs, as in the approach adopted by Hillman Library, would minimize such questions.

Even customers who are fairly sophisticated about using the library get flummoxed trying to find back issues of periodicals. Suddenly issues are gone from the shelves. Taking issues from shelves for binding—and the length of time they remain at the bindery—are a mystery to most customers, even knowledgeable ones. One library shelves all bound periodical volumes by classification number, but unbound issues are held in a "current" periodical section on the ground floor and shelved by title. "Current" can range from the most recent issue to the last three years. Adding to the confusion, some titles are bound with issues for two or three years under the same cover, but this can be determined only by examining the bound volumes.

MORE ON ANXIETY AND FRUSTRATION

A body of research addressing library anxiety—"a psychological barrier to academic success among college students"[17] and perhaps others—underscores that a number of students feel overwhelmed by the vast amount of information that libraries offer and staff whom they perceive as busy and unapproachable. Library anxiety affects student performance and the quality of effort they put into the completion of assignments; quality of effort, George D. Kuh and Robert M. Gonyea argue, "is the single best predictor of what students gain from college."[18] With increased attention being given to active learning and student learning outcomes, this is most likely an exaggeration.

Library Rx: Measuring and Treating Library Anxiety reviews the research on student reactions to the library environment, describes the findings of a research project on library anxiety, and presents ideas to cope with it.[19] Clearly, library staff must be aware of library anxiety and review this work and the strategies it points out. At the same time, anxiety places more pressure on staff to recognize and deal with it. That staff, in part, might suffer from stress and burnout, while having to recognize the difference between library anxiety and customer frustration.

Customer frustration, a rather common occurrence in both academic and public libraries, increases with the time and effort expended in an unsuccessful search for information or materials. Usually, time spent in a library is considered positive, but time spent looking for missing items or trying unsuccessfully to locate a specific piece of information is both unproductive and discouraging. This frustration has several causes. A principal one, inherent in the nature of libraries, is that demand for particular items frequently exceeds supply. Other causes of frustration are the customers' inability to understand the system, library practices that hinder customers from obtaining what they want, and staff members who neglect to ascertain if customers found the information or the items desired. Because most frustrated customers simply leave without complaining, the library has no indication of the magnitude of this frustration. Complicating matters, the library may not be at fault as the customer never approached a staff member. On the other hand, it is important not to dismiss frustration (or the potential for it) as merely the customer's fault. Why did not they ask for help? We are there to assist them.

Figure 2.1 illustrates some of the reasons for frustration. To this list, we would add computer downtime, the inability to borrow equipment such as laptops from the library, restricted borrowing time for that equipment, and the cost of basic services such as having to pay for paper to print downloaded items. Furthermore, the book may not be on the shelf despite the OPAC saying otherwise; the item might be misshelved.

Frustration is the obverse of service quality. Many frustrated customers never return, or if they do, it is infrequently, especially if they find no improvement in the situation. Worse still, they tell friends, family, and colleagues of their experiences, and word of mouth is a powerful factor in shaping the reputation of the library in its community.

As a result, librarians face a difficult task—providing a system that meets multiple needs, perspectives, and expectations. As Maurice B. Line has noted,

> A maxim that should be displayed prominently in every library is "It is better and easier to design systems around human beings than to redesign human beings to fit systems." An ideal system is one that is designed to serve the majority of needs in the most effective and efficient way possible, but that also allows nonstandard needs to be met and nonstandard people to be served.[20]

Although what he proposes may not be easy (or possible) to resolve, librarians should still review his comments and see what solutions they can adopt.

FIGURE 2.1

CUSTOMER FRUSTRATION LIST

1. Customer is unable to locate materials or information.
2. Telephone is not answered promptly when customer calls.
3. Length of time until a reserved material is available seems too long.
4. Library staff are not friendly or helpful.
5. Library staff appear to be busy or unapproachable.
6. Parking is not available nearby.
7. Line at checkout is too long.
8. Librarian is not available to assist in locating material or information.
9. Customers are notified at inopportune times that requested items have arrived.
10. Library staff interpret policies literally and display a lack of flexibility.
11. Library hours are not convenient.
12. Customer must wait at the service desk while staff answer telephone.

Source: Darlene E. Weingand, *Customer Service Excellence* (Chicago: American Library Association, 1997), 73.

A FINAL WORD

Some libraries have erected tall counters between staff and customers. Staff can either stand or sit on high stools. The intent probably was to allow eye contact between staff and customers, which seems perfectly reasonable, but tall counters might make customers feel disadvantaged or feel that asking questions is always part of a formal process. A counter can be a formidable barrier to customers who are short or to those in wheelchairs, who are considerably disadvantaged both by the arrangement and by the reluctance of staff to come from behind the counter to assist.

Darlene E. Weingand makes an important observation: "customer service excellence begins with a restless dissatisfaction with the status quo and the belief that one can do better."[21] The examples noted in this chapter are only intended as a reminder that library staff can always do better. Figure 2.1 offers further evidence that libraries and library staff might do things that confuse, hinder, or frustrate customers. Libraries, like any service organization, should seek to improve their performance and not be satisfied with the status quo. It is always possible to improve. Library staff should look into the library mirror and be certain that they see what customers see. Does this self-examination result in change?

Your customers are your [best] ad agency.[22]

Notes

1. Carla J. Stoffle, Barbara Allen, David Morden, and Krisellen Maloney, "Continuing to Build the Future: Academic Libraries and Their Challenges," *portal: Libraries and the Academy* 3, no. 3 (2003): 377.

2. *The Doctor* was based on the book *A Taste of My Own Medicine* by Ed Rosenbaum (New York: Ballantine Books, 1991).

3. Kirk Kazanjian, *Exceeding Customer Expectations: What Enterprise, America's #1 Car Rental Company, Can Teach You about Creating Lifetime Customers* (New York: Doubleday, 2007), 92.

4. Performance Research Associates, *Delivering Knock Your Socks Off Service*, 3rd ed. Revisions by Ron Zemke (New York: AMACOM, 2003), 103.

5. Marie L. Radford and Gary P. Radford, "Power, Knowledge, and Fear: Feminism, Foucault, and the Stereotype of the Female Librarian," *Library Quarterly* 67, no. 3 (July 1997): 250–266.

6. Patricia Dewdney and Catherine S. Ross, "Flying a Light Aircraft: Reference Service Evaluation from a User's Viewpoint," *RQ* 34, no. 2 (Winter 1994): 217–229; Catherine S. Ross and Patricia Dewdney, "Best Practices: An Analysis of the Best (and Worst) in Fifty-Two Public Library Reference Transactions," *Public Libraries* 33, no. 5 (September/October 1994): 261–266.

7. OCLC, *College Students' Perceptions of Libraries and Information Resources* (Dublin, OH: OCLC, 2005), www.oclc.org/reports/perceptionscollege.htm.

8. In contrast, *Information Searches That Solve Problems* (a report of a national survey jointly conducted with Pew Internet in American Life Project, the University of Illinois, and Princeton Research Associates, December 2007) found that different segments of the American population, including Generation Y, still make frequent use of the public library. Compared to their parents, Gen Y members are most likely to use libraries for engaging in problem solving and for general information gathering. Furthermore, 40 percent of Gen Y said that they will use libraries in the future when they encounter problems, compared with 20 percent of those above age thirty who say they would go to a library.

9. Thomas A. Childers and Nancy Van House, *What's Good? Describing Your Public Library's Effectiveness* (Chicago: American Library Association, 1993), 27.

10. Ibid.

11. See Paco Underhill, *Why We Buy: The Science of Shopping* (New York: Simon and Schuster, 2000).

12. Darlene E. Weingand, *Customer Service Excellence* (Chicago: American Library Association, 1997), 13.

13. Angela Weiler, "Information-seeking Behavior in Generation Y Students: Motivation, Critical Thinking, and Learning Theory," *Journal of Academic Librarianship* 31, no. 1 (January 2005): 46–53.

14. See James A. Buczynski, "Libraries Begin to Engage Their Menacing Mobile Phone Hordes without Shhhhh!" *Internet Reference Services Quarterly* 13, no. 2–3 (2008): 261–269.

15. "New Signage Directs Hillman Library Patrons," *University Times* [University of Pittsburgh] 41, no. 8 (December 4, 2008), http://mac10.umc.pitt .edu/u/FMPro?-db=ustory&-lay=a&-format=d .html&storyid=8442&-Find.

16. Stephen Francoeur, "Why Don't Our Students Ask for Help?" *Digital Reference* (May 2, 2008), www.teachinglibrarian.org/weblog/2008/05/why-dont-our-students-ask-for-help.html.

17. Qun G. Jiao, "Library Anxiety: Characteristics of 'At-risk' College Students," *Library & Information Science Research* 18, no. 2 (1996): 151.

18. George D. Kuh and Robert M. Gonyea, "The Role of the Academic Library in Promoting Student Engagement in Learning," *College & Research Libraries* 64, no. 4 (July 2003): 259.

19. Martina Malvasi, Catherine Rudowsky, and Jesus M. Valencia, *Library Rx: Measuring and Treating Library Anxiety* (Chicago: American Library Association, 2009).

20. Maurice B. Line, "What Do People Need of Libraries, and How Can We Find Out?" *Australian Academic & Research Libraries* 27, no. 2 (June 1996): 79.

21. Weingand, *Customer Service Excellence*, 9.

22. Jeff Jarvis, *What Would Google Do?* (New York: Collins Business, 2009), 46.

Chapter Three

"Your Mission, Should You Choose to Accept It . . ."

The non-profits are, of course, still dedicated to "doing good." But they also realize that good intentions are no substitute for organization and leadership, for accountability, performance, and results. Those things require management and that, in turn, begins with the organization's mission.[1]

Any discussion of meeting or exceeding customers' expectations must occur within a context—that of the organizational mission, goals, and objectives. As libraries explore meeting expectations and perhaps consider the development of customer service standards or plans, they must do so within a larger context. The purpose of this chapter is to provide a context against which libraries can view service quality and customer satisfaction. The information gathered can then be used to revisit mission statements, goals, and objectives to ensure that they meet the needs of a dynamic organization coping with change.

The phrase "Your mission, should you choose to accept it . . ." was always spoken in the first minutes of *Mission Impossible*, a television program popular in the 1970s. The voice on the tape specified clearly and unambiguously what the team of daring adventurers was to accomplish to complete the assignment successfully.

Unfortunately, many libraries have developed mission statements and then *not* accepted them, or at least those missions do not guide planning and decision making.

Most missions are not precisely defined and, even worse, become muddled over time. A number of public libraries have had difficulty in articulating a mission because of the diversity among clientele and the lack of direction from local officials. To fill the void, the public library community itself articulated a mission or set of purposes for the library: information, education, and recreation. Many public libraries, however, wrote their own mission statements and emphasized their purpose as the promotion of such conditions as "creative use of leisure time," "good citizenship," and "democracy." Curiously, most of these statements neglected to mention who was to be affected or who was the focus of these lofty statements—the customers. Fortunately, most local officials never asked for proof of mission fulfillment.

In the 1980s, the Public Library Association promulgated the idea that local libraries, in consultation with members of the community, select and adopt roles (i.e., purposes) from a prepared list. These roles, along with planning instructions, were described in a monograph published by the American Library Association.[2] Charles R. McClure and Paul T. Jaeger cover the change in emphasis for subsequent years, and they show the shift from a focus on the original planning and role-setting process to one emphasizing service responses and service roles.[3] "In simple terms," Sandra Nelson explains,

> a service response is what a library does for or offers to the public in an effort to meet a set of well-defined community needs. Roles are broadly defined categories of service; they describe what the library does in a very general way. Service responses, on the other hand, are very distinct ways that libraries serve the public. They represent the gathering and deployment of specific critical resources to produce a specific benefit or result.[4]

In 2007, the definition of service responses was updated as follows:

> They are . . . designed to describe the most common clusters of services and programs that libraries provide. . . . The descriptions and examples offered are provided to help library planners see the many possibilities that exist for matching their services to the unique needs of their communities.[5]

McClure and Jaeger compare the different service roles developed over time and argue that those roles are "strongly, perhaps inextricably, tied to the provision of Internet access, assistance, and a range of services and applications." They continue their critique by maintaining that "the range of unique applications from the Internet means that it has, and will continue to have, very different impacts on public library service roles and societal expectations of public libraries than did previous technological advances such as video cassettes, computer discs, and microfilm."[6]

Figure 3.1, which reprints the service responses for public libraries, serves as a framework from which libraries can select those responses that they want to consider as priorities. They might engage their community in that discussion. A number of tools exist that enable the staff to probe particular responses. The Urban Libraries Council, for instance, has produced *Welcome Stranger*, whose purpose is to assist public libraries in helping the immigrant population in their transition to a new country and society.[7]

In the case of academic libraries, mission statements usually revolve around the libraries' support for teaching, service, and research for specific constituent groups—students, faculty, staff, and administrative personnel. However, as academe, especially the large universities, has somewhat shifted emphasis from teaching to learning and from research to grantsmanship, the missions of the libraries should reflect the changes. As well, accreditation organizations hold institutions and numerous academic programs accountable for meeting their missions. This is the basis of the movement toward outcomes assessment, as each institution is judged in the context of its declared mission.

THE DIFFERENCE BETWEEN A MISSION AND VISION

The library needs vision and mission statements showing its role and responsibility in supporting the vision and mission of the institution. According to Jann E. Freed and Marie R. Klugman, "a vision statement is a philosophy about values; it is futuristic and optimistic. . . . [It] answers the question: Where do we want to be in five to 10 years and what do we want to be doing?"[8] A mission statement, in contrast, describes the library's purpose, specifies what the library contributes to the overall institution's mission, and "differentiates the institution from other institutions."[9] It does not merely explain what the library does. A statement focusing on providing access to those print and electronic information resources and services required to support the college's or university's teaching and research—or, in the case of public libraries, to meet all the information needs of the public—may create an impression of the budget for building the collection as a bottomless pit, draining precious financial resources. Institution administrators and faculty, or city/town managers, need direction about spending priorities, especially those relating to technology, and the library's vision and service plans.

Most academic and public libraries place their mission on their home pages, most likely under "about the library" or a similar heading. The typical mission statement is very short or else confirms the characterization of cartoonist and humorist Scott Adams that the statement is "a long, awkward sentence [paragraph, or page] that demonstrates management's inability to think clearly."[10] The statement probably also states the obvious, does not issue a challenge to the library, and is not framed within the context of a vision likely to appeal to businesspeople sitting on boards of regents or serving as trustees, or to state legislators trying to gain a sense of the direction and

FIGURE 3.1

LIBRARY SERVICE RESPONSES

Be an Informed Citizen: Local, National, and World Affairs. Residents will have the information they need to support and promote democracy, to fulfill their civic responsibilities at the local, state, and national levels, and to fully participate in community decision making.

Building Successful Enterprises: Business and Nonprofit Support. Business owners and nonprofit organization directors and their managers will have the resources they need to develop and maintain strong viable organizations.

Celebrate Diversity: Cultural Awareness. Residents will have programs and services that promote appreciation and understanding of their personal heritage and the heritage of others in the community.

Connect to the Online World: Public Internet Access. Residents will have high-speed access to the digital world with no unnecessary restrictions or fees to ensure that everyone can take advantage of the ever-growing resources and services available through the Internet.

Create Young Readers: Early Literacy. Children from birth to five will have programs and services designed to ensure that they will enter school ready to learn to read, write, and listen.

Discover Your Roots: Genealogy and Local History. Residents and visitors will have the resources they need to connect the past with the present through their family histories and to understand the history and traditions of the community.

Express Creativity: Create and Share Content. Residents will have the services and support they need to express themselves by creating original print, video, audio, or visual content in a real-world or online environment.

Get Facts Fast: Ready Reference. Residents will have someone to answer their questions on a wide array of topics of personal interest.

Know Your Community: Community Resources and Services. Residents will have a central source for information about a wide variety of programs, services, and activities provided by community agencies and organizations.

Learn to Read and Write: Adult, Teens, and Family Literacy. Adults and teens will have the skills and resources they need to improve their literacy skills in order to meet their personal goals and fulfill their responsibilities as parents, citizens, and workers.

Make Career Choices: Job and Career Development. Adults and teens will have the resources they need to identify career opportunities that suit their individual strengths and interests.

Make Informed Decisions: Health, Wealth, and Other Life Choices. Residents will have the resources they need to identify and analyze risks, benefits, and alternatives before making decisions that affect their lives.

Satisfy Curiosity: Lifelong Learning. Residents will have the resources they need to explore topics of personal interest and continue to learn throughout their lives.

Stimulate Imagination: Reading, Viewing, and Listening for Pleasure. Residents who want materials to enhance their leisure time will find what they want when and where they want them and will have the help they need to make choices from among the options.

Succeed in School: Homework Help. Students will have the resources they need to succeed in school.

Understand How to Find, Evaluate, and Use Information: Information Fluency. Residents will know when they need information to resolve an issue or answer a question and will have the skills to search for, locate, evaluate, and effectively use information to meet their needs.

(cont.)

FIGURE 3.1 (cont.)

Visit a Comfortable Place: Physical and Virtual Spaces. Residents will have safe and welcoming physical places to meet and interact with others or to sit quietly and read and will have open and accessible virtual spaces that support networking.

Welcome to the United States: Service for New Immigrants. New immigrants and refugees will have information on citizenship, English Language Learning, employment, public schooling, health and safety, available social services, and any other topics that they need to participate successfully in American life.

Source: Sandra Nelson, *Strategic Planning for Results* (Chicago: American Library Association, 2008), 47.

---

purpose of the college or university and eager to hold academe to the type of accountability commonly used in business. "Once a vision or mission statement has been developed, it is vital that the statement is communicated to all members of the institution and that members understand the statement and refer to it in their day-to-day work."[11]

According to Betsy Sanders, former vice president and general manager of Nordstrom, Inc.,

> Unfortunately, well-wrought words, even when etched in concrete, do not make a mission statement. That statement is made by the constant, shared redefining of the *why* of the business. For others to share in your success, they, too, must be able to internalize the significance of what it is you are about. The answer to this question ["Why are we in business?"] must be clear, candid, constantly communicated, and dynamic.[12]

Sanders also encourages businesses to develop a vision that articulates where they are going: "Encouraging everyone to share the vision and to become involved in its ongoing refinement is the essence of truly empowering the organization."[13]

A number of academic libraries have developed an organizational mission that aligns with that of the parent organization or institution. They may have separate ones for subunits (e.g., digital centers and information or learning commons) or for special constituent groups (e.g., diversity, including disability).

The Seattle Public Library has a mission that incorporates a vision; in fact the vision is the first part of the mission and service is an integral part of the mission as well as the accompanying "aims":

> Our mission is to become the best public library in the world by being so tuned in to the people we serve and so supportive of each other's efforts that we are able to provide highly responsive service. We strive to inform, enrich and empower every person in our

community by creating and promoting easy access to a vast array of ideas and information, and by supporting an informed citizenry, lifelong learning and love of reading. We acquire, organize and provide books and other relevant materials; ensure access to information sources throughout the nation and around the world; serve our public with expert and caring assistance; and reach out to all members of our community.[14]

The library's eight aims focus on the provisions of high-quality services and a "caring, welcoming, and lively cultural and lifelong learning center" as well as "inviting, safe and well-maintained" facilities. There is also mention, for instance, of

- A highly trained and competent staff that reflects the rich diversity of our community and that works together to provide responsive service to all users

- Appropriate technology to extend, expand, and enhance services in every neighborhood and ensure that all users have equitable access to information

- Careful stewardship of the public trust, which ensures accountability and makes the most efficient and effective use of funds, both public and private; fosters collaboration, cooperation, and co-location where possible with other agencies; and builds public/private partnerships to enhance services to our users.[15]

ACCESS AND ASSISTANCE

No matter the type of library, most librarians can agree with G. Edward Evans and Sandra M. Heft that the primary responsibilities of a library are "to provide access to information in all its many forms and formats . . . [and] to provide assistance in locating specific pieces of information sought by individuals in the service population."[16] These responsibilities—*access* and *assistance*—are constant over time and over all types of libraries and information centers.

Most mission statements, however, do not explain who gets access and/or assistance, and what is to be accessed. In reality, access might be limited to certain categories of people—for instance, residents, students, faculty, and registered borrowers. Access has become more restrictive because of licensing agreements for electronic information, and is limited to particular types of informational or recreational items—those that can be purchased from certain types of distributors. The issues of quantity or quality relating to either access or assistance are ignored. Another important point is that these primary purposes represent the consensus of librarians, and not that of the community to be served, nor that of the community's decision makers.

Both access and assistance are concepts open to wide interpretation. Access can mean entry into the library building, or use of an item owned by a far-distant library. Assistance can mean pointing out the location of an atlas or preparing a long bibliography. The *way* that those responsibilities are carried out distinguishes one organization or information unit from another. The repeated and successful *fulfillment* of these responsibilities constitutes mission accomplishment for the organization.

Access and assistance are basic to the missions of libraries. Without access, none of these other conditions—supporting teaching and research, providing information, education, recreation, or any service role—can be achieved. Access to the materials and information desired is a first step that must be satisfied before any higher-level conditions can occur.

If an academic library accepts a mission to support teaching and research, then customers' expectations about accessing materials for courses and research have validity. Customers of libraries that claim the role of popular materials center should be able to gain access to such materials without difficulty or undue delay. All customers have a right to expect staff to be courteous and knowledgeable and to serve them reasonably promptly.

It is rare that an academic and public library combine. One of the few instances involves the San Jose (California) public and academic library (www.sjlibrary.org). The mission of the former is to enrich "lives by fostering lifelong learning and by ensuring that every member of the community has access to a vast array of ideas and information." That mission is supported by a vision statement that is more of a continuation or elaboration on the mission.

Turning to the academic library, the university dean who oversees the library declares that the library, as the heart of the university, is "a gateway to information. . . . [T]he library prepares SJSU [San Jose State University] students for the future by supporting classroom learning experiences and ensuring that SJSU graduates are prepared for a lifetime of exploration and discovery."[17] The combined library strives to

- Enrich lives by fostering lifelong learning and ensuring that every member of the community has access to a vast array of ideas and information

- Provide students, instructors and the community access to the information they need for educational and personal growth throughout their lives

- Support the San José State University Library's educational mission in expanding the base of knowledge through research and scholarship[18]

A MISSION IS MORE THAN GOOD INTENTIONS

The central part of a mission tends to be highly stable, even though the environment in which the organization operates may change rather dramatically. For example, despite the transition from one-room schools in which students wrote on personal slates to the modern buildings in which students write on personal computers, the mission of schools remains the same—to teach students to read, write, compute, understand, and think well enough to function in contemporary society. The means to accomplish the mission, however, vary depending on local conditions and changes over time.

Continuous improvement in process or product to carry out the mission is essential for organizational well-being. Therefore, plans or concepts on how to accomplish the mission, or how to accomplish it "better," are needed. All plans (activities, whether ongoing or proposed) and decisions need to be scrutinized to determine how they contribute to the library mission—access and assistance.

Guy A. Marco puts library activities and functions into four classes that should be helpful in considering whether or how library activities and practices contribute to access and assistance. These classifications are *ideal*—essential to accomplishment of a given mission

useful—supportive of mission accomplishment, but not essential

useless—irrelevant to mission accomplishment

counterproductive—obstructs mission accomplishment[19]

It may seem strange to list *useless* and *counterproductive* as considerations, but organizations regularly make decisions and plans and take actions that are useless and counterproductive.

Let us consider two common library practices or services and relate them to Marco's classification. Academic librarians might receive release time to work on a research project and to publish the results, but might not relate that research to library planning and decision making. This is counterproductive. In effect, no follow-through occurs between the doing and reporting of research and the use of that research for improving library services and management.

On the other hand, by purchasing AquaBrowser or an alternative, libraries gain a platform for visual, faceted searching that connects to any data source and integrates it with the automation system. As a result, customers can make unexpected finds as items (visual and other) in digitized collections become integrated into the OPAC. The idea of separate silos of digital collections is replaced by the full integration of diverse resources to which the library provides access. Applying Marco's classification, some libraries might consider such an investment as useful whereas others, given their budget, might view it as ideal.

GOALS AND OBJECTIVES

Missions are actualized by goals and objectives. *Goals* are "general descriptions of conditions intended to exist at a future time,"[20] whereas *objectives* are

> descriptions of specific conditions that are intended to exist by certain points in the future, the conditions being measurably different from those conditions that existed when the objectives were set or made. . . . An objective differs from a goal by having measurability: at a certain time (its deadline or expiry date) the objective can be assessed by any rational observer and judged to have succeeded or failed.[21]

Libraries can develop goals and objectives related, for instance, to improving bibliographic accessibility, physical availability, and professional service. Not only should the library have organizational goals and objectives, but each unit within the library should have its own goals and objectives that facilitate the achievement of library-wide goals.

Assuming a goal of "providing high-quality reference and referral services to library clientele," objectives might be to

- increase, by 10 percent, the number of hours that staff members provide public service at the main reference desk within the next six months
- increase, by 5 percent, the accuracy of answers given to library customers within the next fiscal year

Likewise, the library might develop goals relating to the provision of text-messaging reference service and virtual reference service.

For both the library and its composite units, the adoption of goals and objectives is necessary, but they should be accompanied by action and by some way to evaluate the extent of accomplishment. In retail trade, sales personnel have monthly quotas to reach. In some instances, consistent inability to reach these targets results in probation or termination. Department heads or team leaders may work with employees to set targets to be achieved weekly, monthly, annually, and so forth. Thus, managers measure the extent to which agreed-upon objectives are met while employees know which objectives are most important and can focus time and effort on their achievement.

Sanders encourages businesses to set and maintain high standards, through their goals, by demanding the best from their employees. "The expectation of excellence causes everyone to stretch, and the customer is well served in the process."[22] For this reason, it is critical that everyone be involved in: (1) understanding why the organization is in business, and (2) "planning how to move that business forward."[23]

Goals and objectives, in summary, reflect the perspective of the organization and what it wants to achieve. Extrapolating from the work of Sanders, four key questions are

1. To what extent do customers shape the planning framework, including the direction or focus of goals and objectives?

2. To what extent should they shape the framework?

3. Is this framework important to them?

4. How will the organization adopt a systems approach in which all departments work together and are responsive to the information-seeking behavior and requirements of the customers?

An example from the retail industry illustrates how an organization can actively decide to focus on service quality and build customer satisfaction. Nordstrom is renowned for its customer service. Sales associates, who can earn over one hundred thousand dollars a year, specialize in personal service and, even without a customer making a request, will search the store to assemble a selection of items from which to choose. Because of the strong service orientation, customers remember how they were treated and how the organization stands behind its promises and the quality of the products purchased. Nordstrom has been known to accept as returned merchandise items that the store never stocked.[24] The reason is to create or keep a loyal Nordstrom customer. The company maintains a large in-store inventory to ensure that customers find a suitable item, and Nordstrom's catalogs facilitate mail-order purchases. The intent is that, when customers think about purchasing clothes, they automatically associate their need with one department store—Nordstrom.

Keeping shoes properly paired is important to most shoe stores. Nordstrom recognizes, however, that the size of each foot may differ so much that a person might need two different sizes of the same shoe. The store allows customers to pair shoes of different sizes as one purchase for one price. Of course, the store ends up with unmatched pairs of shoes, but expects the difference to balance out over time. Clearly, the needs of the customer are paramount to the service provided.

Such customer-driven practices should not be interpreted to mean that the customer is always right. The organization chooses which expectations it wants to meet as part of its service plan. (See figure 7.4.) (Nordstrom probably goes farther than others with the expectations that it chooses to meet.) There will be situations in which library staff clearly realizes that the expectations of the particular person they are helping are not in the best interest of either the library or other customers.[25]

PHILOSOPHY AND VALUES

Every organization is shaped by both a philosophy and a set of values. These are not necessarily high-minded or erudite. They may not be articulated or even perceived consciously by the people who work in the organization. Philosophy and values are absorbed into organizations in various ways: by the vision articulated by the organization's founder, by a set of widely accepted professional values, by the actions of long-tenured managers, or by the accretion of habits over time. The organization's philosophy and values are revealed by the manner in which it operates, by its interactions with customers or clients, and by the attitudes of the employees toward the organization's work, its customers, and its management.

In essence, the organizational culture, shaped by the organization's philosophy and values, largely determines the quality of its service. The Nordstrom examples clearly show that customers are *valued*, whereas some other organizations seem unresponsive or actually hostile to customers.

Returning to the example of the San Jose Library, the mission is supported by a set of values, namely:

- Our users are not only our customers, they are the reason the library exists. We provide quality service and treat all users fairly and equally. Services are provided in a non-judgmental manner that is sensitive to and supportive of human differences.

- Our employees and volunteers are valued as individuals and for their important contributions to the organization. An open exchange of ideas is encouraged throughout the system. We nurture our talents and each other.

- We are a learning organization that is not afraid to change and take appropriate risks in pursuit of meeting community needs. We constantly reassess our services and methods and try to see ourselves through the public's eyes.

- We maintain high standards in our work and help instill a sense of pride in all employees, as well as a strong sense of responsibility and integrity.

- Both staff and users are encouraged to enjoy their library experience.[26]

The Seattle Public Library provides a succinct but powerful declaration of values, which refers to organizational values: "Service to our users is our reason for being. Those who need us most should be our highest priority."[27]

How should customers respond to the public library that does not permit downloading of files or e-mailing of microfiche that can be digitized from equipment it owns because of fear that customers may use contaminated USB flash drives or the staff does not want to be bothered by having to help customers? Although the answer to this question may be complex, should not the library find solutions that are in the best interests of customers?

THE LIBRARY AS A SYSTEM

A library is composed of a set of units or departments, or teams in the case of some restructured libraries, theoretically working toward a common purpose—accomplishment of the library's and institution's mission. The library is more than the mere sum of these units and teams; it is a system in which the interaction of the parts affects the well-being of the whole, just as one organ affects the overall health of the body, or one mechanism can affect a car's handling or safety.

The *general systems model*, also called an open or dynamic system, provides an important framework for understanding how problems can transcend individual parts and affect many other activities and units. For example, the availability of resources affects an organization positively and negatively, just as the availability of food can affect a human body. How those resources are transformed into products and services, and how well the library meets the information needs and expectations of its customers, are analogous to how a human body might be affected by the nutrients consumed.

General systems theory views organizations as being composed of three parts: input, feedback, and reality. The inputs, of course, strongly influence both feedback and reality. These parts provide "a way to evaluate the relationship among the components of the organization and between the organization and its environment."[28]

Resources are the most commonly considered input. A definite connection exists between the adequacy of resources (personnel, equipment, and physical surroundings) and services, and between services and effectiveness (either good or bad), as viewed from both the organization's and the customers' perspectives. Inputs, however, do not have to be tangible. Attitudes and behaviors can also be inputs that produce positive or negative feedback and, hence, have an impact on reality for both the customers and the organization. For example, a backlog created by one unit or team (input) can create havoc for internal customers throughout the system (feedback) and disrupt service for customers (reality). More positively, libraries used to be adamant that customers not eat or drink inside the building. The consensus was that food and drink would inevitably damage the book collection. Now library cafés are common in public libraries and making inroads into academic libraries. These cafés are magnets for attracting people into the building. Inputs refer to product quality (food) and feedback might involve customer perceptions of product quality; that is, the food and beverages. Meeting spaces are sometimes placed nearby so that participants in library programs can get refreshments. Another change in attitude on the part of librarians is encouraging customers to serve themselves. This trend has accelerated in recent years with customers now expected to check out their own books and pick up their reserved items from an open area instead of having to ask for the item at the circulation desk.

All parts of the organization need to recognize their interdependence and to overcome the belief that one part is more important than the others. Dependence can be recognized by looking at the organization through the customer perspective and asking, "What can the customer expect from the library, regardless of the collection or service used?" and "How can all parts of the library work together to improve the utility of each collection and the quality of each service?"

The key to quality service is that each part, unit, or team discharges its responsibilities so well that the organization creates what some authors have called *seamless service*:

> The service in all of its dimensions and characteristics is delivered without a hitch. It is simultaneously reliable, responsive, competent, courteous, and so forth, and the facilities and tools necessary for it are all put into play smoothly and without glitches, interruptions, or delay.[29]

In essence, customers are not aware that the process of delivering the service might be complex. In fact, they do not care. "Seamless service is something all customers expect."[30]

The general systems model and open systems characteristics offer a "coarse-grained" view of effectiveness.[31] The approach taken here and in the other literature of service quality presents "a finer grained framework," one focusing on what is really important to both customers and the organization: that *the organization should be in harmony with its customers.*[32]

CUSTOMER SERVICE PLANS

According to Arnold Hirshon,

> If an organization expects to deliver high-quality services, it is important to establish a shared benchmark for the library staff and customers to judge what constitutes quality service. To do this, the library must clearly articulate and publicize its service standards.[33]

The analogy is that buyers expect the products they purchase to perform as expected for a reasonable period of time. The product's manufacturer frequently stands by product quality by offering a warranty or guarantee. For libraries, the question becomes: What are they willing to pledge or guarantee concerning the quality of their services? A service plan offers one answer.

A service plan is a promise to live up to the library's mission and goals in a way that is considerate of customers. In some ways, the plan is a vision statement of the type of service or product that the organization considers its highest priority. The plan not only articulates a philosophy of service, but also makes explicit promises to library customers. Adopting a plan is a serious undertaking in that the document, once adopted, cannot be filed and forgotten, as so many mission and goals statements have been.

Hirshon notes:

> There are certain principles that should underlie a customer service statement. The statement should be written from the perspective of the customer, not the staff. The focus should be on frequently used customer-apparent services, not on background operations that may be important for effective function, but of which customers are unaware. The statements should be clear and concise, and avoid the use of jargon. Statements should be unambiguous and phrased positively. Equivocating words or phrases, such as "generally," "usually," or "whenever possible," should be eliminated.[34]

A service plan declares:

- a commitment to high-quality programs and operations
- openness to the concept of change
- responsiveness to the needs and priorities of customers
- a commitment to providing equitable access to library resources and systems
- a willingness to work together as a team
- the availability of training and development opportunities for all staff[35]

A service plan might also contain a declaration that every staff member is accountable for doing effective and efficient work in pursuit of the provision of high-quality services, and recognize that everyone contributes to the fulfillment of the library's service mission.

The plan might contain a "commitment to excellence" that conveys a set of service promises that apply to all service areas within the library:

- respond to customer needs and priorities in a professional, timely, courteous, and helpful manner
- offer programs and services that are responsive to culturally diverse customers and foster an appreciation of diversity among staff
- offer programs and services that are responsive to physically challenged customers, and promote a better understanding of their information-gathering behavior
- maintain open lines of communication and consultation regarding library policies and programs among library management, staff, and customers

Such promises identify a diverse set of responsibilities, many of which might be equated to goals, and serve as a reminder that a library is a customer-focused system, whose whole is greater than the sum of its parts. Where the focus is on activities rather than results, performing an activity—not achieving a result—becomes the standard.

Hirshon reminds us that the service plan should contain a second part: "specific quality measures for each customer service."[36] This part corresponds to objectives and should be measurable; for example, "We will respond personally to your signed suggestions within five working days," or "We will acknowledge you immediately at any service desk and serve you within three minutes or call additional staff."[37] Such examples do not require a survey to measure the extent of compliance. Instead, staff members can check a random sample of signed suggestions and measure the turnaround and outcome (i.e., how satisfied was the customer with the response), or, at random times, they can use a stopwatch to determine how well staff members complied with the three-minute requirement. The library, however, must set the time frame, such as three minutes or five days. A key question is: How do the library's administration and staff agree on that time frame and convey the policy to customers?

On their home pages and in various reports or plans, libraries may explain their standards of (or policy for) customer service, which provide generic standards about what the customer can expect. Such standards might exist for service in general or for a specific service or department such as interlibrary loan or ask-a-librarian (e.g., sending an instant or text message to a reference librarian).[38] They may address, for instance, that customers can expect to

- be acknowledged appropriately
- be treated courteously and respectfully
- receive prompt and timely service

Such statements, however, lack sufficient precision to provide a basis for accountability or measurement. What does "prompt and timely service" truly mean? For such statements, it is impossible to compute a ratio and percentage. Instead, for text messaging, a library might ask customers to indicate their degree of satisfaction or the extent to which they are *completely* satisfied with the service or the actual experience, or to rate the library on the accuracy of the service received. Another example:

$$\frac{\text{Number of questions answered within 2 minutes of receipt}}{\text{Number of questions received in the past 24 hours}} \times 100 = \underline{\quad} \%$$

In order to determine how well promises are being met, the library staff may not need to survey customers or to rely on self-reports of staff members. Rather, both the numerators and denominators can be counted objectively. Such is the case when the measure relates to wait time for the receipt of in-house reference service and the promise is to call for additional staff if wait time exceeds five minutes. Once the staff has constructed a performance measure, at randomly selected times, someone could use a stopwatch to monitor the time and determine whether or not additional staff arrive at the desk in a *prompt* manner—however that is defined.

A FINAL WORD

"In the corporate sector, a customer service strategy has become a vital component of business success," and companies have "engineered their success through formal plans to ensure customer satisfaction."[39] There is no reason that libraries, even those in the nonprofit sector, cannot develop customer service strategies that recognize that "good service adds value to library resources."[40] These strategies must be linked to the mission, vision, philosophy, values, goals, and objectives of the library and the organization within which the library resides.

The emerging plan must be acceptable to and empower all library staff members, as customers learn which of their expectations are of highest priority to the library. The results of meeting the promises of the service plan can and should be measured on a regular basis. Customer-related performance indicators, discussed in the next chapter, provide an excellent framework for measuring the extent to which a library meets its service commitment.

A clearly defined mission will foster innovative ideas and help others understand why they need to be implemented—however much they fly in the face of tradition.[41]

Mission statements have to be operational; otherwise it's merely good intentions.[42]

Notes

1. Peter F. Drucker, *The Essential Drucker: Selections from the Management Works of Peter F. Drucker* (New York: HarperCollins, 2001), 40–41.

2. Charles R. McClure, Amy Owen, Douglas L. Zweizig, Mary J. Lynch, and Nancy A. Van House, *Planning and Role Setting for Public Libraries: A Manual of Options and Procedures*, 2nd ed. (Chicago: American Library Association, 1987).

3. Charles R. McClure and Paul T. Jaeger, *Public Libraries and Internet Service Roles: Measuring and Maximizing Internet Services* (Chicago: American Library Association, 2009).

4. Sandra Nelson, *The New Planning for Results: A Streamlined Approach* (Chicago: American Library Association, 2001), 146.

5. June Garcia and Sandra Nelson, 2007 *Public Library Service Response* (Chicago: Public Library Association, 2007) (e-book), 2.

6. McClure and Jaeger, *Public Libraries and Internet Service Roles*, 14. In chapter 7, they present new roles for public libraries.

7. Rochelle M. Borrett and Danielle P. Milam, *Welcome Stranger: Public Libraries Build the Global Village* (tool kit), 2 vols. and CD-ROM (Chicago: Urban Libraries Council, 2008).

8. Jann E. Freed and Marie R. Klugman, *Quality Principles and Practices in Higher Education: Different Questions for Different Times* (Phoenix, AZ: Oryx Press, 1997), 59.

9. Ibid. See also Triveni Kuchi, "Communicating Mission: An Analysis of Academic Library Web Sites," *Journal of Academic Librarianship* 32, no. 2 (March 2006): 148–152.

10. "Making Them Work Like Roman Orchard Slaves: A Dilbert's-eye View of the Modern Office," *Newsweek* 129, no. 19 (May 6, 1996): 50.

11. Freed and Klugman, *Quality Principles and Practices in Higher Education*, 63.

12. Betsy Sanders, *Fabled Service: Ordinary Acts, Extraordinary Outcomes* (San Diego: Pfeiffer, 1995), 69.

13. Ibid., 71.

14. Seattle Public Library, "Mission," www.spl.org/default.asp?pageID=about_mission.

15. Ibid.

16. G. Edward Evans and Sandra M. Heft, *Introduction to Technical Services*, 6th ed. (Littleton, CO: Libraries Unlimited, 1995), 4.

17. San Jose Public Library, "Message from the Dean," www.sjlibrary.org/about/sjsu/.

18. San Jose Public Library, "Our Vision," www.sjlibrary.org/about/vision/index.htm.

19. Guy A. Marco, "The Terminology of Planning: Part 1," *Library Management* 17, no. 2 (1996): 20.

20. Guy A. Marco, "The Terminology of Planning: Part 2," *Library Management* 17, no. 7 (1996): 18.

21. Ibid.

22. Sanders, *Fabled Service*, 73.

23. Ibid., 72.

24. Robert Spector, *The Nordstrom Way: The Inside Story of America's #1 Customer Service Company* (New York: Wiley, 1995).

25. Ibid., 38.

26. San Jose Public Library, "Mission, Vision, Values," www.sjlibrary.org/about/sjpl/vision.htm.

27. Seattle Public Library, "Mission."

28. Thomas A. Childers and Nancy A. Van House, *What's Good? Describing Your Public Library's Effectiveness* (Chicago: American Library Association, 1993), 14.

29. Benjamin Schneider and David E. Bowen, *Winning the Service Game* (Boston: Harvard Business School Press, 1995), 8.

30. Ibid.

31. Childers and Van House, *What's Good?* 13.

32. Ibid.

33. Arnold Hirshon, "Running with the Red Queen: Breaking New Habits to Survive in the Virtual World," in *Advances in Librarianship*, vol. 20, ed. Irene Godden (San Diego: Academic Press, 1996), 5.

34. Ibid., 7.

35. Ibid.

36. Ibid.

37. Ibid.

38. "Cell phone providers generally charge customers for sending and/or receiving text messages. These charges vary from plan to plan and from telephone provider to provider." See University of Pittsburgh, University Library System, "Ask-A-Librarian," www.library.pitt.edu/reference/.

39. Susan Wehmeyer, Dorothy Auchter, and Arnold Hirshon, "Saying What We Will Do, and Doing What We Say: Implementing a Customer Service Plan," *Journal of Academic Librarianship* 22, no. 3 (May 1996): 173.

40. Ibid.

41. Drucker, *The Essential Drucker*, 43.

42. Jeffrey A. Krames, *Inside Drucker's Brain* (New York: Portfolio, 2008), 47.

Chapter Four

Measuring and Evaluating the Components of Service Quality

The research library is defined by the services provided by the research librarian, not by the physical location of information and collections.[1]

A library and its services, much like a contoured landscape, can be viewed, evaluated, and assessed from a multitude of perspectives. Perspectives commonly referred to in the literature of library and information science (LIS) include inputs, outputs, outcomes, performance measures, effectiveness, and efficiency. Because a number of authors within and outside LIS have defined and used these terms in different ways, we believe that these terms now confuse, rather than clarify, the ways to judge and manage the results obtained from an assessment.

Thomas A. Childers and Nancy A. Van House view "effectiveness very broadly" and believe it deals with "goodness, achieving success, and the quality of performance." They define "effectiveness as impact on the consumer or user and efficiency as the economy with which 'effect' is achieved."[2] When investigating an organization's effectiveness, they suggest the following critical questions:

- To what extent does the organization achieve its goals (input, process, output, or outcome goals)?

- To what extent is the organization a *healthy operating unit?*

- To what extent can the organization capture from the external environment the *resources* needed to survive or thrive?

- To what extent are the various *stakeholders'* priorities met?[3]

Childers and Van House see effectiveness "largely [as] a point of view" and as defying a single definition. They note that "there are multiple groups to be satisfied"; a multiple constituency approach defines effectiveness in terms of meeting "the needs and expectations of strategic constituencies, such as certain user groups or leaders in the community."[4] Libraries serve different constituencies and should not treat them as a monolith. The same applies to evaluation. Although there are multiple perspectives and approaches to evaluation, no single one has gained universal or general acceptance, and no single one will accomplish everything that librarians would like. Equally as important, research in such areas as service quality and satisfaction calls for some reconceptualization and determination about the priorities for evaluation.

This chapter cannot avoid adding some descriptive terms while simultaneously presenting different ways to look at the library landscape. Our intent is to offer a broad overview of some of the possibilities for evaluation for readers to consider and to choose those most pertinent to their particular situations and priorities.

All evaluation is composed of three parts:

1. The thing to be measured

2. The means by which the measurement is taken

3. A judgment about the sufficiency or "goodness" of the thing being measured

These are analogous to a piece of cloth and a yardstick. The cloth is the *what* to measure and the yardstick represents the *how* to measure. Evaluation is a judgment about the sufficiency and suitability of the cloth for the purpose desired.

According to Carol H. Weiss, "What distinguishes evaluation research is not method or subject matter, but intent—the purpose for which it is done." Evaluation, she points out, "is intended for use," and it is an essential aspect of "organizational learning."[5] Evaluators provide evidence to distinguish between effective and ineffective programs, services, and policies, and "to plan, design, and implement new efforts that . . . [are likely to] have the desired impact on community members and their environment."[6] Still, it is critical to decide what to evaluate; among all of the choices, what is highest priority? Goodness, as Childers and Van House view it, deals with organizational effectiveness: "gathering appropriate intelligence [evidence] about the state of the library organization; and *communicating*, or transmitting, that intelligence in a useful and influential way to the library's stakeholders."[7] Similar to Weiss, we add that evaluation has an additional purpose—self-improvement. Thus, some critical questions become: Who answers the question "How good?" when it comes to the library, from what perspective, and using what information and data? What is the quality of that information and those data? Are the information and data interpreted objectively or subjectively, and do they match the question being asked?

WHAT TO MEASURE

It has been stated that almost everything can be the subject of evaluation and measurement, and, as Peter H. Rossi and Howard E. Freeman observe, "systematic evaluations of both existing and new . . . [human services] programs are now commonplace."[8] This book, however, focuses on library and information services and on the factors that reflect different dimensions of those services. Some of these factors are quite traditional and straightforward, whereas others are less common or very complex. Clearly, librarians can assess or evaluate many things about which they can make judgments relevant to planning, decision making, accountability, and documenting their accomplishments.

Library staff and other evaluators can examine the following elements:

Resources

The dollars available to pay for personnel, collections, and equipment are vitally important to any library. Without staff or collections, libraries could not maintain the functions common to all information services. Resources include not only dollars, but also the staff time, materials, services, and supplies that those dollars can buy. Increases and decreases in purchasing power can also affect resources, sometimes quite significantly.

Physical Environment

The library facility must provide a level of comfort acceptable to most customers and to staff. Lighting, temperature, humidity, noise level, seating, and cleanliness influence comfort. Personal safety is another factor necessary for comfort. Discomfort on any of these factors may negatively affect staff performance and customer satisfaction.

Team or Unit

When individuals work in teams or groups, there is interest in their effectiveness and efficiency. Effectiveness has tended to focus on results. Organizational psychologist J. Richard Hackman and management scholar Richard E. Walton see effectiveness as involving three aspects, namely the

- group's productive output (i.e., product or service) meets the standard of quantity, quality, and timeliness of the people who receive, review, and/or use that output (*results*)

- process of carrying out the work enhances the capability of members to work together interdependently in the future (*socialization*)

- groups; experience contributes to the growth and personal well-being of team members (*professional growth*).[9]

Determining how well a team performs is multidimensional. In addition to the results produced, effectiveness includes the continued socialization of team members and their growth as individuals.

Functions

These are major activities common to all libraries. G. Edward Evans and Sandra M. Heft describe nine library functions, which can be assessed separately or in some combination:

- Identification—locating pertinent items

- Selection—deciding which identified items to purchase

- Acquisition—securing the items selected

- Organization—cataloging and indexing the items for ease in retrieval

- Preparation—making the material ready for use

- Storage—placing the items in an accessible location

- Interpretation—helping customers to identify items pertinent to their information needs

- Utilization—providing equipment and space for customers to use materials in the library, and time open (hours of service)

- Dissemination—maintaining a system that allows customers to take materials from the library[10]

To their list, we add *management*, providing the coordination for all the other functions and thereby facilitating service. Management also secures the

resources and makes assessments and decisions about their deployment. At the same time, leaders set the vision that guides the provision of services and that focuses on the contents of the mission statement. Leaders also motivate staff to become change agents, assume responsibility, and accomplish the mission and stated goals.

Processes

These are the separate steps that comprise a function. For example, the preparation function involves placing the call number on the item, sometimes putting on a plastic jacket, stamping the item for library ownership, and, in some cases, pasting in slips or pockets, and/or inserting the bar code. Another example involves the process for making subscription databases accessible on-site or remotely, and how such a resource is introduced to the community. In general, the process includes determining if the purchase is made through the library, consortia, or other partnership agreements; negotiation of a contract if necessary; signing the contract; having staff become familiar with the database and perhaps preparing help guides before placing the URL in an accessible place on the library's home page; informing the community about the new acquisition (public relations), and monitoring the database's use and evaluating its value to the identified information needs.

Customers

These are the recipients of library service. Faculty members and students are the primary customers for academic libraries. By their assignments and course requirements, faculty members directly influence students' use of the library. For a public library, customers encompass community residents, those for whom the library receives outside funding (e.g., from the state), and anyone benefiting from the "open-door" policy. Customer attributes, such as age, gender, occupation, student status, location of residency, and preferences in materials or services, are examples of elements for analysis.

Community

Members of the library's community, both customers and noncustomers, can be the focus of evaluation. In essence, everyone who qualifies for borrowing privileges is a member of the library's community. Data about community members' demographic characteristics, their respective attitudes toward or perceptions of the library, and their reasons for use or nonuse can be explored.

Use

The ways that customers interact with the library constitute use. Use applies not only to circulation but also to interactions, for instance, with the OPAC, electronic resources, equipment, furniture, and staff. The focus is on activities directly generated by library customers. Traditionally gathered measures reflect the volume of business but not perceptions about the quality of the service or customers' satisfaction with the service.

Service

Service represents the sum of functions and their related processes. Typically, services have been specific, and called information service, technical service, children's service, and so forth. However, such terms focus on organizational groupings or isolated activities rather than on what the library is supposed to do for all its customers. Library customers want answers and help, not *reference service*. Or, as a former president of the hardware manufacturer Black and Decker supposedly told his employees, "Customers do not want quarter-inch drills, they want quarter-inch holes." Expressing a similar sentiment, Glenn Miller, former director of the Orange County Library System in Orlando, Florida, wrote, "If the public library is to continue to exist, then the library will necessarily have to develop and serve its customers in the ways they desire."[11]

In order to encourage librarians to think about service in the larger context, we have adopted Evans and Heft's view of service as bibliographic, physical, and intellectual access to library materials.[12] Access and assistance for gaining access are the essence of library and information services because they represent the fundamental requirements that must be fulfilled before any benefits can be derived from the library's efforts, such as support of education, intellectual enlightenment, or knowledge.

Consequence

The focus here is on what happens to customers as a result of interaction with the library. Consequences are sometimes referred to as benefits and are now treated as outcomes and impacts. A key question becomes: Have the resources and services of the academic library, for instance, contributed to the granting of a patent, the publication of a monograph or scholarly article, learning, or the achievement of a particular grade on an assignment? For public library customers, consequences might include enjoyment or enlightenment resulting from reading or viewing library material, resolving a problem with a company by being able to locate the name and address of the chief executive officer, or using recipes from the library for a party. These examples show benefits. Not all interactions with the library, however, are beneficial—sometimes, if the information cannot be obtained, the result to the customer is negative. Therefore, the results of interactions with library services are consequences, rather than benefits.

Impact

Impact relates to mission. The academic institution that funds the academic library expects the library to have a positive and continuous effect on teaching, learning, and research. Local government expects the public library to contribute positively to the educational, intellectual, and cultural life of the community, as well as to support business and economic growth through the services provided.

Summary

Most of the eleven elements identified are somewhat interrelated. In particular, resources—or the lack of them—influence many of the elements. Processes are required for the completion of functions that contribute to service. Use is a subset of service. Consequence depends on use and service.

ANOTHER CONCEPT—ASSESSMENT

Assessment is a type of evaluation that gathers evidence perhaps from the application of evaluation research. The purpose of assessment and evaluation is either accountability or service/program improvement. Both terms, as Hernon and Robert E. Dugan discuss, portray accountability and improvement differently.[13] For librarians, assessment involves partnerships between librarians and others within the organization or community to advance mutually shared goals. In the case of academic libraries, the partnership involves teaching faculty and the requirements specified in the standards set, for instance, by program and institutional accreditation organizations. For public libraries, partnerships extend to those engaged in literacy and other programs in which the library plays a role.

Assessment in this context deals with learning—the creation, implementation, and success of shared learning goals—in the context of the institutional or organizational mission. A number of academic libraries engage in some form of course evaluation or assessment, perhaps looking at how much students learned from an introduction to information literacy (or fluency). Accreditation organizations focus on a higher level of assessment—at the program or institutional level. As discussed later in the chapter, assessment deals with outcomes assessment and ascertaining how much students (and others) have learned over time—perhaps over a program of study. A program is not a collection of individual courses; rather those courses share similar learning goals, which might be framed in terms of critical thinking, problem solving, or enhanced communication skills.

HOW TO MEASURE

What library managers want to know about any of the eleven evaluation elements determines how the measurement should be made. Measurement, a tool in the assessment or evaluation process, "is the collection and analysis of objective data describing library performance on which evaluation judgments can be based. Measurement results are not in themselves 'good' or 'bad'; they simply describe what is."[14] The meaning of the data depends on the goals, objectives, and other expectations of the library and those to whom the library director reports (e.g., provost, mayor/city manager, or board of trustees).

Eleven questions outline the different *hows* of measurement and, in effect, encompass input, output, performance, and outcome measures. The questions can be used singly or in groups. In fact, some of the *hows* are calculated by using data derived from other *hows*. This list of measuring rods progresses from the highly quantitative to the highly qualitative. The focus also shifts from a library or internal perspective to a customer or external perspective. The questions are as follows:[15]

1. **How much?** Cost is the focus. Local, state, and federal government officials and academic administrators, along with tax and tuition payers, are interested in costs. Library personnel are interested in both budget allocations and costs. The amounts designated or spent for personnel, collection, purchased services, and equipment *presume*, rather than demonstrate, the quality of service. In one sense, the resources allocated, coupled with the cost of operation, indicate the importance of the library to the parent institution in higher education or local government. Resources also indicate the confidence that the parent institution has in the library's wise use of those resources to provide good service.

"How much?" can also be used to evaluate the physical facility by measuring the lighting, temperature, humidity, and noise levels, using equipment designed for such measurement and relying on acceptable standards endorsed by the respective professional associations.

2. **How many?** Such questions relate to workload. The numbers of items processed in cataloging, classifying, shelving, and checking in new items are easily counted.[16] Staff members are interested in how busy their team or unit is, as well as in how much work the organization accomplishes. Workloads are one of the most commonly used perspectives in describing libraries. Workload measures are used primarily to justify to decision makers, both those inside the library and those who fund it, the need for resources—staff, equipment, or dollars. Workload measures imply the provision of service, but tell nothing about the actual service delivered.

It is possible to calculate the number of customers that the library encounters during any specified time period. The number of registered customers in relation to the size of the library community reflects what businesses call *market penetration*. It is a credible indicator for public libraries, since registration is a conscious, voluntary action. Two important questions are (1) How many must be counted in order to generalize the results to a population? and (2) How many customers in the sample are counted more than once?

Another aspect of "How many?" is incidences of crime: It is possible to review building security, in part, by the number of incidents reported by category —that is, thefts of customer property, assaults, and so forth.

3. **How economical?** Thrift is the focus. This perspective relates *how much* a service or an activity costs in terms of staff time or materials to *how many* are processed or handled. Efficiency is inferred from the calculation. Customers might ask themselves, "How economical is it for me to borrow a book, especially one that I need for an extended period of time, as opposed to purchasing it?"

4. **How prompt?** This question assesses *speed* in completing processes or functions. Average times for the completion of reference questions, interlibrary loans, or cataloging of materials indicate how promptly the library responds. The data for this evaluation are total time (minutes, hours, days, or months) taken and the number of items completed for any one process or function. Because keeping track of times for every process of interest can be cumbersome, promptness can be calculated by using samples. In addition, promptness refers to the length of the waiting line at a circulation or reference desk.

5. **How accurate?** This is not a question much asked about libraries, with the possible exceptions being vendor profiles for approval plans, the outsourcing of services, the digitization of material in special collections, and unobtrusive testing of library reference services. Yet it can be extremely important. "How accurate?" can be asked about OPAC records, some answers to reference questions in relation to current or historical events, database content and its description, the completeness of information provided for certain factual or bibliographic inquiries, and the shelving of materials. Misshelved items and items that the OPAC designates as *in library* but that are not on the shelves are major sources of customer frustration in many libraries. Sampling is the least cumbersome way to collect data for determining *how accurate.*

6. **How responsive?** The focus here is on how well the library anticipates customer questions and problems and works to eliminate or ameliorate them. Responsiveness, which assesses such functions as management and services, can be examined by counting the number of things that management and staff anticipate customers want (e.g., photocopy machines that take coins as well as cards). Data about responsiveness are usually binary, in that the element or service is either available or not, and these service elements are also countable in terms of the numbers available.

Helpfulness is another indication of responsiveness. Customers perceive staff members who actively assist them, rather than pointing or shrugging, as responsive. Even if a customer does not obtain what was sought, her perception of staff responsiveness might be quite positive. Library failure to be responsive usually causes customer frustration.

7. **How well?** Library staff members might focus on how successfully a function or a service accomplishes its stated objectives and furthers library goals. The comparison is made against established criteria; perhaps the library tracks its performance over time. Users might characterize *how well* in terms of *how promptly, how courteously,* and *how accurately* their requests for information were handled. Customer and staff perceptions may differ sharply about how well a function or a service performs. These perceptions are subjective, but have validity because they influence perceptions and attitudes about the library.

8. **How valuable?** For a customer, measuring the experience against the cost (time, effort, or money) of going to the library instead of doing something else is an assessment of value; for instance, was the trip worth the effort? Tefko Saracevic and Paul B. Kantor examine value in the context of "value-in-use of library and information services based on user assessments."[17] Value, therefore, looks at the customer and how that person approaches a library or one of its services. Among other things, this approach addresses such consequences as (1) the "reasons why a customer came to the library or used the given library service at this time"; (2) "what the customer got out of the use; what benefits did she or he receive"; (3) "what would a customer do otherwise, if the service were not available at that library"; and (4) "elaboration on why did the customer give a particular score on the Likert scales."[18]

Another indication of value is willingness to pay for the service. How frequently that service is used indicates the *value* that customers place on it. Individuals who make decisions about budgets also have their own impressions about which library elements are valuable and which are not. "Value for money" is becoming a commonly heard statement among public librarians. (For a list of readings, see figure 4.1.) The Denver Public Library, for instance, has a "library value calculator" that enables taxpayers to determine "for every $1.00 in taxes you spend on the Denver Public Library, how much do you receive in return?" A note specifies the sources upon which the calculations are made (see http://denverlibrary.org/news/dplnews/roi_calculator.html as well as Maine State Library's Library Use Value Calculator, www.maine.gov/msl/services/calculator.htm).[19]

Some local government officials think that popular fiction should not be provided at taxpayer expense, and others consider the library to be an important cultural asset. Library staff has ideas about the value of certain functions that may or may not match those of most external library customers. Service priorities among the library's customers ought to be a major consideration.

FIGURE 4.1

READINGS ON PUBLIC LIBRARY VALUE

Aabø, Svanhild. "The Value of Public Libraries," presented at World Library and Information Congress: 71st IFLA General Conference and Council, "Libraries—A Voyage of Discovery," August 14–18, 2005. Oslo, Norway. www.ifla.org/IV/ifla71/papers/119e-Aabo.pdf.

Barron, Daniel D., Robert V. Williams, Stephen Bajjaly, Jennifer Arns, and Steven Wilson. *The Economic Impact of Public Libraries on South Carolina*. Columbia, SC: University of South Carolina, School of Library and Information Science, 2005. www.libsci.sc.edu/SCEIS/final%20report%2026%20january.pdf.

Berk and Associates. *The Seattle Public Library Central Library: Economic Benefits Assessment*. Prepared for the Seattle Public Library Foundation, 2005. www.spl.org/pdfs/SPLCentral_Library_Economic_Impacts.pdf.

British Library. *Measuring Our Value*. London, British Library, 2004. www.bl.uk/pdf/measuring.pdf.

Elliott, Donald S., Glen E. Holt, Sterling W. Hayden, and Leslie E. Holt. *Measuring Your Library's Value: How to Do a Cost-Benefit Analysis for Your Public Library*. Chicago: American Library Association, 2007.

Fitch, Leslie, and Jody Warner. "Dividends: The Value of Public Libraries in Canada." *Australasian Public Libraries and Information Services,* 12, no. 1 (1999): 4–24.

Griffiths, José-Marie, Donald W. King, Christinger Tomer, Thomas Lynch, and Julie Harrington. "Taxpayer Return on Investment" in *Public Libraries* (funded under the provisions of the Library Services and Technology Act, from the Institute of Museum and Library Services, administered by the Florida Department of State, State Library and Archives of Florida, 2004). http://dlis.dos.state.fl.us/bld/roi/pdfs/ROISummaryReport.pdf.

He, Leifang, Binu Chaudhuri, and Deborah Juterbock. "Creating and Measuring Value in a Corporate Library." *Information Outlook* 13, no. 2 (March 2009): 13–16.

Holt, Glen E. "On Becoming Essential: An Agenda for Quality in Twenty-First Century Public Libraries." *Library Trends* 44, no. 3 (1996): 545–571. (See the entire issue.)

Holt, Glen E., and Donald Elliot. "Proving Your Library's Worth: A Test Case." *Library Journal* 123, no. 18 (1998): 42–44.

Holt, Glen E., and Donald Elliott. "Measuring Outcomes: Applying Cost-Benefit Analysis to Middlesized and Small Public Libraries." *Library Trends* 51, no. 3 (2003): 424–440. (See the entire issue.)

Holt, G. E., Donald Elliott, and Amonia Moore. *Placing a Value on Public Library Services*. www.slpl.lib.mo.us/libsrc/restoc.htm.

Imholz, Susan, and Jennifer Arns. "Worth Their Weight: An Assessment of the Evolving Field of Library Valuation." *Public Library Quarterly* 26, nos. 3–4 (2007): 31–48.

McClure, Charles R., Bruce Fraser, Timothy Nelson, and Jane Robins. *Economic Benefits and Impacts from Public Libraries in the State of Florida* (Final report to the State of Florida, Division of Library and Information Services). Tallahassee, FL: Florida State University Information. Use Management and Policy Institute. http://dlis.dos.state.fl.us/bld/Research_Office/final-report.pdf.

Missingham, Roxanne. "Libraries and Economic Value: A Review of Recent Studies." *Performance Measurement and Metrics* 6, no. 3 (2005): 142–158.

Morris, Anne, John Sumsion, and Margaret Hawkins. "Economic Value of Public Libraries in the UK." *Libri* 52, no. 2 (2002): 78–87.

San Francisco Public Library. *Providing for Knowledge, Growth, and Prosperity: A Benefit Study of the San Francisco Public Library,* http://sfpl.lib.ca.us/news/berkstudy.htm.

(cont.)

FIGURE 4.1 (cont.)

Urban Libraries Council. *Making Cities Stronger: Public Library Contributions to Local Economic Development.* www.urbanlibraries.org/storelistitem.cfm?itemnumber=1.

Wisconsin Department of Public Instruction. *Economic Impact of Public Libraries,* http://dpi.wi.gov/pld/econimpact.html. This site provides "links to various studies designed to measure the economic impact or taxpayer return-on-investment for public libraries, as well as resources for conducting local studies."

Note: See also "Bibliography of Return on Investment (ROI) Resources," which "was assembled by LTLS Consultants, Michelle Ralston, Pat Boze, and other LTLS staff using both a list that was compiled by Don Reynolds, and ALA's Return on Investment website." Available at www.ltls.org/features/2009-10roibib.html; Stephen Abram, *Stephen's Lighthouse,* http://scanblog .blogspot.com/2009/02/library-roi-brief-webliography.html; American Library Association, "Articles and Studies Related to Library Value (Return on Investment)," www.ala.org/ala/research/librarystats/roi/index.cfm.

Within the business community, value has another meaning, one that might be useful to a public library if members of the board of trustees or city council, or the mayor or city manager, are businesspersons. There might be a desire to increase "the value that technology provides to the business while maximizing IT [information technology] effectiveness and efficiency."[20] Value, as a result, relates to spending on technology and to such questions as "What value are we getting for our money? Are we spending the right amount on technology? Where is the money going?"[21]

9. **How reliable?** Although librarians would like to believe that all customers leave the library with the information or materials they came to obtain, that does not always occur. Although customers know this, they form impressions about how consistently a library's service provides what they want in terms of physical and intellectual access to items or subjects desired. Dependability in terms of bibliographic, physical, and intellectual access is a major component of reliability. Reliability has another dimension: the consistency of treatment received by customers. Do they receive similar treatment over time and from different members of the staff?

10. **How courteous?** Service quality has three parts: expectations for the ideal service, the service actually delivered, and the transaction between the customer and the service organization. When the transaction involves staff members, then the personal interaction becomes important. If the transaction is frustrating or unpleasant, the customer views it negatively. The typical experience for customers becomes, in their minds, the standard of performance for the library.

11. **How satisfied?** "Consumer researchers have moved from the *literal* meaning of fulfillment or satisfaction and now pursue the concept as the consumer [or customer] experiences and describes it."[22] The issue of satisfaction is linked to the concept of service quality and the ever-growing literature on that topic. The focus of service quality is on the match between customer expectations and the service delivered. Expectations, however, have to be confined to those that the library is prepared to meet. Although customers might like to order library materials as they order pizzas for home delivery, such service is infrequently offered; some libraries, however, do provide home or office delivery of books and articles.

Users form perceptions and attitudes about service quality based on their experiences with the library's materials, services, staff, and physical environment, or on the stories told about transactions with the library by people they trust.

Indicators of satisfaction include the willingness to return or to use a service repeatedly, to recommend a service to others, to support a service, or to advocate its support to others. Furthermore, *completely satisfied* customers are much more likely to repeat their business than are those who are *merely satisfied.* Thus, a measure of willingness to return might distinguish between those *completely satisfied* and those displaying lesser degrees of satisfaction.

Perhaps one of the most important of all the questions from a customer perspective is the last one, "How satisfied?" However, satisfaction is not an end unto itself. Rather, the resolution of an information need or the question of "*How valuable?*" become more important. Undoubtedly, aspects of the other questions contribute to meeting customer expectations and to making library customers satisfied and willing to use a service or the library again. The goal is not merely to meet their expectations; it is to exceed them—forming customer loyalty or individuals who constantly recommend the library and its services to friends, colleagues, and acquaintances.

MORE ON "HOW WELL?"

"How well?" might also be defined in terms of outcomes assessment, which involves student and student learning outcomes. Student or similar outcomes are actually outputs; they report the number of people who attended a session on information literacy or a workshop on the use of technology in the public library. Student learning outcomes focus on impact assessment and what students are expected to know and be able to do by the time they graduate. For a public library engaged in literacy education, what are the learning goals and what have participants actually learned? The evidence gathered to answer this question provides a basis to view and improve learning. (Figure 3.1 identifies the full array of services responses from which public libraries can select areas to develop outcomes.)

Rhea Joyce Rubin views outcomes as part of a progression from inputs and outputs.[23] In fact, outcomes, especially those involving student learning outcomes, may bypass outputs and proceed directly from inputs to outcomes. This is true where accreditation organizations are unwilling to recognize customer or student satisfaction as a factor contributing to learning.

THE RANGE OF OPTIONS FOR EVALUATION

Figure 4.2, which outlines the elements pertinent for each of the eleven "How . . . ?" questions, serves as a reminder that there is no "one-stop shopping" for evaluation or assessment. Depending on what they want to know, library managers have choices. Furthermore, some of the questions focus more on the organization and its perceptions about the services offered, whereas others directly take customer perspectives into account and do not infer customer satisfaction. Viewed from another perspective, does the library assume it knows what customers want and need, as well as knowing what their preferences are, or does it ascertain the information directly from the customers and respond accordingly? Needs, wants, preferences, and satisfaction represent different perspectives and elements. It merits repeating that no one-stop approach encompasses all these perspectives.

WHO DECIDES WHAT IS IMPORTANT?

A number of stakeholders, besides the staff and library administrators, have an interest in the library. These include customers, decision makers who oversee and fund the library, and the community at large, whether the library is academic or public. Taxpayers and those who pay tuition fees have a stake even though they may never enter the library.

Library staff can best address issues related to economy, workload, and volume of use, since these matters are of considerable interest to them. Customers, however, determine issues of consequences, expectations, and satisfaction. Both the library and its customers have an interest in and opinions about issues relating to responsiveness, value, and reliability; these may not be congruent. The library and the customers also may not have the same opinions about the qualities of promptness, accuracy, and courtesy. Each has a different perspective, requirements, and expectations.

In 2002, the *Journal of Academic Librarianship* published a paper in which Robert E. Dugan and Hernon attempted to broaden the discussion of relevant measures for academic and other types of libraries. They commented:

> Libraries tend to view data collection from one of three distinct perspectives: the user in the life of the library, the user and the library in the life of the institution, and the library and institution in the life of the user. Each perspective has its proponents and provides useful information to enhance institutional effectiveness. Clearly, inputs and outputs do not reflect all three perspectives, and the profession needs to develop knowledge, measures, and data-collection techniques that cut across perspectives. The result is a more complete view of a "jigsaw" puzzle entitled "the library as a partner and contributor to advancement of the institutional mission."[24]

Viewing Library Metrics from Different Perspectives looks at those three perspectives while adding a fourth: the library and the institution in the life of stakeholders (e.g., parents of students, the executive and legislative branches of government, accreditation organizations, and donors and others contributing funds to support libraries).[25] As academic libraries collaborate with a wide assortment of campus partners, be they teaching faculty or units that operate complementary services (e.g., those associated with a campus learning commons), there are increased opportunities to expand the range of measures—input, process, output, and outcome—that might be compiled, reported, and used for purposes of accountability and improvement in the educational experience and the quality of services provided to the community. Clearly, the eleven questions apply to evaluation and assessment and can be examined from different perspectives.

FIGURE 4.2

COMPONENTS OF THE "HOW . . . ?" QUESTIONS: THE LIBRARY AND CUSTOMER PERSPECTIVE

LIBRARY CONTROL

How much?	How many?	How economical	How prompt?
Magnitude Percentage of change last year Percentage of overall change Costs	Magnitude Change	Resources used Units processed	Cycle times Turnaround time Anticipatory

LIBRARY AND CUSTOMERS DECIDE

How valuable?	How reliable?	How accurate?	How well?
Effort expended Cost Benefit obtained	Dependability Access Accuracy Currency	Completeness Comprehensiveness	Accuracy Promptness Courtesy Expertise

CUSTOMERS DECIDE

How courteous?	How responsive?	How satisfied?
Attentive Welcoming	Anticipatory Helpful Empathetic	Expectations met Materials obtained Personal interaction Ease of use Equipment used Environment Comfort Willingness to return/ use again

---

THE Q WORDS: QUANTITY AND QUALITY

Because libraries engage in many activities that can be easily counted, librarians have tended to focus on *quantities* of use as indicators of the "goodness" of the service. Even though the prevailing professional philosophy asserts that interaction with library materials (i.e., reading) has a beneficial effect upon people, the emphasis has remained on quantity. Nevertheless, quantity alone is seldom of concern to customers. Rather, they judge the library by how well it meets their particular expectations. Customer expectations can be quite different from those of the librarians. It is becoming increasingly important to have measures that reflect some aspects of quality—that is, service quality—and indicate how customers respond to services or functions.

A common concern is the value that different units provide to the sponsoring institution. Many special libraries are increasingly concerned with proving their value to avoid closure or outsourcing. Now, questions about value are being raised in higher education and local government. Some measures need to be adopted solely for the library that place it within the broader context of issues—beyond cost—important to the parent organization. Unlike measures for resources or use, they need to examine other facets of the picture, those of primary concern to the parent institution grappling with determining and demonstrating quality. In the case of academic libraries, the focus might be on the quality of teaching and learning and the role of the library in enhancing critical thinking, information literacy, or the educational agenda of classroom faculty, or in assisting the institution in retaining students—avoiding their transfer to other institutions and the consequent loss of revenue (student outcomes and student learning outcomes).

Figure 4.3 offers examples of measures that are of considerable interest to both the academic library and the institution's administrators, as well as an example of a measure for public libraries. These examples reflect important issues. Clearly, there is a need for indicators relating to customer loyalty (translated into donations and fund-raising, and the amount of money received), student retention, and student learning. Some of these issues (e.g., loyalty) have a direct relationship to the library and can provide a highly visible means for demonstrating the value of the library to the overall institution. (See chapters 9 and 12.)

Given the amount of time that a number of academic and public library directors devote to fundraising, it would seem that more library services might be patterned after the private sector and encourage customer loyalty, willingness to return or reuse, and satisfaction. Such a focus on quality might have some ultimate relationship to donations and financial support for the library after students graduate.

Judgments about the library may vary among and within stakeholder groups, and certain interests important to one may conflict with the interests of another. For staff, those interests include job security and salary issues. For decision makers, the interests may be staying well within the budget or cutting costs, including those related to personnel. Customers want their service expectations to be met, while taxpayers and those who write tuition checks prefer that costs either do not increase or, if they must, do so minimally. Figure 4.4 shows the level of interest each stakeholder group has in some of the "How . . . ?" questions. Note that the figure moves from quantitative questions on the left to qualitative questions on the right. The qualitative assessments are based on opinions, experiences, and expectations.

Both the library and its customers should be interested in the intersection between "How well?" and "How valuable?" The library has some control over "How well?" but customers really decide about service performance and its value.

RELATING *WHAT* TO MEASURE WITH *HOW* TO MEASURE

It is important that library managers understand the ways that the elements in the things to measure can relate to the different *hows* of measurement. Figure 4.5 shows these relationships. It is not necessary to answer all the "How . . . ?" questions related to any particular thing that can be measured.

Some, indeed many, library activities can be evaluated in several ways and from different perspectives. Information literacy, for example, can be evaluated in terms of the number of sessions offered ("How many?"), the number of students attending ("How many?"), and cost per session and per student ("How economical?"). The library might evaluate value by comments from faculty about the success of that instruction in their classes or by an increase in the number of faculty members requesting similar instruction for their stu-

dents. Faculty might determine "How well?" by an increase in the number of references to scholarly articles or works cited in students' papers or by a perceived improvement in the quality of completed assignments. For students, the grade achieved from the assignment completed with the information literacy instruction influences the perception of value. From the vantage point of assessment, "How well?" might deal with programs of study and the extent to which students' knowledge, skills, and abilities improve throughout the duration of the program. (See figure 4.6 for a partial depiction of

FIGURE 4.3

MEASURES OF INTEREST TO ACADEMIC LIBRARIES AND CENTRAL ADMINISTRATION

1. Number of graduates donating money for the library in relation to the total number of graduates. (The number of graduates must reflect those for whom the institution has current addresses and those who, of course, are still alive.)
2. Amount of donations for the library in relation to total donations (not grants) for parent institution.
3. Number of graduating students who are active library borrowers in relation to number enrolled.
4. Number of graduating seniors who are accepted by the graduate program of first choice in relation to the number of graduating seniors wanting to attend graduate school. (Regarding this measure, the library could factor in the number who were extensive library borrowers.)
5. Number of community users of the library who are "completely satisfied" with the library and its services in relation to the number expressing lesser degrees of satisfaction.
6. Ratio of gifts from Friends' groups to those of the parent institution, or the ratio of alumni gifts to library versus alumni gifts to parent institution.

Note: For public libraries, a good measure is the number of borrowers who do not live in the service area. Here the county or state pays the libraries to issue cards to nonresidents. Libraries can tell how many nonresidents have cards by the amount of money collected.

evaluation and assessment.) Faculty, perhaps in partnership with librarians, might view the information literacy competencies of the Association of College and Research Libraries in terms of a scoring rubric that reflects a progression of skills and abilities from the novice to the mastery stages.[26]

COMPARED TO WHAT?

Absolute numbers—"How much?" or "How many?"—represent data collected by librarians in many categories, such as circulation, serials received, and expenditures for certain items. The "How much?" or "How many?" question is usually followed by a desire for a comparison that places the numbers in some context and makes them more meaningful. The comparison can be against past years, peer institutions, or past procedures, or it can be on a per capita basis.

Although absolute numbers can be compared, usually the magnitude of the numbers is greater than most people can comprehend. A simple way to understand the data is to use *rankings*, comparing such similar factors as budget, staff, collections, or subsets of each of these. Another way to simplify understanding is to compare one year's data with those of another—perhaps the percentage of increase or decrease in local funding for each library compared with the previous year. Percentage measurement requires two absolute numbers, because one is dependent on the other. *Ratios*, which are simply variants of percentages, are another means of making numbers more relevant.

Figure 4.7 identifies thirty ratios that primarily reflect resources. *Input measures* indicate what libraries "put in" to the system. The percentages relating expenditures on staff, serials, library materials, binding, and operations to the total spent are slices in a pie called expenditures. A number of the measures reflect capacity or, regarding service, "How much?" or "How many?" There is no indication of the quality of any aspect of service, with the exception of the percent of customer satisfaction. In the absence of profit or other financial indicators, library administration may view the ability to obtain resources as an indicator of success.

SOME SOURCES OF NUMBERS
Academic Libraries

The Council for Aid to Education (CAE) has the Voluntary Support of Education (VSE) survey, which covers private giving to higher education and private

K–12, "consistently capturing about 85 percent of the total voluntary support to colleges and universities in the United States." Conducted online, it provides comparative data with CAE's VSE Data Miner service, a web-based service for subscribers, predominantly schools, colleges, and universities, to gain access to three hundred data variables about private giving collected over the past decade. The latest report, for the 2008 fiscal year, "demonstrated that private contributions to America's higher education institutions increased by 6.2 percent to $31.6 billion. The level of giving represents an increase in contributions for current operations and also for capital purposes, such as endowments and buildings."[27]

The International Archive of Education Data (IAED) is a project formerly sponsored by the National Center for Education Statistics (NCES), the primary federal entity for collecting and analyzing data related to education in the United States and other nations. The IAED

> acquires, processes, documents, and disseminates data collected by national, state or provincial, local, and private organizations, pertaining to all levels of education in countries for which data can be made available. Data will encompass the "inputs" to education (funding, personnel, teaching resources, facilities, teacher and student preparation, etc.), the variety of processes by which teaching and learning occur, and the "outputs" of education (graduation and matriculation rates, drop-out rates, test scores, job placements, life histories, life assessments, etc.).[28]

The NCES also has the Integrated Postsecondary Education Data System (IPEDs), which gathers and reports data "in areas including enrollments, program completions, graduation rates, faculty, staff, finances, institutional prices, and student financial aid. These data are made available on our website to students, researchers and others." Through its College Navigator, "college students, prospective students, and their parents understand the differences between colleges and how much it costs to attend college" by data related to

- Admissions
- Room and board charges
- Graduation rates
- Accreditation status
- Student financial aid awarded
- Enrollment and completions

An individual can select and compare colleges and universities by location, programs, and degree offerings.[29]

The Association of College and Research Libraries provides summary data in print and electronic form from more than eleven hundred institutions from its annual *Academic Library Trends and Statistics* (www.acrl.org/ala/mgrps/divs/acrl/publications/trends/index.cfm). (See chapter 11.) Published annually since 1961–1962, the Association of Research Libraries (ARL) provides *ARL Statistics*, a series of annual publications that describe the collections, expenditures, staffing, and service activities for ARL member libraries.[30]

Association of Research Libraries

Historically ARL has relied on descriptive data, largely expressed in terms of inputs, for drawing comparisons and tracking trends of investment in member libraries. Realizing that such data have limitations (neither fully reflect their activities and services nor their impact on the communities they serve), ARL is exploring ways to generate supplementary data. In 1999, the ARL New Measures Initiative emerged as a way to indicate how well research libraries meet institutional and community information needs and how often their resources and services are used. The E-Metrics Project offers a set of inputs and outputs to describe electronic services and resources in member libraries. Other initiatives, such as one related to LibQUAL+ (see chapter 11), expand coverage of outputs; service quality and satisfaction are outputs and not widely accepted as conveying outcomes or the impact of services on the communities served. Still, some of the emerging measures deal with cost-benefit or cost-effectiveness, and the value of such measures should not be minimized.

Public Libraries

The Public Library Data Service Statistical Report, a project of the Public Library Association, published annually since 1988, provides data from more than eight hundred public libraries across the United States and Canada on finances, library resources, annual use figures, and technology. In addition, each year's edition contains a special survey highlighting statistics on one service area or topic (www.pla.org/ala/mgrps/divs/pla/plapublications/pldsstatreport/index.cfm).

NCES began a nationwide library statistics program in 1989 that included the Public Library Survey. In 2007, that survey, together with the State Library Agencies Survey, was moved to the Institute of Museum and Library Services (IMLS). IMLS collects data from more than nine thousand public libraries (http://harvester.census.gov/imls/publib.asp). Data are available for individual public libraries and are aggregated to state and national levels.[31]

It merits mention that the Information Use Management and Policy Institute, Florida State University, under the direction of Charles R. McClure, conducts a number of relevant surveys about public library use of the Internet.

When any data involve rankings, the comparison with peer institutions has been the traditional way that libraries have shown their "goodness" and how they keep up with peers or competitors.

FIGURE 4.4

STAKEHOLDER INTEREST IN CERTAIN QUESTIONS ABOUT THE LIBRARY

Stakeholder Group	How Much?	How Economical?	How Well?	How Valuable?	How Satisfied?
Library Staff	High	High	High	High	High
Customers	Low	Low	High	High	High
Decision Makers	High	Medium	Medium	Medium	Medium
Community	Medium	Medium	Low	Low	Low

FIGURE 4.5
RELATING *WHAT* TO MEASURE WITH *HOW* TO MEASURE

| Question | WHAT TO MEASURE | | | | | | | | | | |
| | Internal Perspective | | | | | External Perspective | | | | | |
	Resources	Physical	Team/Unit	Process	Function	Customer	Use	Service	Consequences	Community	Impact
How much?	x	x	x							x	
How many?	x	x	x	x	x	x	x			x	
How economical?			x	x							
How prompt?			x	x							
How accurate?			x	x							
How responsive?			x		x		x	x			
How well?			x	x	x		x	x	x	x	x
How valuable?			x	x	x		x	x	x	x	
How reliable?						x	x	x			
How courteous?						x		x			
How satisfied?									x		x

COUNTER

Launched in March 2002, COUNTER (Counting Online Usage of Networked Electronic Resources) is an international initiative involving librarians, publishers, and intermediaries that sets standards for the facilitation of the recording and reporting of online usage statistics. The first COUNTER Code of Practice, covering online journals and databases, was published in 2003. In 2006, the Code was extended to online books and reference works.[32] This project has helped to create a set of criteria by which vendors can be designated as COUNTER-compliant and thus acknowledge accountability for the performance of their product. The goal is to let librarians compare performance among competing vendors. Still, the focus is on input and output metrics. (See chapter 9.)

USING THE INFORMATION ABOUT WHAT AND HOW

Change, uncertainty, and complexity have been endemic over the past twenty years and two economic recessions. Only the most nimble organizations have prospered. In addition to their ability to adapt to the changing climate, these organizations are aware of the need to concentrate on continuous quality improvement in products and/or services. Libraries have certainly concentrated on information technology and electronic resources. Perhaps it is time to focus on other areas needing improvement. This can be done through practices including benchmarking and reviewing best practices. An advantage of engaging in such endeavors is that librarians can determine what works well in their library and elsewhere, and incorporate the findings into changing the organizational culture to better meet the stated mission and goals. The library should continue to challenge itself to meet the changing expectations of its customers.

Benchmarking

Continuous quality improvement requires that organizations address such questions as

- Are we performing better than we did in the past?
- Are we performing as well as, or better than, other units on campus or in local government?
- Are we performing better than our competitors?

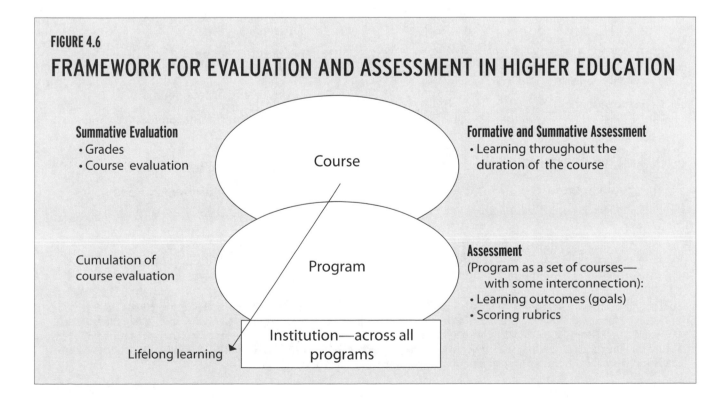

FIGURE 4.6

FRAMEWORK FOR EVALUATION AND ASSESSMENT IN HIGHER EDUCATION

Summative Evaluation
- Grades
- Course evaluation

Course

Formative and Summative Assessment
- Learning throughout the duration of the course

Cumulation of course evaluation

Program

Assessment
(Program as a set of courses— with some interconnection):
- Learning outcomes (goals)
- Scoring rubrics

Lifelong learning

Institution—across all programs

- Are there other libraries or organizations that are performing well and from which we can learn?

These questions are not new to the thoughtful library manager. The process of gathering information to make such types of comparisons has, however, acquired a trendy name: benchmarking. Benchmarking comparisons are usually based on time, cost, and quality as measured against previous performance, others in the organization or profession, or the best in that class. These focuses are called: *internal, competitive,* and *functional* or *comparative.*

Internal Benchmarking

The most common way to begin is with internal benchmarking done within the library. New processes can be compared with old; closely related teams or

---

FIGURE 4.7

SELECTED NUMBERS, PERCENTAGES, AND RATIOS

GENERAL

Percentage of institutional dollars allocated to the library

COLLECTIONS

Number of electronic books

Number of electronic full-text journals

Cost of electronic full-text journals

Number citations/abstracts accessed

Library expenditures for bibliographic utilities, networks, and consortia

Size of library digital collection (e.g., title count)

LIBRARY AS A PLACE

Visits per opening hour

Seat occupancy rate

Shelving accuracy rate

INTERNAL OPERATIONS

Acquisition speed

STAFF

Expenditure on staff per user

Expenditure for training per staff member

USE, INCLUDING VIRTUAL VISITS

Peak use (by day of week)

Number of log-ins

Number of turn-aways

Number of electronic reference transactions

Number of log-ins (sessions) to electronic databases

Number of customer visits to the library's website or catalog from outside the library premises without regard to the number of pages viewed

Percentage of annual e-reference transactions to total reference transactions

Number of virtual library visits out of all library visits

Downloads (average) per e-journal

Percent of customer satisfaction

Visits per capita

Attendance at training sessions per capita

Full-text article requests (by month and journal)

Total searches and sessions (by month and database)

Sources: Association of Research Libraries, *Measures for Electronic Resources (E-metrics),* 3 parts; Roswitha Poll and Peter te Boekhorst, *Measuring Quality: Performance Measurement in Libraries,* 2nd rev. ed. (Munich, Germany: Saur, 2007); Oliver Persch, "Project COUNTER and SUSHI: An Overview" (Philadelphia, PA: NFAIS Forum: Online Usage Statistics: Current Status and Future Directions, 2006), www.niso.org/workrooms/sushi/info/NFAIS-COUNTER-SUSHI.ppt#17; WilsonWeb, "Enhanced Usage Statistics," www.hwwilson.com/Documentation/WilsonWeb/usagestats.htm.

units using common or shared performance parameters can be matched. Teams divided by subject, whose other duties are similar, could be compared according to how many, how much, how economical, how prompt, how responsive, and/or how well. The best-performing team or unit sets the benchmark (standard) for the others to attain. Relying only on internal analysis, however, reinforces an inward focus that can engender complacency or set up rivalries within the organization that become counterproductive.

Competitive Benchmarking

Competitive benchmarking generally focuses on direct (so-called peer libraries and institutions) or indirect (related organizations, such as bookstores) competitors. Historically, comparisons involved resources and workload measures. Externally oriented benchmarking, especially with a best-in-class organization, makes staff aware of improvements that are many times greater than they would have thought possible. Nonetheless, before embarking on such benchmarking, it is essential to determine the degree of comparability—comparing like, not unlike, items.

Functional or Comparative Benchmarking

Benchmarking might also be functional—targeted at organizations in other fields to see how a particular function is carried out—or generic—going beyond a particular function and identifying the ways in which other organizations, libraries or otherwise, operate. For example, Xerox had a problem with its warehousing operations that caused customer dissatisfaction. For solutions, Xerox managers looked to L. L. Bean, a retail company that sells clothing by mail. L. L. Bean is noted for its high customer satisfaction, which largely depends on the efficiency and effectiveness of its warehousing operation. Many of their techniques were applicable to Xerox's situation.[33]

Areas of Benchmarking

Benchmarking can be undertaken in almost any area of organizational endeavor. The basic requirements are that key performance variables be identified, measured, analyzed, and compared to provide a basis for planned performance improvement. As well, benchmarking can be applied internally to reflect change over time and changes in processes in order to determine whether or not the services to customers are improving. Businesses commonly identify their core services—those expected to provide high degrees of customer satisfaction—and set benchmarks for other services that they intend to develop as core services. Thus, they target the areas to benchmark as they improve the quality of service provided. The key is to be clear about the organization's needs and the areas and processes to improve. The general aim should be to keep it simple by concentrating on a few chosen measures and following through on needed changes.

Using internal benchmarking, library managers, together with staff, can set the baseline for service performance as reflected through a particular measure—for example, the time to respond to an information request sent via e-mail. Initially, performance might be set at "75 percent of all e-mail reference questions will be answered within twenty-four hours"; once that target has been achieved consistently, the expectation level might be raised.

Benchmarking that is done well has been characterized as a positive process that emphasizes excellence in performance, not simply improvement. As a first step, however, the key is to improve, and continue to do so, rather than to be satisfied with the status quo. Should resources decline, the approach is to look for ways to do the right things smarter, rather than to continue routine processes that contribute little to service quality or customer satisfaction. A caution about internal benchmarking is necessary: library managers should first ask if a process needs to be done at all or if every step is necessary. Clearly, the value of such benchmarking and the instances in which it is used must be reviewed.

Figure 4.8 identifies the steps in benchmarking. A key is to set targets and measure achievement against them. Based on the data gathered, library managers

---

FIGURE 4.8

STEPS IN BENCHMARKING

1. Select activity for benchmarking.
2. Determine what to compare (internal or external).
3. Select the measure and the target to achieve.
4. Determine how to gather the data—quantitative and/or qualitative.
5. Collect, analyze, and interpret the data.
6. Implement change (in context of goals, objectives, or other expectations).
7. Revisit the expectations and decide whether to set new targets.
8. Revisit steps 5 through 7.

can introduce change as needed and set new targets to improve service. They should not, however, expect staff simply to work harder!

Best Practices

The U.S. General Accounting Office, now called the Government Accountability Office, has viewed best practices in terms of "best management practices," which refers to the processes, practices, and systems identified in public and private organizations that performed exceptionally well and are widely recognized as improving their organization's performance and efficiency in specific areas. Further, "successfully identifying and applying best practices can reduce business expenses and improve organizational efficiency."[34]

Anne Wilson and Leeanne Pitman note that best practices and quality are not used synonymously; however, they note that best practices emerge in

> the pursuit of world class performance. It is the way in which the most successful organisations manage and organise their operations. It is a moving target. As the leading organisations continue to improve the "best practice" goalposts are constantly moving. The concept of continuous improvement is integral to the achievement of best practice.[35]

Best practices are beneficial to learning organizations that seek proven solutions that have application to them.[36] There are best practice guidelines in library and information science for areas such as Web 2.0 applications and digital collection.

A QUESTION OF BALANCE

The drive to cut costs and obtain "value for money," especially during economic recessions, is as pervasive in higher education and government as it is in large corporations. Reductions of resources have a systemic effect on an organization—the goodness or badness of the effect has to be acknowledged and considered in the light of its impact on the library's quality and ability to fulfill its mission. In times of fiscal stringency, it is common for libraries to cut hours of service. In response to a city budget crisis, Phoenix Public Library, for instance, cut Sunday hours in all but a few of its branches and main facility. This is an inconvenience to customers who can only come on Sundays. Another cost-cutting measure that might seem effective is to cancel paper copies of serials that

are also available online. This assumes that all customers are computer literate—which is still not true in a public library, at least. Canceling paper copies prevents customers from browsing through an issue or back issues.

QUALITATIVE ANALYSIS: THE MISSING PORTION OF THE PICTURE

Most measures tell only a part of the story; that part may involve a minor story line or be unimportant in meeting the organization's mission. Rankings, percentages, and ratios are useful for things that are countable, but they all need some context to make the meaning more understandable. As well, certain measures might be used in combination. Not everything worth knowing can be counted precisely and reduced to a rank, percentage, or ratio; many aspects of information service are intangible, and must be evaluated in other ways. Herein is the value of qualitative analysis. Satisfaction, like service quality, is subjective, and certain attitudes or opinions cannot necessarily be reduced meaningfully to a quantitative measure.

No local government ever agreed to fund a public library merely to circulate books. The intent was always something more edifying, and the edifying part was used to convince local officials that the library would be a community asset. Even golf courses and swimming pools are established and maintained partly because of the health benefits—fresh air and exercise—accruing to golfers and swimmers. The expectation for the library has been, and continues to be, the *opportunity* for education and self-improvement as well as the economic benefits both to individuals and to the community derived from an educated, well-informed, and employed citizenry.

Taxpayers who never use the library have been willing to fund libraries for the same reasons, and also for the *opportunity* of possible benefits to their children and grandchildren. Clearly, something more than the mere number of items circulated is expected.

Such perspectives are important, but they underscore that *impact* is separate from the other types of evaluations. Impacts are important to the sponsoring organization because they relate to the purpose (mission) of the library and to the direct or indirect effects or consequences resulting from achieving program or service goals and objectives. Impacts, which are outside the scope of this book, are extremely difficult to measure.

WHAT NOW?

Counting and measuring are useful, but another element is needed to assess service quality—*judgment*. It is necessary, but insufficient, to know that a library has 60 percent of the items that customers need and that it takes three weeks for a book loaned by another library to arrive. The real question should be: Is such performance acceptable to both the library and the customer?

Because there are no universally accepted standards or norms for performance on any aspect of library processes, functions, or service, senior staff in each library has to decide on the acceptable level of performance. The next step is to communicate the standard to the staff whose work directly influences performance. Unless these steps to set standards are taken, each staff member determines his own standard for acceptable service. That standard may be unacceptable or insufficient to customers.

It is neither necessary nor desirable to set standards for every process, function, or service all at once, or even within a short period of time. Indeed, that would be counterproductive. It is important to set a standard for one area or for each team to work on achieving a common standard. Slow and steady improvement will be more readily accepted and better implemented than swift and large-scale changes.

Organizations can adopt more than one perspective. They can pick and choose those that meet their particular needs. For instance, library managers might want to determine how effective (including cost-effective) a particular service is. They might also want to judge it in the context of customer expectations and satisfaction, knowing that the insights gained will help to reshape and revitalize that service.

The intention of this book is not to advocate one perspective over another, but rather to explain customer-driven perspectives and show how librarians can gather useful data for meeting customers' expectations and ensuring their satisfaction. They might even create a customer value chain, "defined as moving from customer satisfaction to customer loyalty."[37]

MEASURES OF CONSEQUENCES

Consequences are the results of interactions with the library service. Interactions with library materials can and do affect individuals' lives—both positively and negatively. Academic librarians, for example, might like to believe that (1) students who are frequent borrowers earn higher grades than students who seldom come to the library, and (2) students who cannot obtain materials when they need them receive poor grades. Consequences can also be affected by components of service quality, in particular promptness and reliability. If the customer's deadline for receipt of the information is not met, or if the answer given to an important question is incorrect, then consequences are likely to be negative.

The library may gain some indication of negative consequences by tracking unsatisfactory transactions—materials desired but not obtainable, interlibrary loan items that arrive too late for course or research deadlines, and reference questions that the library was unable to answer. Additional problems arise when a library cannot provide material that faculty needs to complete a grant application before the submission deadline or when a member of the business community needs to file a business plan before the filing date expires.

A FINAL WORD

One other means of gathering information is known as *mystery shopping*. A number of librarians new to the profession and library school students have prior work experience as mystery shoppers. These anonymous shoppers make a particular purchase in a store or restaurant, for example, on a periodic or irregular basis and then report on the experience; these reports focus on issues such as courtesy, responsiveness, and their satisfaction with the experience. Most likely, the subject is also judged on "up-purchasing," being persuaded to buy more than they had intended. Unobtrusive testing does not focus on customer expectations, whereas mystery shopping often includes a more subjective component. Some libraries have experimented with mystery shopping and linked the results to staff development and improved service delivery.[38] (See also balanced scorecard, chapter 1.)

"Library use is largely self-service."[39] For this reason (if not for others), it is important to review the issues depicted in figure 4.9 and assessment as portrayed in figure 4.6. Such a review should lead to judgments and actions that will improve the organization's service performance and image. Other chapters will build on this foundation and indicate how to examine both service quality and satisfaction. As a result, librarians will gain better insights about customers' wants and needs as well as the gap between service expected and service provided.

The library community has embraced such terms as *input, output, performance,* and *outcome measures,* and explored impact measures—how a service has made a difference to learning, to job or classroom performance, to scholarly production, and so on. These terms, however, lack universal acceptance and have been defined in various ways. Input, output, and performance measures present the organizational or library perspective and what that entity considers important: often, resource allocation and volume of business. Outcome measures might examine outputs or quality assurance, but the term also implies results and perhaps even impacts.

Clearly, libraries need to adopt a customer focus and to concentrate on what is important to customers. (See figure 4.10.) We refer to the types of indicators discussed in this book as *customer-related indicators.* Such indicators provide insights into

- effectiveness
- attributes of timeliness and accuracy
- customer satisfaction
- quality (customer perceptions and expectations)
- complaint, comment, and compliment analysis
- processes (queuing, making contact with service personnel, and performance of tasks essential for producing satisfied and delighted customers)

Later chapters will offer examples of customer-related measures and present new ways of looking at and evaluating library services.

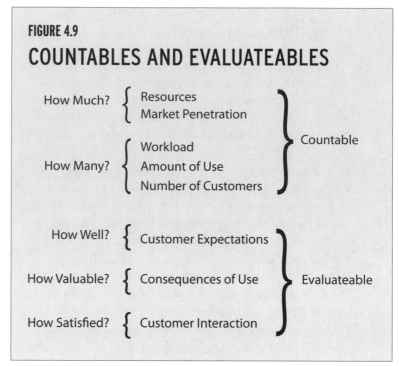

FIGURE 4.9
COUNTABLES AND EVALUATEABLES

Nonprofit institutions tend not to give priority to performance and results. Yet, performance and results are far more important and far more difficult to measure and control in the nonprofit [institution] than in a business.[40]

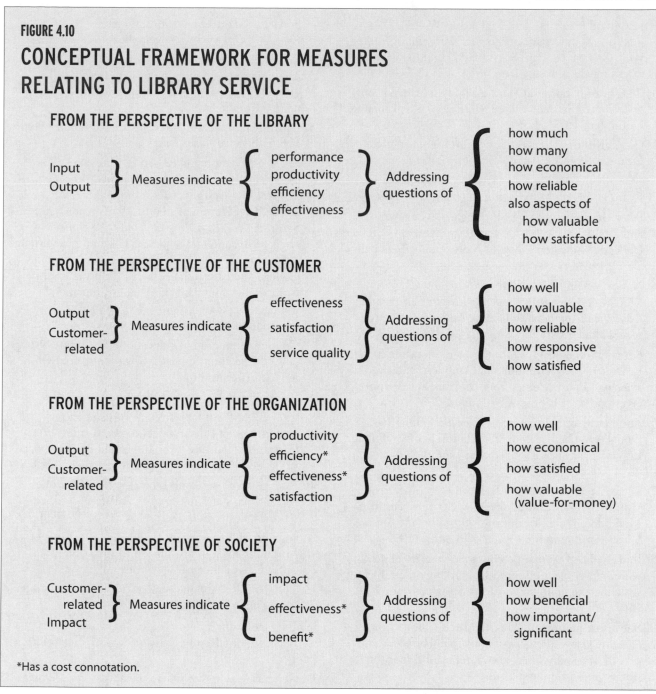

FIGURE 4.10

CONCEPTUAL FRAMEWORK FOR MEASURES RELATING TO LIBRARY SERVICE

FROM THE PERSPECTIVE OF THE LIBRARY

Input
Output } Measures indicate { performance
productivity
efficiency
effectiveness } Addressing questions of { how much
how many
how economical
how reliable
also aspects of
how valuable
how satisfactory

FROM THE PERSPECTIVE OF THE CUSTOMER

Output
Customer-related } Measures indicate { effectiveness
satisfaction
service quality } Addressing questions of { how well
how valuable
how reliable
how responsive
how satisfied

FROM THE PERSPECTIVE OF THE ORGANIZATION

Output
Customer-related } Measures indicate { productivity
efficiency*
effectiveness*
satisfaction } Addressing questions of { how well
how economical
how satisfied
how valuable
(value-for-money)

FROM THE PERSPECTIVE OF SOCIETY

Customer-related
Impact } Measures indicate { impact
effectiveness*
benefit* } Addressing questions of { how well
how beneficial
how important/
significant

*Has a cost connotation.

Notes

1. Association of Southeastern Research Libraries, "Shaping the Future: ASERL's Competences for Research Librarians," www.aserl.org/statements/competencies/competencies.htm.

2. Thomas A. Childers and Nancy A. Van House, *What's Good? Describing Your Public Library's Effectiveness* (Chicago: American Library Association, 1993), 5.

3. Ibid., 7.

4. Ibid.

5. Carol H. Weiss, *Evaluation: Methods for Studying Programs and Policies* (Upper Saddle Road, NJ: Prentice Hall, 1998), 5, 15, 26.

6. Peter H. Rossi, and Howard E. Freeman, *Evaluation: A Systematic Process*, 4th ed. (Newbury Park, CA: Sage, 1989), 18.

7. Childers and Van House, *What's Good?* 1.

8. Peter H. Rossi and Howard E. Freeman, *Evaluation: A Systematic Approach*, 5th ed. (Newbury Park, CA: Sage, 1993), 4.

9. J. Richard Hackman and Richard E. Walton, "Leading Groups in Organizations," in *Designing Effective Work Groups*, ed. Paul S. Goodman and Associates (San Francisco: Jossey-Bass, 1986), 72–119.

10. G. Edward Evans and Sandra M. Heft, *Introduction to Technical Services*, 6th ed. (Littleton, CO: Libraries Unlimited, 1995), 4.

11. Glenn Miller, *Customer Service and Innovation in Libraries* (Fort Atkinson, WI: Highsmith Press, 1996), 9.

12. Evans and Heft, *Introduction to Technical Services*, 4.

13. Peter Hernon and Robert E. Dugan, "Assessment and Evaluation: What Do the Terms Really Mean?" *College & Research Libraries News* 70, no. 3 (March 2009): 146–149.

14. Nancy A. Van House, Beth T. Weil, and Charles R. McClure, *Measuring Academic Library Performance: A Practical Approach* (Chicago: American Library Association, 1990), 4.

15. For additional insights into these questions see Robert E. Dugan, Peter Hernon, and Danuta A. Nitecki, *Viewing Library Metrics from Different Perspectives* (Westport, CT: Libraries Unlimited, 2009).

16. Another measure relates to book circulation. See Douglas A. Galbi, "Book Circulation per U.S. Public Library User since 1856," *Public Library Quarterly* 27, no. 4 (2008): 351–371.

17. Tefko Saracevic and Paul B. Kantor, "Studying the Value of Library and Information Services. Part II. Methodology and Taxonomy," *Journal of the American Society for Information Science* 48, no. 6 (1997): 543.

18. Ibid., 545. A Likert scale consists of a series of items to which the subject responds by marking on an intensity scale the extent to which he or she agrees or disagrees with each item.

19. See also Chelmsford (Massachusetts) Public Library, "Library Use Value Calculator: Calculate the Value of YOUR Library Use," www.chelmsfordlibrary.org/library_info/calculator.html.

20. Howard A. Rubin, "In Search of the Business Value of Information Technology," *Application Development Trends* 1, no. 12 (November 1994): 24.

21. Ibid., 23.

22. Roland T. Rust and Richard L. Oliver, *Service Quality: New Directions in Theory and Practice* (Thousand Oaks, CA: Sage, 1994), 4.

23. Rhea Joyce Rubin, *Demonstrating Results: Using Outcome Measurement in Your Library* (Chicago: American Library Association, 2006). See also Texas State Library, "Outcome Measures," www.tsl.state.tx.us/outcomes/; Institute of Museum and Library Service, "Grant Applications: Outcome Based Evaluation," www.imls.gov/applicants/faqs.shtm.

24. Robert E. Dugan and Peter Hernon, "Outcomes Assessment: Not Synonymous with Inputs and Outputs," *Journal of Academic Librarianship* 28, no. 6 (November 2002): 380.

25. Dugan, Hernon, and Nitecki, *Viewing Library Metrics from Different Perspectives*.

26. See Peter Hernon and Robert E. Dugan, ed., *Outcomes Assessment in Higher Education: Views and Perspectives* (Westport, CT: Libraries Unlimited, 2004); Peter Hernon, Robert E. Dugan, and Candy Schwartz, ed., *Revisiting Outcomes Assessment in Higher Education* (Westport, CT: Libraries Unlimited, 2006); American Library Association, Association of College and Research Libraries, "Information Literacy Competency Standards for Higher Education," www.acrl.org/ala/mgrps/divs/acrl/standards/informationliteracycompetency.cfm.

27. Council for the Aid to Education, "Voluntary Support of Education Survey." www.cae.org/content/pro_data_trends.htm.

28. International Archive of Education Data, "Welcome," www.icpsr.umich.edu/IAED/welcome.html.

29. Department of Education, National Center for Education Statistics, "The Integrated Postsecondary Education Data System," http://nces.ed.gov/IPEDS/.

30. Association of Research Libraries, "ARL Statistics," www.arl.org/stats/annualsurveys/arlstats/. A historical set of data extends the series back to 1907–1908.

31. For a list of the variables included, see Institute of Museums and Library Service, "Library Statistics," (http://harvester.census.gov/imls/pub_questdefs.asp).

32. COUNTER, "About Counter," www.projectcounter.org/contact.html.

33. Tony Hope and Jeremy Hope, *Transforming the Bottom Line* (Boston: Harvard Business School Press, 1996), 102–103.

34. General Accounting Office, *Best Practices Methodology: A New Approach for Improving Government Operations*, GAO/NSIAD-95-154, www.gao.gov/archive/1995/ns95154.pdf.

35. Anne Wilson and Leeanne Pitman, *Best Practice Handbook for Australian University Libraries* (Canberra Department of Education, Training and Youth Affairs, Evaluations and Investigations Programme, Higher Education Division, 2000), www.dest.gov.au/archive/highered/eippubs/eip00_10/00_10.pdf.

36. "Library Success: A Best Practices Wiki," which covers a wide range of topics, offers content from different types of libraries on a worldwide basis. www.libsuccess.org/index.php?title=Main_Page.

37. National Performance Review, *Serving the American Public: Best Practices in Customer-Driven Strategic Planning* (Washington, DC: Government Printing Office, 1997), 38.

38. See Mary W. Jordan, "What Is Your Library's Friendliness Factor?" *Public Library Quarterly* 24, no. 4 (2005): 81–99.

39. Childers and Van House, *What's Good?* 26.

40. Peter F. Drucker, *Managing the Nonprofit Organization: Principles and Practices* (New York: Harper-Collins, 1990), 107.

Chapter Five

What Can Go Wrong with Numbers?

[I]t is not enough to know the results of a study, survey, or experiment. We also need to know how those numbers were collected and who was asked.[1]

Examining service elements in the library can be very useful to management, but must be done with care and foresight about what might go wrong. The purpose of this chapter is to provide a cautionary note about the use of any performance indicator, especially measures of input (reflecting those resources essential to providing library services) and output (conveying the amount of service provided).

Any measure, including customer-related ones, should be linked to performance targets and outcomes, which monitor, and are intended to improve, the quality of service over time. Nonetheless, any data reported as performance indicators might be used for political purposes, ones not always aimed at developing and improving library services. As Peter Hernon and Charles R. McClure note, "Information is a tool useful for acquiring and retaining power. Information may enable an organization to advance its image and role as dynamic and meet its mission, goals, and objectives."[2]

Although the increasing use of the Internet as an information resource has caused librarians and vendors to ponder how to measure and report statistics from electronic data in a way meaningful to key stakeholders, there are other changes in both the larger society and in education that are affecting the future of libraries. In 2006, the Research Committee of the Association of College and Research Libraries conducted an extensive review of the literature and talked with numerous librarians about the future of academic libraries. Based on the review, committee members developed a list of ten assumptions ranked in order of importance. The list merits recounting, as it "underscore[s] the dominant roles that technology and consumer expectations are increasingly playing in libraries."[3] (See figure 5.1.)

OBJECTIVES AND ACTIVITIES

Given the assumptions and the experiences at a number of institutions, it is no wonder that the number of performance measures for e-resources is expanding

FIGURE 5.1

TEN ASSUMPTIONS ABOUT THE FUTURE OF ACADEMIC LIBRARIES AND LIBRARIANS

1. There will be an increased emphasis on digitizing collections, preserving digital archives, and improving methods of data storage and retrieval. Academic libraries have an opportunity to make their unique collections available to the world in unprecedented ways. In fact, the digitization of unique print collections may emerge as one of the primary missions of academic libraries in the 21st century. . . .

2. The skill set for librarians will continue to evolve in response to the needs and expectations of the changing populations (students and faculty) that they serve. Changes in skill sets among library professionals are well underway. Entry level salaries are increasing, due in part to the increased expectations of a new generation of professionals who have other career options. . . . Libraries that are open to creating new career paths within their organizations are in an optimal position to embrace the future.

3. Students and faculty will increasingly demand faster and greater access to services. Statements such as "print journals are to today's students what microfiche was to the previous generation" are becoming increasingly common. Similarly, the refrain "print journal material is becoming invisible" can be heard. What implications do information-seeking behaviors and attitudes have for the selection of materials, and in what format?

4. Debates about intellectual property will become increasingly common in higher education. While this is not a new issue, what is new is the increased opportunity for infringement upon intellectual property rights brought about by online access.

5. The demand for technology-related services will grow and require additional funding. The digital revolution is in its infancy; academic libraries are still operating in a predominantly print world. Futurists predict that both the supply and demand for print material will continue to increase in the near future, but a tipping point will inevitably occur. Tipping points are often followed by an abrupt decline in interest in out-of-favor technologies. Consider: What library products and services will decline over the next ten years? Will libraries be able to reallocate resources into new technologies? Which products and services are already effectively dead, but are being kept on "life support," hence are slowing efforts to embrace new technologies?

6. Higher education will increasingly view the institution as a business. Today, universities are extremely focused on fundraising and grant writing, maximizing revenue, reducing costs, and optimizing physical space. Do academic libraries have sufficient data to defend how their resources are allocated?

7. Students will increasingly view themselves as customers and consumers, expecting high-quality facilities and services. Today's students are increasingly paying the true cost of their education and demanding to be treated as customers. This has profound implications, ranging from how teaching faculty interrelate with students to the quality of residential housing and library facilities. Universities are becoming more aware of the importance of attractive library facilities as an effective recruitment tool. Is your library a strong advocate for high-quality, customer-friendly library facilities and services?

8. Distance learning will be an increasingly more common option in higher education, and will coexist but not threaten the traditional bricks-and-mortar model. Throughout higher education, technology has made possible the rapid proliferation of online instruction. The "just-in-time" model of [e]mbedding library tutorials into Web-based courses complements traditional "just-in-case" library instruction, and may surpass it in the future. Libraries will want to continue to develop products and services that scale, i.e., are easily replicated, in an increasingly resource-stretched environment.

9. Free public access to information stemming from publicly funded research will continue to grow. This is perhaps the most unpredictable and exciting of the ten assumptions, and legislation will play a key role here. Finished research will still need to be vetted, edited, organized, and dissemi-

nated in logical ways. It could be advantageous for the academic community to return to the scholarly publication business if it can be proven to address the soaring cost of access to published scientific research. Libraries could and should play a leading role, understanding that it may require reallocation of institutional resources.

10. Privacy will continue to be an important issue in librarianship. This is another assumption that has taken on greater attention and importance due to advances in technology. The debate becomes even more of an issue for libraries that are moving toward authentication and/or password access to electronic workstations located in public areas of the library.

Source: James L. Mullins, Frank R. Allen, and Jon R. Hufford, "Top Ten Assumptions for the Future of Academic Libraries and Librarians: A Report from the ACRL Research Committee," *College & Research Libraries News.*

and that libraries have included in their strategic plans objectives and activities such as these:[4]

Objective 1.2: evaluate, select, organize, and facilitate the availability/accessibility and retrieval of information in a multiplicity of formats to meet undergraduate, graduate and faculty needs.

Activity 1.2.1: increase the total of accessible e-monographs including reserves from 28,000 in 2005 to 100,000 volumes by 2010

Activity 1.2.2: increase the availability of e-reference sources

Activity 1.2.3: increase the availability of e-reserves through the online catalog

Activity 1.2.4: increase the availability of Web-based help guides

Activity 1.2.5: evaluate the feasibility of merging the "free elected Web sites" guides into the "help and research guides" eliminating the former as a genre of guides

Activity 1.2.6: increase the availability of media-based information news throughout the library.[5]

DO MORE RESOURCES MEAN HIGHER QUALITY AND BETTER SERVICE?

A widespread assumption exists that resources equal quality service; ergo, with more resources, the library automatically provides more and better service. Library directors have been using that argument for years. Sharon A. Weiner "showed that there is a relationship between the ARL [Association of Research Libraries] Index and services . . . [as well as] between the number of undergraduate students and services . . . and between instructional presentations and operating expenditures." (See www.arl.org/stats/index/index.shtml.) Service was defined in terms of three outputs: reference transactions, instructional presentations, and attendees at group presentations.[6] The

index, she notes, considered the following inputs: volumes owned, volumes added, number of serial subscriptions, number of staff, and total expenditures.[7]

In a more recent study, Weiner found that the academic library contributes to the reputation of a university. She "used quantitative variables that reflected library service activities, not library collection measures." Library collection measures, she maintains, are no longer sufficient to describe the value of the library to an institution.[8] The services measured included library expenditures, reference transactions, library presentations, attendees at library presentations, and library professional staff. Using multiple regression analysis, she discovered that only library expenditures were consistently significant among the service and institutional variables studied.

Roswitha Poll reviewed and compared the performance indicators that groups in different countries (Germany, Australia, Sweden, the United Kingdom, and the Netherlands) use. Some of the indicators have wider acceptance than others, but all of them reflect the library's perspective.[9]

Turning to public libraries, Hennen's American Public Library Ratings (HAPLR) Index includes fifteen variables that focus on circulation, staffing, materials, reference service, and funding levels. A cautionary note is that the index

does not include data on audio and video collections, or interlibrary loan, among other items that could have been calculated from the FSCS [Federal-State Cooperative System] data. Perhaps most prominently absent from the data are any measures of electronic use or Internet service. While such measures would have been desirable, the FSCS data . . . are simply not sufficient for such comparisons at this time. Internet, electronic services and audiovisual services are excluded because there is simply not enough data reported by enough libraries to make comparisons meaningful. What remains are fairly traditional data for print services, book checkouts, reference service, funding and staffing.[10]

The LJ (*Library Journal*) Index, sponsored by Baker and Taylor's Bibliostat, draws on the 2006 public library statistical data published by the Institute of Museum and Library Services. (See chapter 4.) Later editions of the data set will continue to draw on those public libraries with total expenditures of at least ten thousand dollars that serve populations of at least one thousand. Library ratings are based on per-capita service indicators (library visits, circulation, program attendance, and public Internet use) and a set of inputs such as funding. The ratings divide libraries into comparison groups based on total operating expenditures.

The creators of the Hennen Index and the LJ Index appear to disagree about which method is better.[11] The former is more input-based and the latter includes more outputs. Still, missing from the variables covered by the Weiner and Poll articles as well as the Hennen Index and the LJ Index are outputs reflecting customer interests and outcomes, defined as "benefits to the end user that demonstrate the effectiveness of a [library] program or service."[12] Improved service assumes quality and, from the perspective of this book, customers will make their own determination about quality. That perspective, together with the ability of libraries and their parent institutions to demonstrate the extent to which they meet their missions, become central to evaluation and assessment. For academic institutions, outcomes reflect opportunities to become partners with faculty in the learning process and demonstrate how libraries make a difference in the lives of their constituent groups.

RANKINGS CAN BE NOT ONLY MISLEADING BUT ALSO DANGEROUS

Most library directors would be delighted to announce that they presided over the best-funded library in the area, the state, the region, or the country. But in the late 1990s, the city councilors who funded one such library were horrified to learn that they were supporting the most expensive public library in New Zealand. The reaction was not pride, but determination to cut the library's resources. These councilors did not want to have the best-supported library in the country. For them, one slightly-better-than-average library would be just fine. As a result, the library's budget was slashed and the full-time staff was cut by one-third.

This case is a good example of how rankings and resource statistics can be more harmful than helpful. (In today's fiscal environment, this example may not be extreme. Look at the number of administrators—outside the library—who firmly believe that the Internet is a viable substitute for a library and its collections and services.)

Information about the New Zealand library's high level of financial support was included in statistical reports that compared the largest public libraries in the country on a number of factors, including cost per circulation, circulations per staff member, and volumes per capita. In comparison with the other libraries mentioned in the report, this library had a higher cost per circulation and a lower number of circulations per staff member. Upon external review, these ratios were taken as indicators of excess and waste in the system and low productivity on the part of staff. The city councilors used volumes per capita as an indication of the materials budget being overgenerous.

The real situation was somewhat different. The city in this example used a total charge-back approach in calculating the library's expenditures. The library was charged more than $1 million for depreciation on its central building and over $3 million for debt service on the building, and had many other charges that the other cities did not assign to their libraries. In fact, because the charges to the libraries differed from city to city, the comparison of expenditures among this group of libraries was faulty. Nonetheless, using noncomparable data, other comparisons were made. Of course, costs per circulation were higher for the library in the example; all expenses were higher because of the charge-backs.

Another misleading statistic was the high volume count per capita. This library had not weeded its collection for many years. When it moved into a new central building, the staff moved books from storage to fill the empty space. These books were still in the collection some years later, although, because of their age and poor physical condition, few circulated.

SOME STATISTICS BECOME DOUBLE-EDGED SWORDS

The number of volumes in the collection has been presumed to indicate quality. In some cases, it may. This number, however, can be interpreted as reflecting a collection so extensive that few new materials are needed. Complicating any tally is the number of digital resources in library collections. Even some university libraries that are ARL members are willing to see a dramatic decline in the size of their print collections as their directors accept the previously mentioned ten assumptions and support changing patterns of information gathering.

The preceding example about books per capita shows how some statistics can be double-edged swords. If the library described earlier now gets rid of all those titles that it should have discarded long ago, the city government is likely to accuse it of manipulating the number of volumes to make a case for an increase in the materials budget.

Another library placed a bar code on each serial issue received because it circulated serials. The city council hired a consultant to evaluate the library, and he asked the systems librarian for the number of titles that had not circulated in the past five years. The number was obtained by matching bar codes to circulation records using the OPAC. The number was quite high—over five hundred thousand—because each issue of a serial had been bar coded and, thus, recorded as a separate item. Yet, only the number—five hundred thousand—not the explanation, appeared in news reports about the need to streamline the library.

The amount of time spent in the library is sometimes considered an indication of use on the part of the customers. Time spent certainly can imply reading and using materials, but time can also be spent trying to find materials and having other frustrating experiences. On the other hand, a library whose system is transparent, one that makes it easy for customers to find what they are looking for quickly and to leave the building perfectly satisfied—or even not have to come in for every transaction—will come out low on time spent. Therefore, time as an indicator can also be a double-edged sword, and should be used very carefully.

ALL ACTIVITIES ARE NOT EQUAL

When activities are lumped together in one report, it is difficult for the reader to understand that these are not necessarily comparable in terms of staff used, time expended, or impact on customers. For example, it takes only a few seconds to charge or discharge an item, whereas making a presentation to a class or visiting a school library can take a lot of time. Nor are all requests for assistance equal. Directional questions are quickly answered, whereas some questions can be quite complicated and require multiple sources to answer. Some library activities never show up

in library statistics at all. Of course, all the costs do appear, but they are spread over other activities.

COUNTING THE SAME ITEMS TWICE INFLATES AND MISLEADS

In various reports, libraries may give an unrealistic picture of many performance indicators' elements. For example, volumes held per student, volumes held per faculty, expenditures per student, expenditures per faculty, serials per student, and serials per faculty are all based on the total. Using expenditures as an example of distorted statistics, let us consider a library that spends $4,550,000. The service population includes 21,889 students and 1,222 faculty members. To report that the library spends $208 per student and $3,723 per faculty member overstates reality. In truth, the library spends about $197 per capita on its likely customer population ($4,550,000 divided by 23,111—the combined total of students and faculty).

ARE ALL THESE REALLY APPLES?

To make comparisons meaningful and fair, it is necessary to agree on definitions about what is being compared and on a standard procedure for comparison. In most instances, that is not done. Take a simple thing like volumes in a library. There is no consensus in the profession about uniformity in reporting volumes. Here are some of the issues/questions about volume counting:

- Should volumes be counted as bibliographic or physical items?
- Is an encyclopedia one volume, or is each part a volume?
- Should CD-ROMs be included in the volume count, and if so, as bibliographic or physical items?

Further complicating matters, some libraries collect and report volume counts, whereas others either maintain title counts or both volume and title counts.

Comparability issues can be found in every area of library activity. Unfortunately, too many comparisons are made without taking into account that not every library is counting the same way. These counting practices are not, however, usually stated or questioned when comparing libraries.

A FINAL WORD

Library managers must be certain about what they want and need to know: what use they will make of the data collected, how they will interpret the data, what decisions the data will impact, and how the data will be used to improve library service. As Richard L. Lynch and Kelvin F. Cross explain,

> performance measures must help managers and workers:
>
> - Measure what is important to . . . customers;
>
> - Motivate operations to continually improve against customer expectations;
>
> - Identify and eliminate waste—of both time and resources;
>
> - Shift the focus of their organizations from bureaucratic, vertical empires to more responsive, horizontal business systems;
>
> - Accelerate organizational learning and build a consensus for the change when customer expectations shift or strategies call for the organization to behave differently.[13]

As a result, meaningful evaluation might focus on the overlapping dimensions covered in SERVQUAL, LibQUAL+, or other variations of SERVQUAL. LibQUAL, a frequently used instrument in academic and some other libraries, has some core dimensions; the particular ones vary in library reports based on survey results.

Although the research is still in the preliminary stage, it appears that specific dimensions apply for certain constituency groups, namely students with disabilities and those for whom English is their secondary language.[14]

Using LibQUAL dimensions but a different set of questions, figure 5.2 offers examples of questions meaningful to customers, for whom the library could develop performance indicators and, in reports and elsewhere, relate the findings to a customer service plan and to organizational goals and objectives. (See chapter 3.) An overarching question is, "What is the reputation of the library, individual units in the library, and specific services?" After all, a library, like other organizations, operates in a political context and may have to collect and report input and output measures. Nonetheless, it should also "stay close to . . . [its] customers,"[15] while becoming more engaged in outcomes assessment.

Most of the metrics that the customer service industry has captured and tracked over the past twenty years are rubbish.[16]

FIGURE 5.2

SERVICE DIMENSIONS THAT CAN BE CONVERTED TO PERFORMANCE INDICATORS AND REPORTED

AFFECT OF SERVICE

How long does it take staff members to answer the telephone?

Are telephone calls returned when promised?

Are errors made in overdue and fine notices?

Are reference questions answered correctly?

Are new periodicals and newspapers checked in promptly?

Are books reshelved promptly?

Is turnaround time for interlibrary loan requests minimized?

Are customer complaints quickly resolved?

Are staff members courteous to customers?

Are staff members familiar with the equipment and the technology?

Are senior managers accessible when customers need them?

How long is the waiting time at the circulation and reference desks, as well as at computers?

Do staff members avoid the use of unnecessary jargon?

Are staff members good listeners?

Are customers who complain assured that their problem or concern will be addressed?

How much faith can customers place in the information provided by the library?

To what extent are regular customers recognized and treated accordingly?

To what extent do staff members understand customer expectations and try to satisfy them?

INFORMATION CONTROL

Does equipment work when it has been repaired?

Are the OPAC and other equipment functional?

LIBRARY AS A PLACE

Is the library an attractive place to visit?

Is the building too hot or too cold? Is the lighting adequate?

What is the condition of the equipment?

Are handouts attractive and clear?

How safe is it to be in and nearby the library?

Is furniture comfortable?

Note: If the focus is on websites and digital resources, numerous other questions emerge. For an extensive list, see Peter Hernon and Philip Calvert, "E-service Quality in Libraries: Its Features and Dimensions," *Library & Information Science Research* 27, no. 4 (2005): 377–404.

Notes

1. Jessica M. Utts, *Seeing through Statistics*, 3rd ed. (Belmont, CA: Thompson Brooks/Cole, 2005), 10.

2. Peter Hernon and Charles R. McClure, *Evaluation and Library Decision Making* (Norwood, NJ: Ablex, 1990), 214.

3. James L. Mullins, Frank R. Allen, and Jon R. Hufford, "Top Ten Assumptions for the Future of Academic Libraries and Librarians: A Report from the ACRL Research Committee," *College & Research Libraries News* 68, no. 4 (April 2007): 246.

4. See Association of Research Libraries, *Measures for Electronic Resources (E-metrics)*, www.arl.org/stats/initiatives/emetrics/index.shtml; Robert E. Dugan, Peter Hernon, and Danuta A. Nitecki, *Viewing Library Metrics from Different Perspectives* (Westport, CT: Libraries Unlimited, 2009).

5. Suffolk University, Sawyer Library, *Long-Range Plan: Strategic Directions, July 1, 2005–June 30, 2010* (Boston: Suffolk University, 2005), www.suffolk.edu/files/SawLib/2005-2010-strat-plan.pdf.

6. Sharon A. Weiner, "Library Quality and Impact: Is There a Relationship between New Measures and Traditional Measures?" *Journal of Academic Librarianship* 31, no. 5 (September 2005): 432.

7. Ibid., 436.

8. Sharon Weiner, "The Contribution of the Library to the Reputation of a University," *Journal of Academic Librarianship* 35, no. 1 (2009): 9–10.

9. Roswitha Poll, "Benchmarking with Quality Indicators: National Projects," *Performance Measurement and Metrics* 8, no. 1 (2007): 41–53.

10. Hennen's American Public Library Ratings, "Rating Methods," www.haplr-index.com/rating_methods.htm. The actual variables included are expenditures per capita, percent of budget to materials, materials expended per capita, full-time employed staff per one thousand population, periodicals per one thousand residents, volumes per capita, cost per circulation (low to high), visits per capita, collection turnover, circulation per full-time employed staff hour, circulation per capita, reference per capita, circulation per hour, visits per hour, and circulation per visit.

11. "Alternative System Rates Public Libraries," *American Libraries* (April 2009): 21; Thomas J. Hennen Jr., "HALPR vs. LJ Index," *Library Journal* (April 1, 2009): 10.

12. Rhea Joyce Rubin, *Demonstrating Results: Using Outcome Measurement in Your Library* (Chicago: American Library Association, 2006), 2.

13. Richard L. Lynch and Kelvin F. Cross, *Measure Up! Yardsticks for Continuous Improvement* (Cambridge, MA: Blackwell, 1991), 8.

14. See Peter Hernon and Philip Calvert, ed., *Improving the Quality of Library Services for Students with Disabilities* (Westport, CT: Libraries Unlimited, 2006).

15. Lynch and Cross, *Measure Up!* 98.

16. Bill Price and David Jaffe, *The Best Service Is No Service: How to Liberate Your Customer from Customer Service, Keep Them Happy, and Control Costs* (San Francisco: Jossey Bass, 2008), 253.

Chapter Six

Managing the Three Cs (Comments, Complaints, and Compliments)

Customers who take time to complain have at least a little confidence in the organization.[1]

Once upon a time when a library wanted to evaluate its service and operations, it invited a distinguished librarian to visit and determine how well it was doing. The consultant spent several days in the library, and usually based his recommendations on his own library's exemplary service. Hence the old joke: "How I run my library good." In retrospect, hiring a consultant who knew nothing of local needs and preferences seems not to be a good idea. Why do this when the library has access to people who have firsthand knowledge of the service and who are a great resource—the library's own customers?

Customers have a right to express their opinions about what they would like the library to do, about mistakes, and about perceived quality of the service, good or bad, as well as the right to make specific complaints (e.g., about the length of time that equipment does not work or material is at the bindery, the length of time it takes to receive material through interlibrary loan, and borrowed material that has been returned but is still shown in the OPAC records as checked out). Smart managers recognize, accept, encourage, and profit from customer comments and complaints. They do not equate complaints with problem patrons.

WHAT ARE COMMENTS AND COMPLAINTS?

A comment and a complaint differ. A comment is more value neutral, points something out, or raises an issue, but, if it is critical, it is still expressed with a mild or nonhostile tone. The customer, for instance, may request the purchase of an item, the placement of more wastebaskets, action be taken to regulate heating in the building, or an extension of library hours. That person might also comment on the lack of parking or study space. Clearly, action cannot be taken on every issue, but there is an opportunity to create a dialogue with constituent groups. A customer complaint indicates that a service does not meet customer expectations. This definition is broad, so let us examine it more closely.

Customer disappointments in libraries center around perceived staff behavior, problems related to downtime for nonworking equipment, the inability to download some items, access to digital material, and so on. Having people serve themselves as they do in most libraries has obvious advantages, but also certain disadvantages, the most serious of which is loss of information about unmet needs, wants, or demands. Customers who do not find what they want, unless the need is urgent, may simply leave the building or terminate an online session, some never to return.

Teenagers and undergraduate students often associate libraries with print books and fail to realize that the databases they use reside on the library's web pages. Complicating matters, they become so dependent on those databases that they fail to realize or appreciate the OPAC. If they discover a source in a database that does not provide access to full text, they may not realize that the same journal might be included in the OPAC and available from alternate databases.

In some instances, customers unable to locate the desired item or information are likely to approach the first person who seems to be an employee and ask for help. In the stack area of a large library, that employee is probably a part-time shelver whose knowledge may be insufficient to be helpful. More persistent customers, perhaps driven by the importance of the search, might go to the reference or circulation department for assistance. If the request concerns a missing item, the staff will likely check the OPAC record. Should the record indicate that the item is in, the customer will be told to search again—looking on tables and book carts—and be sent back to the stack area where the item is supposed to be. If the item is still not found, the customer either leaves without the desired item or information, or must accept alternatives. In the case of such departing customers, the library may be missing an opportunity to learn how it might better meet their expectations, assuming that they will return.

Complaints are not all the same. They can range from minor annoyances to major problems. Items being unavailable may seem minor. Yet, unavailability represents a "situation where customers are deprived of the specific satisfaction [the library's] service was supposed to give them."[2] Unless library managers establish some mechanism to capture and record data about items or information desired but unavailable, they have no way of knowing if availability is a minor or major problem, nor do they have any information about how to improve availability.

In some libraries a complaint has to be specifically labeled as such to make it official. The dissatisfaction or disappointments of people who just grumble to the staff are seldom brought to management's attention. Thus, problems that might have been corrected remain unnoticed except by the customers. The people who complain or just grumble about the service should be thanked and appreciated because they may be reporting flaws in the system, and because they may represent only a fraction of the disappointed customers.

WHY PEOPLE DO NOT COMPLAIN

The consensus in the business literature is that 96 percent of all dissatisfied customers will never complain, but 90 percent of them will not return either. In addition, each one of that 90 percent will tell at least nine other people about their unsatisfactory experience with the organization. Another 13 percent will tell twenty or more people about the poor service they received. One writer estimated that if an organization had just ten unhappy customers a month, that as many as 101 people would become aware of poor service quality in that organization.[3] In other words, one person complained; nine other people were just as unhappy, and now as many as 101 people could have a poor opinion of the service. The reasons why people do not complain have been repeatedly verified:

- You do not care about me.
- You make it hard for me to tell you that I am dissatisfied (which proves you do not care about me).
- Why should I do your work for you, such as finding mistakes? You do not even deserve my comments.[4]
- You will not do anything about my problem anyway.

You Do Not Care about Me

The viewpoint that "you do not care about me" is reflected in three ways:

1. The system itself is not customer friendly.

2. A policy regarding dissatisfied customers is not known or understood by frontline staff.

3. Staff seems disinterested or unhelpful in solving the customer's problems.

A lot of customer frustration arises from an inability to understand the "system" or because the system itself is not working properly. How to use the library and how to find desired items may be unclear to many customers, especially new ones. With the inclusion of digital archives, numerous databases, and assorted other collections in different formats, the public can easily fail to find the items in library collections that meet their needs. For this reason, libraries are creating software or investing in software such as AquaBrowser that make a high percentage of content in library collections available using a single query.

Many libraries have no policies for dealing with complaints. Rather, each complaint is treated on an ad hoc basis. As a result, managers have not thought about such basic elements as what is a complaint, how customers are informed about the complaint policy, the mechanisms by which complaints can be made, who is responsible for responding, and how responsive the library wants to be.

Customers who feel annoyed or frustrated tend to vent their feelings to the first library employee they encounter. The reaction from the staff greatly influences the customer's perception of the service. The worst, and most common, enemies of responsive customer service are indifference and defensiveness. When people have trouble finding materials in the stacks, they may go to the main floor and report the item as missing. Staff, especially part-time staff and students in academic libraries, usually have not been trained how to respond, so they simply shrug off the customer with the attitude, "It is not my job" or "It is probably stolen." In some libraries, staff is not permitted to leave the service area to help customers in the stacks, or customers might be instructed to go to a particular service area for assistance. If they do so, they might find the area unstaffed, understaffed, congested, or the staff unhelpful.

One major problem is that all too often employees receiving a complaint or negative comment about the service react defensively. This is shown by body language that bristles although no verbal response is made. "When a frontline person reacts negatively to a customer, . . . [that person] communicates not that the customer has a problem, but that he [or she] is the problem."[5] Others try to make the customer feel guilty for complaining by responding with the cliché,

"We are doing the best we can!" Such a comment is an admission that the library's service is less than excellent—and likely to stay that way.

Both customers and library staff members, as Ann Curry explains, have rights. She analyzes eleven rights, which, by the way, would make an excellent discussion document for library staff. For instance, she notes that customers have "the right to be treated equally" and "to dislike libraries," while the staff have "the right to dislike a customer. . . . [That right] is acceptable as long as the rights of those customers are not infringed."[6]

You Make It Hard for Me to Tell You That I Am Dissatisfied

Sometimes customers wander around in the stacks trying to find a desired item. If the customer is in a multistoried library and all the visible staff is on the first floor, seeking help is difficult. Libraries expect customers to understand the system; customers, especially those unfamiliar with the intricacies of the system, can easily feel frustrated. Every day somebody comes to the library for the first time, yet only the unusual library consciously tries to make navigating the system easy for inexperienced customers. How many libraries post signage explaining what the OPAC is and how to use it? How many libraries post signs asking customers to tell their good and bad experiences at a service desk? How many libraries have telephones on each floor that connect to a service desk to answer queries from "lost" customers?

If customers grumble or complain at the library's public service desk, will a staff member try to solve the problem, or at least promise that the complaint will be passed on to the person responsible for resolution? Or do customers have to go to another desk or office to file a complaint formally? How many times do customers have to explain the problem? If they want to see a manager or supervisor, is one available?

Organizations that actively discourage complaints require that the complaint be submitted in writing—sometimes with extra copies. Ideally, every complaint should be recorded in order to track it to resolution or stalemate, but should the customer actually have to write out a statement? Responsive organizations make complaining easy. Complaint forms are available at every public service point, but using the form is not required. (Figure 6.1 offers a sample form.) Complaints can be made online through the library's home page. Complaints can be phoned in and the specifics taken either through audio equipment or by an employee filling out a form. Staff is encouraged to pass along customer grumbles, even though a customer may have declined to make a formal complaint. Figure 6.2, the Problem Report Form, is an example of how staff can report problems and complaints. The form can also be put on a template for the library's internal computer network.

Why Should I Do Your Work for You?

Just as the staff considers that supervisors get paid to deal with certain situations, customers think that library personnel should be responsible for library service performance and that they should look for and correct problems. A factor inhibiting customers from mentioning mistakes, such as misshelved items, is that they are unsure of the staff's reaction to the report. Staff who welcome being told about problems encourage reporting, but other staff may react stiffly, causing customers to vow never to mention another mistake.

FIGURE 6.1
COMPLAINT FORM

Something Wrong? Missing? Out of Place?
Let us know so we can fix it.

Today's date: _____

Nature of the problem (Please be as specific as you can. Tell us when, where, and how you encountered the difficulty.):

[ ]

If you'd like a response, let us know how to reach you. (Optional)

Name: _____
Address: _____
Phone: _____
E-mail address: _____

You Will Not Do Anything about My Problem

Believing that nothing will be done about the problem is one of the most common reasons that customers do not complain. They believe that the library does not operate for them. They feel like outsiders, having to cope with rigid rules and procedures, and staff who are not there to serve them.

ATTITUDE AND ACTIONS

Simply announcing that the library wants to satisfy customers is insufficient. The real task is to turn satisfied customers into loyal ones, customers who will return often to use library services. Creating loyal and delighted customers requires both an attitude and action. The attitude is recognition that keeping customers is important and that the entire organization has a commitment to customer service. The actions are steps for developing and maintaining a system for handling complaints. Such a system should also deal with compliments. Compliments reinforce good service performance and make staff feel that they make a difference and that they are appreciated. Thus, the library should have a compliment form (figure 6.3) as well as a complaint form (figure 6.1).

Some pointers culled from reading numerous books on customer service can serve as guides to action:

- Make it easy for customers to complain, and they will make it easy for the organization to improve.
- Respond to complaints quickly and courteously with common sense. The purpose is to improve customer loyalty.
- Resolve complaints on the first contact and (1) save money by eliminating unnecessary, additional contacts that escalate costs, and (2) build customer confidence.
- Develop an automated compliment and complaint handling system.
- Recruit and hire the best (approachable, people-oriented, and wanting to fill information needs) staff members to fill customer service jobs.

FIGURE 6.2

PROBLEM REPORT FORM (FOR STAFF USE)

Problem Report Form [#_____]

Date of incident: _____

Reported by: ❑ Patron   ❑ Library staff   ❑ Other

Location in library: _____

Description of problem:

Action taken:

User satisfied?   ❑ Yes   ❑ No
If no, why not? Is further action required? If so, describe it.

Comments?

Optional: Complete if user wishes to be notified of actions taken.

Name: _____

Address: _____

Phone: _____ E-mail: _____

Today's date: _____ Recorded by: _____

ESTABLISHING A COMPLIMENT AND COMPLAINT TRACKING SYSTEM

Key ingredients for a compliment and complaint tracking system are

- management commitment
- publicity for the system
- accessibility of complaint management staff
- promptness and courtesy of response
- personalized response, whenever possible
- simple, clear communication with customers
- objectivity and flexibility in determining the proper resolution
- uniform, consistent, and computerized record keeping[7]

A computerized system enables management to monitor the efficiency and effectiveness of a comment, complaint, and compliment management system and can provide evidence about trends.

A library that wants a first-rate tracking system should follow these five steps:

1. Establish an implementation team with diverse representation—both managers and nonmanagers—to oversee the development of the system.

2. Develop a policy statement that says that the organization embraces complaints and views them as opportunities for improvement. For example, "The library embraces complaints and thrives on compliments. Let us know what you like and dislike. We view complaints as opportunities to improve. We may not always be able to resolve your complaints, but we can sure try. Compliments tell us that we are going in the right direction."

3. Identify each step necessary for creating a useful tracking system and then establish the system. The staff should record and classify comments, compliments, and complaints so that the data can be analyzed and reported to top management.

4. Develop recommendations to improve core processes and empower frontline employees to resolve complaints on first contact.

5. Develop an action plan for implementing approved customer recommendations and for publicizing the value of customer input.[8]

The implementation team must consider ways to draw attention to the tracking system. To this end, it should interact with various stakeholders to determine the most effective ways of encouraging customers to express their compliments and complaints. The team should also consider the inclusion of staff comments and possibly develop ways to ensure that any suggestions are anonymous and the person does not feel threatened by making suggestions.

Many businesses reward employees for good service by maintaining employee of the week or month awards. Some of the rewards are as simple as being able to use a parking spot with a sign reading "Reserved for the Employee of the Month." The library need not adopt the same reward system, but the implementation team should consider various options, as it works with library administration and other staff members to shift the focus from collections to customer services.

FIGURE 6.3

COMPLIMENT FORM

**Something Right? Well Done?
Let us know so we can thank
the people who did it.**

Today's date: _____

Describe what we did that you thought we did well:

[ ]

*If you'd like a response, let us know how to reach you.
(Optional)*

Name: _____

Address: _____

Phone: _____

E-mail address: _____

ISSUES TO CONSIDER

The questions listed in figure 6.4 serve as a basis for developing the building blocks of the compliment and complaint tracking system. The implementation team should invite library staff, library managers, and library customers to express their views and perspectives. It is important that the managers and staff do not become defensive, no matter what customers have to say. Discussions might consider these questions:

- What types of complaints and problems should be addressed?
- What changes in the library—its services and operations—have resulted from financial and resource stringencies?
- Are certain problems caused by problem or disorderly patrons, or by problem staff?
- Does the library act on complaint data?

- How does it act on such data?
- To what extent are customers' complaints heeded?

These questions should guide the implementation team as it interacts with internal and external customers, and develops the compliment and complaint tracking system. The team might meet with customers in groups and listen to their discussion of certain questions. (See chapter 8 on focus group interviews.)

The questions in the figure can be answered by all the regular staff members as an indication of the organizational climate for handling complaints, and as a means of enlightening managers about staff knowledge and attitudes in helping customers solve problems. The discussion of these questions serves a dual purpose. First, it indicates the extent to which library staff members are prepared to deal with the community they serve as valued customers. (If they are not

---

FIGURE 6.4

DISCUSSION QUESTIONS FOR LIBRARY STAFF

1. What has the department [or library] done to make sure it listens to the voice of the customer?
2. How does the organization listen to the voice of the employee who directly serves the customer?
3. How do the leaders in the organization view complaints?
4. How does the organization make it easy for customers to complain?
5. What does the organization do to make it easy for employees to solve customers' problems?
6. How does the organization support frontline employees so that they can serve customers with complaints?
7. Will staff receive incentives for participation and not be put "on the spot"—when each episode or encounter becomes public or known throughout the organization?
8. How does the organization currently track and analyze complaints?
9. How does the organization use information about complaints to identify and address underlying problems?
10. How well are resource decisions aligned with the desire to meet customer expectations and to ensure customer satisfaction?
11. How does the organization train frontline employees to handle complaints and to produce satisfied customers?
12. How do you delight customers who have problems?
13. What access do customers have to the organization so that it is easy for them to complain?
14. How do you make sure that you understand what customers want?
15. How do you manage customer expectations?
16. How does the organization design its complaint-handling processes?
17. Does the organization invest in the infrastructure needed to make the complaint-handling process effective both in customer recovery and minimizing costs?
18. How does the organization use complaint information to make operational improvements?

Source: Adapted from the National Performance Review, *Serving the American Public: Best Practices in Resolving Customer Complaints* (Washington, DC: Government Printing Office, 1996).

prepared, steps should be taken to remedy the situation.) Second, the discussion helps staff to understand the benefits of monitoring customer responses voiced as complaints or compliments.

It merits repeating that the assumption is not that customers are always right and must be given whatever they ask. Rather, the purpose is to review those customer expectations that the library wants to meet and the extent to which it does so. In cases where the library cannot act on complaints, it might be important to explain why. Of course, special attention must be given to the forum in which the explanation is provided. How effective is it? How well was the message explained and received? These discussions will reveal the extent to which managers are willing to act on the results—to build them into goals and objectives.

The next step (and it may not be an immediate one) is for the implementation team to develop a policy statement. Again, the statement should be widely discussed and everyone should realize the benefits of having it. The next step (and again, it may not be immediate) is to review the procedures involved in tracking complaints and compliments. Customers, through selected individual and group interviews, should provide feedback into the process.

CONSIDERING PROCESS AND PROCEDURE

The library must adopt a systematic strategy for complaint and compliment management. In developing the procedures for the system, the implementation team needs to consider the following questions:

- Will it be easy for customers to complain or give a compliment?
- Will the system be decentralized, with each employee responsible for resolving complaints; centralized in one location; or a "combination of both, with larger or more serious complaints resolved in a central office"?[9]
- What training will complaint management staff receive? Will that training be adequate?
- How will the library periodically survey customers to ensure that they are satisfied with the complaint management system? Will the library encourage feedback?
- Will the system be regularly reviewed to make necessary improvements? Will the

computer program be flexible enough to accept any revisions?
- Will the system be used (and how will it be used) for quality control and problem prevention more than settling individual complaints?
- Does the system generate on-demand systematic information about causes of complaints and provide trends? Do the data meet the needs of managers?
- Will regular reports be generated from the system, and what will be the nature of those reports?

USING THE TRACKING SYSTEM

It is important to analyze complaints and compliments to see what patterns emerge. Just as FedEx tracks all shipments, identifies bottlenecks, and provides customers with feedback on the delivery status of their packages, so libraries can monitor complaints and how the staff dealt with them. The purpose is to identify problems and, when necessary, develop an effective mechanism to explain why something cannot be done. Furthermore, complaints should not be treated as isolated instances; rather, the library should analyze the reasons, look for patterns, and ensure that the organization learns from both complaints and compliments.

Data from complaints can be "scattered, biased, and fragmentary and [are] as apt to be misleading as to be helpful. Not everyone likes or dislikes the same things."[10] To help sort out patterns and minimize the impact of isolated minor instances, the compliment and complaint tracking system should be automated. Any database or spreadsheet package can be used. The important thing is to enter all compliments and complaints, and assess the patterns for improving the system and service.

Figure 6.5 outlines sample categories for inclusion in a compliment and complaint system that covers both internal (staff) and external customers. The system recognizes that both stakeholder groups must be listened to and respected, and their concerns addressed. Categories should be coded by number for ease of data processing.

Using the information provided in the Problem Report Form (figure 6.2), the following data must be entered into the spreadsheet: the date the complaint was made, status of complainer, type of problem, action taken, the extent to which the customer professes satisfaction, and length of time taken to resolve the problem. (Speed to resolution is an issue, especially if fines are accruing.) Figure 6.6 is an example of a Problem Resolution Tracking Database form. Regarding compliments, the system should monitor the reasons and extent to which the same items gain repeated praise. Library managers can also gauge the extent of *mixed signals*—comments about, as well as complaints and compliments for, the same service.

MAKING THE AUTOMATED SYSTEM AVAILABLE

Library staff must be apprised of progress in developing the system, participate in the field test, and be informed of system procedures. Once the system is installed, all staff members in the library should be able to access it. The reasons are quite simple: looking at how similar problems were handled may be a guide for new staff or for staff dealing with a problem for the first time. Other reasons are accountability and encouraging staff to participate in maintaining a compliment and complaint tracking system.

CONTINUOUS IMPROVEMENT

Figure 6.7 provides a framework for maximizing customer satisfaction and loyalty. The focus here is on continuous improvement within the context of stated goals and objectives, in which the library sets benchmarks and seeks to improve service delivery and staff interactions with customers. "The key to continuous improvement is to refine, redesign, and improve . . . [the] process while putting the customer first."[11] Thus, the compliment and complaint process is

> viewed as a loop with the customer at the beginning and at the end and with the core operating processes in the middle. Constant feedback from both customers and employees and constant reevaluation based on satisfaction measurement assure constant improvement.[12]

As figure 6.8 indicates, organizations can compute and include in regular reports various measures that reflect customer satisfaction with the complaint resolution process, and the timeliness and efficiency of the resolution. As well, complaint managers should monitor employee satisfaction with the results of the measures and the effectiveness of staff training in cus-

tomer service. They should determine the number of hours spent in customer service training per employee and per department or organizational unit, and monitor attrition rates among the staff and the reasons for leaving.

"As complaint data and other customer feedback are used to eliminate underlying problems, the number of complaints should decline."[13] At the same time, the library should strive to stimulate the number of compliments given. The measures depicted in figure 6.8 can reflect a marked improvement in the quality of service performance and in repeat business.

APPLICATION ON THE LIBRARY'S HOME PAGE

The suggestions offered in the previous sections of the chapter should be supplemented with a suggestion or comment box on the opening screen of the library's home page. Figure 6.9 reprints the suggestion box of the Sawyer Library, Suffolk University (Boston), which could easily be adapted to fit the needs of any library. On the opening screen, a user survey appears above the suggestion box and affords students and others an opportunity to provide details about their information needs and expectations. (Some libraries may want to delete question five, as some customers might consider "for verification purposes only" as threatening.)

Instead of (or in addition to) the topics covered in figure 6.9, the online suggestion box might ask the date of the visit, which location they visited, "Please share your views with us," "Do you have any ideas for improvement?" "Are there any staff members who deserve a special mention?" the extent of satisfaction with the visit (perhaps on a five-point Likert scale ranging from *very satisfied* to *very dissatisfied*), and whether the customer would appreciate a written, telephone, e-mail response or even no response.

In those instances in which libraries do not have online suggestion boxes, off-site customers wanting to make a comment or complain would have to locate the staff or departmental directory and find the appropriate person to contact. If they have a more generic comment and do not expect a speedy reply, they might use "contact us" on the home page. The web master would then refer the query to the appropriate department or person and then replay that response back to the inquirer.

As an alternative to an online suggestion box, some libraries gather similar information from their blogs.

FIGURE 6.5

SAMPLE CATEGORIES FOR A COMPLIMENT AND COMPLAINT TRACKING SYSTEM

	COMPLIMENTS	
	Internal Customers	External Customers
System		
Appreciated instruction in use		
Policies consistently applied		
Service delivery: meet or exceed expectations		
Environment		
Good ambiance		
Attractive building		
Spacious		
Staff		
Helpful		
Knowledgeable		

	COMPLAINTS (SUGGESTIONS FOR IMPROVEMENT)	
	Internal Customers	External Customers
Resources		
Item		
Not owned/purchased		
Owned but missing		
Mutilated		
Delays in making it available (e.g., still in process)		
On order; not received		
In poor physical condition		

	COMPLAINTS (SUGGESTIONS FOR IMPROVEMENT)	
	Internal Customers	External Customers
Inappropriate for library or age group		
Inaccurate or missing OPAC information about it		
Insufficient number of copies held		
Prefer its availability in electronic form		
Why no longer held in library?		
Delays in its receipt from storage		
Outdated holdings		
Reserve material		
Long wait for their return		
Insufficient copies		
Mutilated		
Lost		
Too slow in placing material on reserve		
Need more videos and recordings		
Intralibrary loan delays		
Fines erroneously charged		
Charges too high for		
Fines		
Interlibrary loans		
Reserves		
Photocopies		
Rental items		
Videos		
Policies		
Information required for registration too personal (e.g., age or Social Security number)		
Policy not to give children's record of current borrowing to parents		

(cont.)

FIGURE 6.5 (cont.)

	COMPLAINTS (SUGGESTIONS FOR IMPROVEMENT)	
	Internal Customers	**External Customers**
Policy not to restrict children's borrowing to children's materials		
Other customers using inappropriate Internet materials		
Internet access not filtered or restricted for children's use		
Have to wait in line too long		
Problems with phones (e.g., getting through, cut off, placed on hold, or getting a recording instead of a person)		
Need for Internet/OPAC/database instruction		
Environment		
Parking problem		
Lighting		
Temperature		
Too hot		
Too cold		
Too noisy		
Other customers talking on cell phones		
Children running around unsupervised		
No seats available		
No seminar or conference rooms available		
Other customers who smell, stare, or are distasteful		
Concern about personal safety		
Theft of customer belongings		
Equipment		
Insufficient number		
Not in working order		
None available at moment (in use)		

	COMPLAINTS (SUGGESTIONS FOR IMPROVEMENT)	
	Internal Customers	**External Customers**
Hard to use		
Screens hard to read		
Keyboards dirty		
Poor quality printing		
Water fountains/restroom facilities not working or dirty		
Reader area messy		
Too many unshelved items		
Garbage from people eating and drinking		
Elevators not working		
Hours library open		
Staff		
None present in service area		
Long queue for service		
Circulation desk		
Information desk		
Do not seem to know collection or sources		
Not helpful		
Discourteous/rude		
Aloof/uninterested		
Unresponsive (e.g., using OPAC without saying a word)		
Too busy talking with each other		
Answer telephone before helping customers awaiting service		

FIGURE 6.6

PROBLEM RESOLUTION TRACKING DATABASE

Problem Number	Date	Problem Type	Location	Reported By	Responsible Person	Action Required?	Action Taken	Date Taken	Reply Required?	Date Sent

Problem Number: Assigned by staff

Date: Date incident was reported

Problem Type: Mechanical (copier, computer, etc.), shelving error, etc.

Location: Where in building(s) the problem occurred

Reported By: Staff member who filled out problem report

Responsible Person: Name of person responsible for fixing this kind of problem.

Action Required: Is any further action needed to fix this problem?

Action Taken: If action is required, what was done?

Date Taken: If action was taken, when?

Reply Required: Did patron request a response?

Date Sent: If so, when was it sent?

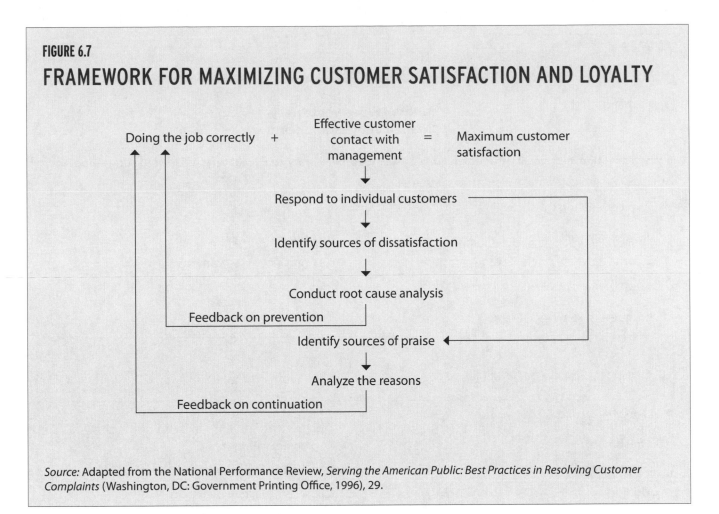

FIGURE 6.7

FRAMEWORK FOR MAXIMIZING CUSTOMER SATISFACTION AND LOYALTY

Doing the job correctly + Effective customer contact with management = Maximum customer satisfaction

→ Respond to individual customers

→ Identify sources of dissatisfaction

→ Conduct root cause analysis

Feedback on prevention

→ Identify sources of praise ◀

→ Analyze the reasons

Feedback on continuation

Source: Adapted from the National Performance Review, *Serving the American Public: Best Practices in Resolving Customer Complaints* (Washington, DC: Government Printing Office, 1996), 29.

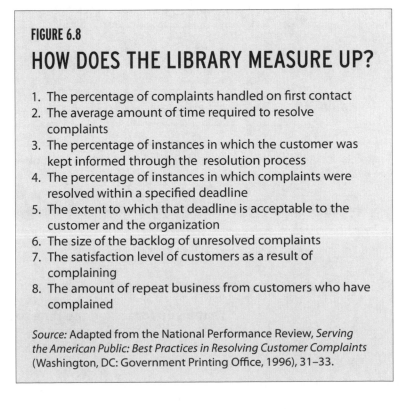

FIGURE 6.8

HOW DOES THE LIBRARY MEASURE UP?

1. The percentage of complaints handled on first contact
2. The average amount of time required to resolve complaints
3. The percentage of instances in which the customer was kept informed through the resolution process
4. The percentage of instances in which complaints were resolved within a specified deadline
5. The extent to which that deadline is acceptable to the customer and the organization
6. The size of the backlog of unresolved complaints
7. The satisfaction level of customers as a result of complaining
8. The amount of repeat business from customers who have complained

Source: Adapted from the National Performance Review, *Serving the American Public: Best Practices in Resolving Customer Complaints* (Washington, DC: Government Printing Office, 1996), 31–33.

FIGURE 6.9

SUGGESTION BOX (LIBRARY HOME PAGE)

Mildred F. Sawyer Library
"Make a Suggestion" Form

If you are a Suffolk University student, faculty or staff member, library staff are interested in your suggestions.
An asterisk * indicates that a response is required.

* 1. I am completing this form:

❑ in the Sawyer Library   ❑ from my work place

❑ from elsewhere on the Boston campus   ❑ from another SU campus

❑ from home

* 2. I suggest the Sawyer Library:

* 3. I am a:

❑ freshman   ❑ graduate student

❑ sophomore   ❑ full time faculty member

❑ junior   ❑ part time faculty member

❑ senior   ❑ University staff member

4. My major/department is ("none" if no major chosen at this time):

* 5. Last name (for verification purposes only):

* 6. Suffolk University Identification Number (seven digit number—for verification purposes only):

7. If you would like to be contacted by the Sawyer Library staff, please include your e-mail address:

Thank you for taking the time to make a suggestion!

Source: Suffolk University, Sawyer Library, "Suggestion Box," http://fs3.formsite.com/sawyerlibrary/form409839305/index.html.
Reproduced with permission.

They might even move some of the comments to a testimonial or news page on their website. As an alternative, there might be separate sections for testimonials and news, thereby bypassing the blogs.

In the case of academic libraries, requests for feedback serve another purpose. They enable the library to provide evidence to accreditation organizations about their responsiveness to constituent groups and institutional effectiveness: One accreditation organization, for instance, defines institutional effectiveness thus: "The institution regularly and systematically evaluates the adequacy, utilization, and impact of its library, information resources and services, and instructional and information technology and uses the findings to improve and increase the effectiveness of these services."[14]

A FINAL WORD

By making it "easy for customers to complain," including internal customers, and handling "complaints quickly and courteously with common sense," organizations not only "save money by eliminating unnecessary additional contacts that escalate costs [but also] build customer confidence."[15] That confidence produces or improves customer satisfaction and loyalty. Effective complaint handling, therefore, "sustains and strengthens" customer loyalty to a service or organization.[16] Loyalty is interrelated with satisfaction, and the correlation can be either positive or negative; if the latter, the number of complaints increases—or at least does not decrease—and the organization may become more resistant to customer grievances. A concept known as *vicious circle complaints* may emerge: The more complaints that an organization receives, the less responsive it becomes. Instead of making use of customer complaints, the organization behaves dysfunctionally.[17] Furthermore, more customers may be lost as they desert the library and go elsewhere for the resolution of their information needs, and as they convey their negative experiences to friends and colleagues.

In summary, two objectives of complaint handling are to: (1) turn a dissatisfied customer into a loyal customer, and (2) reduce barriers or problems that might have a negative impact on other customers. After all, if complaints indicate, for instance, that a service fails to meet customers' expectations or that customers feel they have not been heard or treated fairly, it might be appropriate to approach complaints more as opportunities for improved service delivery and to accept the challenges of creating a more customer-focused, service organization.

Paul Hawken, author and specialist in garden and horticultural mail-order businesses, has specified how to be a good customer:

- Complain
- Praise
- Be articulate in expressing needs/wants
- Demand quick service
- Be quick yourself (complain immediately)
- Be kind
- Be persistent[18]

To this list, we add *be knowledgeable*—know what you are talking about and where to go to make your voice heard. Library staff, therefore, should avoid saying, "If only customers knew about . . ." and perpetuating the status quo. The library should constantly strive to improve its services and should let customers participate in shaping those services of highest priority to them. For this reason, it is important to respond to comments and complaints in a timely manner; after all, librarians want to demonstrate that they listen to their customers. The more that they are perceived as listening to customers, the more likely customers will reciprocate by participating in surveys and other means of data collection.

Complaints should gain more attention from the library than is provided through notices on a bulletin board or in a centrally located notebook. Complaint data should not be ignored as library staff deals with issues of evaluation and assessment.[19]

Complaining customers are giving us an opportunity to find out what their problems are so we can help them and they will be encouraged to come back, use our services . . .[20]

It is estimated that only 10 percent of customer complaints are ever articulated.[21]

Notes

1. Janelle Barlow and Claus Møller, *A Complaint Is a Gift: Recovering Customer Loyalty When Things Go Wrong* (San Francisco: Berrett-Koehler Publishers, 2008), 20.

2. Clay Carr, *Front-Line Customer Service: 15 Keys to Customer Satisfaction* (New York: Wiley, 1990), 26.

3. Ibid., 20–21. See also Keki R. Bhote, *Beyond Customer Satisfaction to Customer Loyalty* (New York: American Management Association, 1996), 28.

4. Carr, *Front-Line Customer Service*, 21.

5. Ibid., 79.

6. Ann Curry, "Managing the Problem Patron," *Public Libraries* 35, no. 3 (May/June 1996), 183.

7. Department of Commerce, Office of Consumer Affairs, *Managing Consumer Complaints: Responsive Business Approaches to Consumer Needs* (Washington, DC: Government Printing Office, 1992), 5.

8. National Performance Review, *Serving the American Public: Best Practices in Resolving Customer Complaints* (Washington, DC: Government Printing Office, 1996), 2. See also Darryl A. Griffin, "A Manual for Turning Customer Complaints into Opportunities to Improve Customer Service and Satisfaction in the Service Industry," Master's thesis (California State University, Dominquez Hills, 2009), AAT 1461578. Available from *Dissertations and Theses Full Text*.

9. Ibid., 29.

10. Carr, *Front-Line Customer Service*, 135.

11. National Performance Review, *Serving the American Public*, 8.

12. Department of Commerce, *Managing Consumer Complaints*, 13.

13. National Performance Review, *Serving the American Public*, 6.

14. New England Association of Schools and Colleges, Commission on Institutions of Higher Education, *Standards for Accreditation: Standard Seven: Libraries and Other Information Resources*, item 7.12, http://cihe.neasc.org/standards_policies/standards/standard_seven/.

15. National Performance Review, *Serving the American Public*, 1, 2.

16. Ibid., 6.

17. See Claes Fornell, "A National Customer Satisfaction Barometer: The Swedish Experience," in *Performance Measurement and Evaluation*, ed. Jacky Holloway, Jenny Lewis, and Geoff Mallory (London: Sage, 1995), 113.

18. Paul Hawken, *Growing a Business* (New York: Simon and Schuster, 1987).

19. See Peter Hernon and Robert E. Dugan, "Assessment and Evaluation: What Do the Terms Really Mean?" *College & Research Libraries News* 70, no. 3 (March 2009): 146–149.

20. Barlow and Claus Møller, *A Complaint Is a Gift*, 27.

21. Shep Hyken, *The Cult of the Customer: Create an Amazing Customer Experience That Turns Satisfied Customers into Customer Evangelists* (New York: Wiley and Sons, 2009), 36.

Chapter Seven

Listening to Customers through Surveys

Active listening . . . involves far more than simply hearing your client's spoken words.[1]

[T]he very act of surveying customers conveys a very positive message: the organization is interested in its customers' well-being, needs, pleasures, and displeasures.[2]

Libraries concerned about how well they are satisfying their customers need to make a strong effort to listen to what customers tell them about their experiences using the library. There are various ways of reaching out; some take little effort, others take considerably more, and all require thought about what to ask and how the information solicited might be used to improve services. Figure 7.1 identifies various ways in which libraries can listen to customers, identify their expectations, and compare their expectations to perceptions of service delivery or to the actual service provided. Library staff members or outside evaluators might collect data *actively* (from customers directly), perhaps through a survey or focus group interview. (See chapter 8.) In so doing, they request a *favor* of or make an *imposition* on respondents. As an alternative, they might collect data *passively*— "meaning (a) any solicitation of feedback . . . done without direct customer interaction, and (b) the customer initiates any response given."[3]

According to Scott E. Sampson, examples of passively solicited customer feedback "include customer comment cards (left on a table, a wall display, etc.), toll-free telephone numbers, and comment links on . . . Web pages."[4] He notes that, "passive methods generally have lower response rates and are inherently biased, but have cost and sample frame advantages when used to monitor quality on a continuing basis."[5] Passive methods are less time consuming, do not require a major campaign to invite response, and can more easily be assumed as part of regular staff duties and responsibilities. The findings, however, require great caution in interpretation and application, in part because customers must be motivated to respond. Because those customers who are the most satisfied or dissatisfied are the most likely to respond, there is a risk of response bias.

Sampson, who surveyed customers staying at a hotel, concludes that, "customers who spontaneously register complaints generally record higher ratings of the service provider than customers who complain in response to a complaint solicitation."[6] This important finding, if transferable to library settings, is a reminder to encourage customers to complain or to compliment, in such a way that libraries ensure spontaneity and prompt resolution of problems, when feasible.

FIGURE 7.1

SOME WAYS TO LISTEN TO CUSTOMERS

SUGGESTION BOXES, FORMS, AND COMMENT CARDS

These are customer initiated and tend to focus on problems. The survey might take the form of comment cards similar to those found in hotels and restaurants. Such methods, however, lack the tracking and management features of complaint tracking systems. (See chapter 6.) The suggestion or comment box might appear on a library's home page or at the institution's "my.portal," which provides the customers of an institution with personalized access to helpful information and services. The institution may prefer to place the online comment form on its home page to ensure that only its direct constituents reply.

Advantages

- Information can be collected with little effort and low cost.
- Data come in continuously.
- Constituent groups may respond whenever they choose.

Disadvantages

- Data are subject to extreme bias.
- There may be few responses.
- There may be no linkage to a tracking and management system.

LIBRARY BLOGS AND WIKIS

Many blogs provide commentary or news on a particular subject. They might combine text, images, and links to other sources. The ability for readers to leave comments in an interactive format is an important part of library blogs. A wiki is a collaborative project in which anyone can add, edit, or delete pages. Librarians might also collect perceptions from online social networks such as Facebook and/or MySpace.[a]

Advantages

- Develop an ongoing but irregular dialogue with individuals.
- Opportunity to test ideas and announce services.
- Information can be collected with little effort and low cost.
- Constituents may respond at their choosing.
- Data come in continuously.

Disadvantages

- Only a small proportion of a library's constituency will participate.
- The extent of their participation varies.
- Data are subject to extreme bias.
- There may be few respondents.
- There may be no linkage to a tracking and management system.

CUSTOMER SURVEYS

The intent is to identify customers' expectations and perceptions—presumably those that the library is willing to meet. Such surveys might be repeated as part of customer follow-up over a predetermined time frame. Methods might include rating cards placed in a service area or near the exit. Customers can then rate the quality of service they received and comment on the extent to which their expectations were met. Library home pages might also contain brief surveys that rate services and the extent to which expectations were met; any questions eliciting background information should not infringe on customers' privacy.

QUESTIONNAIRES

These must be constructed carefully and distributed according to a sophisticated sampling plan.

Advantages

- Can explore many aspects of service.
- Usually obtain some demographic information about respondents.
- Sampling is controlled by the researcher.
- High rates of response are possible.
- Data may well reflect the characteristics and opinions of the customer population.
- Costs less than interviewing.
- Can be self-administered.
- May survey large numbers of people.

Disadvantages

- Produces a snapshot of the situation at a particular point in time.
- May be time consuming to analyze and interpret results.
- Produces self-reported data.
- Data lack the depth resulting from interviewing.

FOCUS GROUP INTERVIEWS

Libraries can use focus groups to gather insights into customer expectations, the willingness of library staff members to meet those expectations and embrace customer service plans, and the ability to regain lost customers or to attract first-time customers.

Advantages

- Unstructured nature can allow for deeper exploration of customers' views.
- Sampling is controlled by the researcher.
- Groups can represent one type of customer or customers in general, depending on what the library wants to know.
- See chapter 8 for other advantages.

Disadvantages

- Requires a skilled moderator able to be objective in data collection; such an individual may be difficult to find.
- See chapter 8 for other disadvantages.

IN-PERSON OR TELEPHONE INTERVIEWS

Interviews gather customers' opinions on a service, product, or issue on a one-on-one basis. In one type of telephone survey, customers calling the library are asked to participate in a short interview while on the line. An alternative is the telephone recontact, in which the staff member asks if the customer would agree to being called later and, if so, obtains the person's name and phone number. Or, instead of getting the phone number for telephone recontact, the customer might be asked to provide an address for a mail survey or comment card.

Advantages

- Sampling is controlled by the researcher.
- Data may be representative of the population.
- More topics can be explored than by passive data collection (not surveying customers directly).
- In-person interviews permit in-depth probing of opinions and elaboration of issues; telephone surveys may not.
- Permits interaction with respondents.

Disadvantages

- Cost is high to medium.
- Chance for error in transcription is medium to high.
- Time-consuming to set up and administer.
- Interviewers must be well trained.
- Data collected may be self-reports.
- May produce low response rate.
- May be hard to find interviewers who have the voices and verbal skills to gain compliance and high-quality data.
- Not all households may have telephones.

TOLL-FREE OR SPECIAL TELEPHONE NUMBER(S)

As a companion to other methods for registering complaints, offering compliments, or identifying special expectations, library staff might provide a toll-free or local telephone number. Such numbers might be listed on brochures (e.g., service pledges) and on signs scattered throughout the library.

Advantages

- Data collection is quick and continuous.

Disadvantages

- May produce response bias if most customers are angry.
- Cost of maintaining phone line may be high.

(cont.)

FIGURE 7.1 (cont.)

WEB-BASED SURVEYS

Through the library's home page, or independent of it, customers can communicate directly with library staff and convey problems, expectations, and degree of satisfaction.

Advantages

- Information can be collected with little effort and low cost.
- Data can be collected continuously.
- Method is self-administered.
- May provide an opportunity for interaction and follow-up with subjects.

Disadvantages

- Population may be unknown.
- Responses are all self-reported.
- Risks self-selected sample.

E-MAIL

E-mail can also be used as a means of conducting customer surveys.

Advantages

- The survey reaches a geographically dispersed group of customers.
- The method is faster and cheaper than mailed, telephone, and in-person surveys.
- The likelihood of a prompt response is high.
- The survey can target a specific group of customers.

Disadvantages

- Respondents may not be representative of the population.
- Respondents are likely to be better-educated, urban, white-collar, and technologically literate.
- Problems may occur in telecommunications transmissions.
- Response rate, if it can be determined, may be low.
- It is more difficult to show legitimacy of the study (e.g., demonstrate authority of those doing the investigation).
- Customers may resent receiving surveys among their e-mail communication.

COMPLAINT TRACKING SYSTEMS

As discussed in chapter 6, these systems track responses to inquiries and complaints, for the purpose of improving response time, resolving problems, and creating and maintaining customer loyalty. Data received from suggestion boxes, e-mail, and special phone lines can be incorporated into the compliment and complaint tracking system.

Advantages

- Data are useful for tracking quality on a continuous basis.

Disadvantages

- Some costs are incurred to establish and maintain the system.

SOME READINGS

Bertot, John C. "Web-Based Surveys: Not Your Basic Survey Anymore." *Library Quarterly* 79, no. 1 (January 2009): 119–125.

Best, Samuel J., and Chase H. Harrison. *Measuring and Adjusting for Survey Nonresponse.* Thousand Oaks, CA: Sage, 2010.

Fink, Arlene. *How to Conduct Surveys: A Step-by-Step Guide,* 3rd ed. Thousand Oaks, CA: Sage, 2006.

Gaiser, Ted J., and Anthony E. Schreiner. *A Guide to Conducting Online Research.* Thousand Oaks, CA: Sage, 2009.

Gregory, Vicki L., and Nahyun Kwon. "The Effects of Librarians' Behavioral Performance on User Satisfaction in Chat Reference Services." *Reference and User Services Quarterly* 47, no. 2 (Winter 2007): 137–149.

Herring, Susan C., Lois Ann Scheidt, Inna Kouper, and Elijah Wright. "A Longitudinal Content Analysis of Weblogs: 2003–2004," in *Blogging, Citizenship, and the Future of Media,* ed. M. Tremayne, www .blogninja.com/brog-tremayne-06.pdf.

James, Nalita, and Hugh Busher. *Online Interviewing.* Thousand Oaks, CA: Sage, 2009.

Kittleson, Mark J., and Stephen L. Brown. "E-mail versus Web Survey Response Rates among Health Education Professionals." *American Journal of Health Studies* 20, no. 1–2 (Winter/Spring 2005): 7–14.

Krueger, Richard A., and Mary Anne Casey. *Focus Groups: A Practical Guide for Applied Research,* 4th ed. Thousand Oaks, CA: Sage, 2008.

Sue, Valerie M., and Lois A. Ritter. *Conducting Online Surveys.* Thousand Oaks, CA: Sage, 2007.

Yin, Robert K. *Case Study Research: Design and Methods,* 4th ed. Thousand Oaks, CA: Sage, 2009.

[a]See Ruth S. Connell, "Academic Libraries, Facebook and MySpace, and Student Outreach: A Survey of Student Opinion," *portal: Libraries and the Academy* 9, no. 1 (January 2009): 25–36.

Another way to collect information about customers is to train library staff members to make objective observations and consult records that provide insights into potential problem areas. For instance, they might monitor the number of busy signals received on a telephone line, connectivity problems to the library's home page, and the working condition of equipment. The focus of such methods is less on the identification of customer expectations and more on the condition or state of the actual service delivered. Thus, by comparing active methods to other methods, library staff members can monitor discrepancies between expectations and the service provided. They can then seek to reduce the gap between the two. Whatever methods the library uses for characterizing the service actually delivered must be objective and must produce valid comparisons to customer expectations.

Librarians can engage in data collection that produces *quantitative* results (in which numbers are reduced to measurement) or *qualitative* results (which lack that reduction). Whenever possible, they should collect both types of data about operations, services, and customers. Each one provides a portion of the picture; together, they provide rich insights useful for better serving customers and attracting new or lost ones. This chapter fills in a portion of the picture—that part requiring quantitative data collection. Together, chapters 6 through 8 and chapter 10 offer strategies for evaluating service quality and satisfaction. A library needs to select those strategies most relevant to its particular situation. (See figure 7.1.)

MEASURING SERVICE QUALITY

Expectations, a theoretical concept, cover both service quality and satisfaction. Service quality deals with the interaction between actual customers and service providers such as libraries. In the 1980s and 1990s, most marketing and library and information science researchers tended to view service quality in terms of meeting and/or exceeding expectations. This definition is all-encompassing and applies across service industries, but expectations change and may be shaped by experiences with other service providers.

The Gaps Model of Service Quality offers service organizations a framework to identify services in the form of the gaps that exceed (or fail to meet) customer expectations. The model posits five gaps that reflect a discrepancy between

- customers' expectations and management's perceptions of these expectations (gap 1)
- management's perceptions of customers' expectations and service quality specifications (gap 2)
- service quality specifications and actual service delivery (gap 3)
- actual service delivery and what is communicated to customers about it (gap 4)
- customers' expected services and perceived service delivered (gap 5)[7]

Although all five gaps may hinder an organization in providing high-quality service, the fifth gap is the basis of a customer-oriented definition of service quality that examines the discrepancy between customers' expectations for excellence and their perceptions of the actual service delivered. Expectations are *desired* wants—the extent to which customers believe a particular attribute is *essential* for an excellent service provider,[8] and perceptions are a judgment of service performance.

Jeffrey E. Disend, who correlates the Gaps Model with the concept of service quality, maintains that poor service results if the gap, or the difference, is large between what is expected and what is delivered. When what is delivered matches what is expected, customers find the service acceptable. If the service is better than what they expected, exceptional service materializes.[9] Consequently, when expectations and perceptions are ranked on a scale, the gap is a number reflecting the difference between the two—expectations ranking minus perceptions ranking. If there is a poor service gap, a negative number occurs. If the number, by chance, is zero, service is acceptable (expectations match perceptions). If a positive value emerges (perceptions exceed expectations), the service provider has achieved exceptional service.

The definition of service quality presented in the Gaps Model recognizes that expectations are subjective and are neither static nor predictable. Before using a service, a customer has certain expectations about it. These expectations become a basis against which to compare actual performance. After having gained some experience with a service, customers can compare any expectations with the actual performance; expectations are

1. *Confirmed* when perceived performance *meets* them

2. *Affirmed* (reinforced by positive disconfirmation) when perceived performance *exceeds* them

3. *Disconfirmed* (failed by negative disconfirmation) when perceived performance *falls short* of them[10]

SERVQUAL

The literature on measuring service quality has tended to focus on the use of SERVQUAL, which was developed originally through marketing research in the profit sector. It measures the fifth gap—the difference between customers' perceptions of what a service should deliver and how well that service meets idealized expectations.

In her dissertation, Danuta A. Nitecki adapted the SERVQUAL instrument to measure the quality of interlibrary loan, room reserve services, and reference services.[11] She also applied that instrument to reference services at Sterling Memorial Library at Yale University, and Joan Stein adapted Nitecki's instrument to examine interlibrary loan services at Carnegie Mellon University. The *Proceedings of the 2nd Northumbria International Conference on Performance Measurement in Libraries and Information Services* reproduces both the Nitecki and Stein instruments.[12]

Believing that SERVQUAL does not sufficiently address local expectations and priorities, Peter Hernon and Philip Calvert developed a generic set of expectations from which individual libraries could select the subset of interest and plug them into the SERVQUAL format.[13] They supplemented these lists with an extensive array of statements for the online environment.[14] Central to their approach is the belief that whatever expectations are probed should result from local review and the input of library staff and presumably of some customers (perhaps through a customer advisory panel). Their research has focused on one library or service location and has not attempted to determine the relevancy of the statements across institutions or over time.

Figure 7.2 represents a partial list of the various statements they developed and pretested, and that were affirmed by a number of librarians. The set of statements, although far-reaching, do not cover every conceivable aspect for which customers from any stakeholder group might form expectations. Further, that set might be modified. Discussions with a library's internal and external customers may reveal additional choices for possible statements to include in a survey.

Nitecki and Hernon combined the local approach to identify service factors with a version of SERVQUAL. Their study took place at Yale University libraries, and the success of the projects suggests that it can be replicated elsewhere.[15] Central to this approach is that the statements require modification from setting to setting, as determined by the priorities for service improvement established by service providers and managers. The goal, after all, is local diagnosis built around statements that have importance to both libraries and their customers.

LibQUAL+

In 1999, twelve libraries affiliated with the Association of Research Libraries led by Fred Heath, Colleen Cook, and Bruce Thompson of Texas A and M University adapted the SERVQUAL instrument and structure into what has become known as LibQUAL+. From this beginning, the instrument has been applied in more than one thousand libraries, including colleges and universities, community colleges, health sciences libraries, law libraries, and public libraries. In addition to the United States, these studies have been conducted in Canada, the United Kingdom, Africa, Asia, Australia, and Europe.

LibQUAL+ aims to

- foster a culture of excellence in providing library service
- help libraries better understand user perceptions of library service quality
- collect and interpret library user feedback systematically over time
- provide libraries with comparable evaluation information from peer institutions
- identify best practices in library service
- enhance library staff members' analytical skills for interpreting and acting on data

Participating libraries receive institutional reports and data enabling them to determine whether their library services meet expectations; receive aggregate reports allowing them to compare their results with peer institutions; gain access to a digital library of research articles, presentations, and resources focused on library evaluation; join a community interested in developing excellence in library services; receive survey data that help the library identify best practices, analyze deficits, and allocate resources.

Conducting the LibQUAL+ survey requires little technical expertise, as participating libraries use the designers' online Management Center to set up and track survey progress. The libraries invite their primary constituency groups to take the survey, distributing the URL for their library's web form via e-mail or posting a link to the survey on the library's website. Respondents complete the survey form and their answers are sent to the LibQUAL+ database. The data are analyzed and presented in reports describing respondents' service expectations.

The fee-based instrument consists of twenty-two core questions which are rated on a Likert scale of one to nine, along with some demographic questions.[16]

There are also some other questions, including a few that address general satisfaction:

- In general, I am satisfied with the way in which I am treated at the library.
- In general, I am satisfied with library support for my learning, research, and/or teaching needs.
- How would you rate the overall quality of the service provided by the library?

Each of the twenty-two questions asks respondents to express their minimum and desired expectation and their perceived level of service. There are two gap measures; one is the difference between the perceived level of service and the minimum expectation, and the other is the difference between the perceived level of service and the desired expectation. A positive gap implies high service quality and a negative gap poor service quality.[17]

The designers of the LibQUAL+ survey process provide a time line and action plan with critical milestones, and provide participating libraries with a survey process. As part of that process, they receive a report that analyzes survey findings.[18] As with any survey, it is important to consider the time of the school term to conduct the study, the type of incentive to offer, ways to bolster the response rate, and effective strategies to promote the study and the value of survey completion.

A concern is that response rates tend to be low—often between 12 and 22 percent. The survey designers argue that even such response rates can produce findings representative of the population, but is that population the institution's population or the population of actual library users? A generic characterization of respondents as reflective of the freshman class ignores the composition of that class by race, ethnicity, disability, and so forth. To argue for the latter ignores that the study population is not users but members of the institution.

The Association of Research Libraries has a complementary suite of data-collection processes, one of which is known as StatsQUAL, which

> is a gateway to library assessment tools that describe the role, character, and impact of physical and digital libraries. Through StatsQUAL®, libraries gain access to a number of resources that are used to assess library's effectiveness and contributions to teaching, learning, and research. StatsQUAL® presents these tools in a single powerful interactive framework that integrates and enhances data mining and presentation both

FIGURE 7.2

SAMPLE STATEMENTS (SERVICE QUALITY)

CUSTOMER GUIDANCE/ASSISTANCE

Library Website

Allows me to find out about library hours, locations, services, and policies.

Arranges library databases by general subject/discipline.

Arranges links to websites by general subject disciplines.

Enables me to download material:

Onto the computer screen quickly.

And print a copy with ease.

Enables me to have access to:

Download material onto removable media (e.g., USB memory device).

Online guides to information about my subject interests.

Has links that function (no dead links or redirected links that do not work).

Includes online request forms (e.g., for reference/interlibrary loan).

Is easy to navigate.

Is easy to return to after using other websites/online resources.

Is well structured with:

Consistent headings and labels on every page.

Links that provide access to relevant information, allowing the serendipitous discovery of sources.

Menus that help me understand how information/content is organized.

Uses colors, backgrounds, fonts, icons, images, text size, and layout that are easy to view.

Online Catalog

The online catalog is an accurate source of information about all material held by the library.

The online catalog computer is in good working order. (It is not "down" when I want to use it.)

The information displayed on the online library catalog computers is clear and easy to follow.

Waiting Times

I do not have to wait more than three minutes when I

ask for assistance at a reference or information desk.

phone the library for assistance or information.

borrow material.

use the closed reserve collection.

use microfilm and microfiche readers.

use photocopiers.

use self-issue machines.

use the online library catalog.

use electronic resources (e.g., databases).

need to print from a computer.

Library Staff

Library staff is

approachable and welcoming.

willing to leave the desk area to help me.

available when I need them.

courteous and polite.

friendly and easy to talk to.

All public service desks throughout the library are served by knowledgeable staff.

Knowledgeable staff is available to assist whenever the library is open.

Finding Materials

The materials I want are in their proper places on the shelves.

Materials are reshelved promptly.

It is easy to find where materials are located in the building.

THE BUILDING AND THE LIBRARY ENVIRONMENT

Comfort

I find the

humidity in the building is comfortable.

temperature in the building is comfortable.

ventilation in the building is comfortable.

Lighting

The lighting in the building is adequate to my needs.

Furniture

Library furniture is

available (e.g., I can find a seat or study desk).

comfortable.

functional.

OTHER UTILITIES

Online library catalog keys are clean.

Online library screens are clean.

The drinking fountains are clean.

The number of drinking fountains in the building is sufficient.

The toilets are clean.

The machinery that opens, closes, and locks compact shelving is in good working order.

---

within and across institutions. StatsQUAL® includes instruments and data such as . . . [LibQUAL+], DigiQUAL®, and MINES for Libraries®, as well as a growing dataset of survey results.[19]

DigiQUAL modifies and repurposes LibQUAL+ protocol to evaluate the services provided by digital libraries.

In summary, from an extensive review of the literature on LibQUAL+, some participating libraries mischaracterize the instrument as one measuring satisfaction or as useful in providing evidence of student learning outcomes. This instrument actually measures service quality, and accreditation organizations do not consider either satisfaction or service quality as more than outputs. Survey findings do not reflect what students learn through their program of study. Furthermore, the final satisfaction question (asking for an overall rating) does not really address satisfaction. (See chapter 10.)

A FORM TAILORED TO INDIVIDUAL LIBRARY NEEDS

All of the uses of SERVQUAL have been for the general population of library customers. The percentage of undergraduate students with a disability has been put at approximately 10 percent nationwide, with more high school students with disabilities planning to continue their education in postsecondary schools. Given this situation, to serve as an effective tool for such a population, SERVQUAL needs a drastic revision. Hernon and Calvert, together with librarians and disability specialists, rewrote the questionnaire for a disability audience. They developed two versions of the instrument, which were widely pretested. In part, the procedures and the dimensions probed had to be simplified.[20] The point is that librarians should not consider that there is only one way to measure service quality (as covered in the next section).

A more recent version of SERVQUAL asks respondents to comment on a series of statements from the same three contexts: *minimum* service expectations, *desired* service expectations, and the *perception* of service performance using a nine-point scale. (See figure 7.3.) The three-column format reconceptualizes expectations into desired and minimum expectations at either end of a continuum; a *zone of tolerance* falls in between. This zone encompasses the service performance that customers consider *satisfactory*.

There are advantages and disadvantages to either the two- or three-column format. As a result, librarians have an option. If the goal is to include some statements from LibQUAL+ and make comparisons, obviously the three-column format is preferred. Librarians may prefer to substitute the dimensions from LibQUAL+ and not probe the more general set or the set tailored to the digital environment. Those dimensions are

Affect of service, the human aspect, relates to the extent to which library staff is courteous, knowledgeable, helpful, and reliable.

Information control measures how users prefer to interact with the library and whether the needed information is delivered in the format, location, and time of their choosing.

Library as a physical place covers the usefulness of space, the symbolic value of the library, and the library as a refuge for work or study.[21]

As this book reflects, library staff members have choices about the types of comparisons they make. First, they might use a modified version of SERVQUAL to compare customer expectations and perceptions of service performance. Second, they might compare customer expectations to objective indicators of service quality. Or third, they might compare customer expectations to staff members' or management's perceptions of service performance.

Although this book does not emphasize the first approach, it is still a viable choice. (Readers who want to use this approach can adapt the ideas discussed in this chapter.) This book focuses on the second choice and shows that libraries can pursue various choices and develop customer-related indicators. The third choice is the most risky, if library staff members assume that they already fully understand service performance and become defensive in responding to customer expectations. Any use of the third choice must seek ways to minimize rationalization of the status quo and the attitude that the customer is never or seldom right.

Whatever the choice, librarians should remember that customers are not merely recipients of the services offered; they are "partners in the development and implementation of services" to make library experiences more successful from their perspective.[22]

If a library decides to proceed with an adaptation of SERVQUAL, in addition to or in place of LibQUAL+, the staff should review the set of statements such as those appearing in figure 7.2, select those most relevant, and add other potentially important statements. They can consult the Nitecki and Hernon article, which reprints the SERVQUAL instrument.[23] That form consists of twenty-two pairs of statements about factors that a service provider delivers. The first set of statements measures the customer's expectations by asking each respondent to rate how essential each factor is for a service to be excellent. The second set of twenty-two statements formulates the same factors into descriptions about service delivered and ascertains the respondent's perception of the level of service given. For each pair of statements, the difference between the ranked perception minus the ranked expectation

is calculated; the average of these gap scores is the SERVQUAL overall quality score.

As an alternative, the staff might align data collection with LibQUAL+ by asking respondents to express their minimum and desired expectation, and their perceived level of service. More than likely, this adaptation of SERVQUAL would focus on actual library customers and their expectations.

Valarie A. Zeithaml, A. Parasuraman, and Leonard L. Berry maintain that their set of twenty-two statements encompasses five interrelated dimensions that customers most value when they evaluate service quality in a service industry: *tangibles* (the appearance of physical facilities, equipment, personnel, and communication material); *reliability* (ability to perform the promised service dependably and accurately); *responsiveness* (willingness to help customers and provide prompt service); *assurance* (knowledge and courtesy of employees and their ability to inspire trust and confidence); and *empathy* (the caring, individualized attention that a firm provides its customers).[24] Complicating matters, the dimensions for e-service quality at this time appear to differ and encompass

- ease of use (navigation, search, download speed, remote access)
- website aesthetics (colors, graphics, size, etc.)
- linkage (connectivity to relevant information, avoid broken links, regularly update the accuracy of links, etc.)
- collections (quality, relevance, and deep collections of electronic material to meet my immediate needs)
- reliability (frequency of updating, proper technical functioning of website or electronic product, etc.)
- support (help pages, section on frequently asked questions, technical help if there is a problem, etc.)
- security/privacy/trust (belief the site is relatively safe from intrusion, personal information is protected, etc.)
- ease of access (log on/off quickly, etc.)
- flexibility (different search procedures: basic and advanced, etc.)
- customization/personalization (receive e-mail announcements about the arrival of new books on topics of personal interest, etc.)[25]

Another choice then is to use the SERQUAL or LibQUAL+ dimensions or to experiment with the special e-SERVQUAL dimensions. The staff might even prefer not to probe dimensions in their survey.

HOW TO PROCEED

As the first step—before conducting any survey—library staff, meeting in departments or teams and across departments/teams, should review the organization's mission for its coverage of customer-based services, as well as any strategic planning documents. Everyone should understand that customers comprise "one of the key drivers in planning for the future."[26] Any customer-driven organization

> maintains a focus on the needs and expectations, both spoken and unspoken, of customers, both present and future, in the creation and/or improvement of the product or service provided. . . . Spoken and unspoken means that not only must the expressed needs and expectations of the customers be listened to, but also that information developed independently "about" customers and their preferences . . . will be used as input to the organizational planning.[27]

Such planning and the resulting information that managers and others obtain might be called "an investment in success."[28]

In preparation for conducting a survey of external customers or a population such as faculty or students (consisting of present [infrequent to high-volume] customers, lost customers, and never-gained customers), the library should review its customer service plan and the staff should engage in self-assessment. Self-assessment reveals the extent to which the library is oriented toward satisfying and delighting customers. Figures 7.4, Customer Service Inventory, and 7.5, Reasons and Remedies for Customer Dissatisfaction, offer sample questions that libraries can adapt as the staff engage in an internal dialogue about their service role. Such a discussion, especially if customers are brought into it, may delay the necessity of surveying external customers.

Asking customers to rate more than twenty-two statements is excessive, and not all the statements in figure 7.2 and the sources cited in endnotes eleven through sixteen reflect priorities that a library has the resources to meet. Thus, this section describes how to query customers so that the results will be meaningful to library planning and decision making. As a first step, it is important to determine the extent of the staff's customer orientation. If they do not understand the importance of customer service, that lacuna must be addressed first. Do the library's mission statement

---

FIGURE 7.3
RESPONSE CHOICES (THREE COLUMNS)

Minimum—the number that represents the *minimum* level of service that you would find acceptable

Desired—the number that represents the level of service that you *personally* want

Perceived—the number that represents the level of service that you believe this library *currently* provides

For each statement, rate it in all three columns OR identify the statement as not applicable (NA).

When it comes to . . .	My minimum service level is		My desired service level is		Perceived service performance is	
	Low	High	Low	High	Low	High
The library is a safe and secure place	1 2 3 4 5 6 7 8 9		1 2 3 4 5 6 7 8 9		1 2 3 4 5 6 7 8 9	
Opening hours meet my needs	1 2 3 4 5 6 7 8 9		1 2 3 4 5 6 7 8 9		1 2 3 4 5 6 7 8 9	
Etc.						

FIGURE 7.4

CUSTOMER SERVICE INVENTORY (TO BE COMPLETED BY STAFF)

I am interested in providing the best customer service that the library and I can.

Using the scale of 1 to 5, with 5 being the best, please rate how well you and other staff members provide each of the following services.

	Myself	Other Staff
1. Courteous answering of telephone		
2. Accurate responses to telephone queries		
3. Courteous and friendly service to in-person customers		

Place a mark in the box that most clearly corresponds to your level of agreement with the statement. Do not attach your name or department to the form. Thank you for your participation.

	Strongly Agree	Agree	Neutral	Disagree	Strongly Disagree
4. Only rarely do customers have to wait in line longer than a few minutes for service.					
5. The telephone is answered by the fourth ring.					
6. Customers are placed on hold for no more than one minute.					
7. The atmosphere of the library is warm and inviting.					
8. Customer complaints are resolved quickly and satisfactorily.					
9. I like my job.					
10. The staff demonstrates a caring attitude toward each other.					
11. Other staff demonstrate a caring attitude toward customers.					
12. The library has a good reputation in the community.					
13. The customer pays my salary.					

	Strongly Agree	Agree	Neutral	Disagree	Strongly Disagree
14. Top management puts the customer first.					
15. Middle management puts the customer first.					
16. The rest of the staff puts the customer first.					
17. Management asks, "What is best for the customer?" and makes decisions based on hard data relating to customer expectations and satisfaction.					
18. Staff know how to transfer calls without cutting off the caller.					
19. The customer is the ultimate judge of quality and, ultimately, determines quality collections and services.					
20. There is a strong commitment to product/service quality in the library.					
21. The morale among staff in the department is excellent.					
22. The morale among staff in the library is excellent.					

23. Do you think your job has an impact on how satisfied customers are about using the library?
❑ Yes, most definitely   ❑ Somewhat   ❑ Not sure   ❑ Definitely no

24. Over the past year, do you think the library has done better or worse in providing high-quality customer service?
❑ Much better   ❑ Better   ❑ About the same   ❑ Worse   ❑ Much worse

25. The three things I like MOST about working here are:
a. _____
b. _____
c. _____

26. The three things I like LEAST about working here are:
a. _____
b. _____
c. _____

27. If I could change ONE thing about how the library helps customers, it would be:
_____
_____
_____

and strategic planning documents contain statements about service? If so, the library has a starting point for emphasizing the need to learn how well a service meets customer expectations.

Staff should identify those statements they regard to be the highest, second-highest, and third-highest priority. Such a list of priorities serves as a reminder that the intent is to identify those expectations that staff believes are most essential to meet and to lay the foundation both for expanding the list over time and for deciding where to set benchmarks. Perhaps, together with selected customers, they might select an initial pool of, say, thirty statements and rewrite them or make substitutions as they desire. Then, using a nominal group technique, each staff member might vote for her three *most important* priorities.[29] The statements that receive the most votes become the basis for conducting a customer survey such as figure 7.6.

The review discussed above will take time and may require administrative leadership to support the development of a customer-service commitment and to supply the necessary resources to maintain that commitment. The intended outcome is achievement of the managerial perspective depicted in figure 7.7. The review should encourage staff to

- become more customer-focused
- finalize the set of expectations they want to meet
- feel a sense of empowerment
- pursue strategies for seeking a relationship with customers and for gaining their loyalty
- identify the data-collection strategies to be pursued, such as a survey
- ensure that customers can easily provide feedback
- relate findings to actions, policies, and processes that the library can follow to make improvements

The initial stage will probably require customer service training and sensitivity to issues that are important to customers, as well as the selective involvement of some *valued* customers in the discussions.

To recap, this procedure enables the organization to involve the staff in deciding on priorities for service

---

FIGURE 7.5

REASONS AND REMEDIES FOR CUSTOMER DISSATISFACTION (TO BE COMPLETED BY STAFF)

Customers become dissatisfied for various reasons. Please identify the three *most important* reasons why you think customers become dissatisfied with library services. Also, please suggest ways to overcome those points of dissatisfaction.

INTERNAL CUSTOMERS

Reasons	Possible Remedy
One:	
Two:	
Three:	

EXTERNAL CUSTOMERS

Reasons	Possible Remedy
One:	
Two:	
Three:	

quality. The staff discusses potential priorities among themselves, sharing what they consider important as internal customers and what they are prepared to do for external customers. They do not, however, want to develop expectations that are unimportant to customers or are unrealistic to attain. Data collection becomes a means to test the importance of specific expectations to customers, as the library determines which expectations have the highest priority and which ones the organization will consistently provide the resources to meet.

Once these decisions have been made, the staff can move to the next phase—surveying customers about selected expectations and measuring the gap between those expectations and the actual service provided. They can then work on reducing that gap. To begin, however, they need to frame relevant customer-related indicators, decide on how to interpret the results (benchmarking), and set the time frame for retesting and for interpreting later benchmark results. As the next step, they need to decide on the survey method and develop guidelines for ensuring an acceptable response rate.

CUSTOMER-RELATED MEASURES

One way to view outputs is through the voice of customers and issues of satisfaction, expectations met, materials obtained, and willingness to return, as an organization sets long-term targets and strives to achieve them. As shown in figure 4.9, libraries have choices about which data they collect. Customers cannot provide meaningful feedback in every instance; however, when libraries focus on questions of "How well?" "How valuable?" and "How satisfied?" they can. Also, as previously discussed, the answers to these questions can be analyzed through the use of customer-related indicators. Thus, as the staff develops the questionnaire, they can determine the types of indicators to develop. For example, if they are concerned about customers having to queue at service desks, they might decide customers should not have to stand unacknowledged at a desk for more than three minutes. Before reassigning staff to accommodate the three-minute limit, they might want to verify its importance to customers. (As a note of caution, library staff should avoid raising false expectation and should be willing to act on any survey statements they include.) Let us assume that the survey discovers that the time limit is very important to customers; then the staff could develop

a customer-related measure. Thus, a survey becomes the basis for determining what is important to customers and what would be meaningful to develop into performance indicators.

Using the preceding example, a measure might be

$$\frac{\text{Number served within three minutes}}{\text{Number of people waiting in line}} \times 100 = \underline{\hspace{2cm}} \%$$

Given the focus of the ratio, the percentage should be large and, over time, should increase even more.

The survey tests the importance of certain expectations to customers. Library staff must then translate the findings into something measurable. Again using the example of waiting in line, the staff can periodically monitor service areas, count the number of people in line, and use a stopwatch to monitor the three-minute limit. Thus, data collection is not an imposition on customers, and the results, if properly gathered, comprise a "reality check."

Figure 7.8 provides some examples of measures that have direct implications for customers and for which customers can provide insights. Producing meaningful results requires that such data be collected over a reasonable period of time. Otherwise, the data provide only a snapshot of a single time. Survey statements pertaining to the amount of time in line or to material awaiting reshelving produce yardsticks that are quantifiably measured, whereas statements about the staff have a more subjective focus. Having a subjective base does not mean that the data should not be collected, but, rather, that greater caution should be used in the interpretation.

Within the survey itself, specific time frames such as three minutes should not be set arbitrarily. Such numbers must come from extensive discussion among the staff and managers as they develop a time frame that is realistic for them to achieve. Further, as the figure illustrates, there are different types of customer-related measures; chapters 9 and 12 offer more choices.

DEVELOPING THE SURVEY INSTRUMENT
Target Audience

Customers are either internal or external. Internal customers are fellow staff members—it is they who must feel empowered and appreciated by the organization if they are to go out of their way to meet the needs and preferences of customers, and, thus, maintain satisfied and loyal customers. All staff members

FIGURE 7.6

LIBRARY CUSTOMER SURVEY

We ask you to spare a few minutes of your time to identify what you think are the most important indicators of high-quality service that you expect a library to provide. Some items are probably *more important* to you than others. The information that you provide will enable us to understand and respond to your service needs and priorities.

Please circle the number that indicates how important each of the following points is for the high-quality service that you expect a library to provide. (The range is from 1 = *of no importance* to 7 = *of highest importance*.)

If you don't use a particular service, please DO NOT circle a number for that statement.

	No Importance						Highest Importance
1. The OPAC allows me to find out about library hours, locations, services, and policies.	1	2	3	4	5	6	7
2. The OPAC enables me to download material:							
Onto the computer screen quickly.	1	2	3	4	5	6	7
And print a copy with ease.	1	2	3	4	5	6	7
3. The OPAC enables me to have access to download material onto removable media (e.g., USB memory device).	1	2	3	4	5	6	7
4. I do not have to wait in line more than three minutes when I ask for assistance at an information desk.	1	2	3	4	5	6	7
5. I do not have to wait in line more than three minutes when I borrow material.	1	2	3	4	5	6	7
6. Library staff are:							
a. Approachable and welcoming.	1	2	3	4	5	6	7
b. Willing to leave the desk area to help me.	1	2	3	4	5	6	7
c. Available when I need them.	1	2	3	4	5	6	7
d. Courteous and polite.	1	2	3	4	5	6	7
e. Friendly and easy to talk to.	1	2	3	4	5	6	7
7. Library staff:							
a. Communicate with me using terms I understand.	1	2	3	4	5	6	7
b. Give accurate answers to my questions.	1	2	3	4	5	6	7

	No Importance						Highest Importance
c. Encourage me to come back to ask for more assistance if I need it.	1	2	3	4	5	6	7
d. Demonstrate cultural sensitivity.	1	2	3	4	5	6	7
8. Materials are reshelved promptly.	1	2	3	4	5	6	7
9. Equipment is in good working order:							
a. Computer printers	1	2	3	4	5	6	7
b. Microfilm and microfiche readers	1	2	3	4	5	6	7
c. Photocopiers	1	2	3	4	5	6	7

Thank you for your participation.

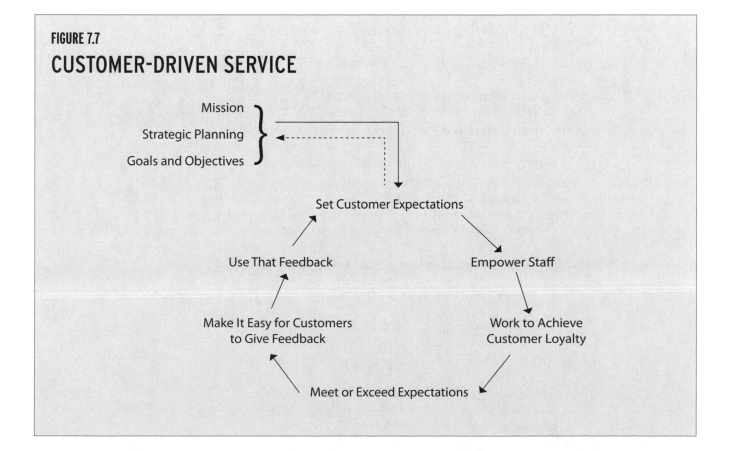

FIGURE 7.7

CUSTOMER-DRIVEN SERVICE

Mission
Strategic Planning
Goals and Objectives

Set Customer Expectations

Use That Feedback

Empower Staff

Make It Easy for Customers to Give Feedback

Work to Achieve Customer Loyalty

Meet or Exceed Expectations

must agree on a minimal set of expectations they will meet; individual members may go beyond this, but they will require a supportive organization.

Although internal staff might be the first surveyed, they need not be. Chapter 8 offers another method for seeking information from internal customers. In either case, a draft of the survey should be shared with staff as a discussion document; paraprofessional staff, student workers, and volunteers should also be brought into the process.

External customers can include a wide assortment of stakeholder groups, especially for public libraries that serve a community of broad interests, educational and income levels, lifestyle preferences, and age groups. Academic libraries traditionally have served faculty, staff, administrators, students, and sometimes

FIGURE 7.8

CUSTOMER-RELATED MEASURES

$$\frac{\text{Number of customers served within three minutes}}{\text{Number of customers seeking reference desk service}} \times 100 = \underline{\hspace{1cm}} \%$$

$$\frac{\text{Number of customers served within three minutes}}{\text{Number of customers waiting to check out items}} \times 100 = \underline{\hspace{1cm}} \%$$

$$\frac{\text{Number of staff approachable/welcoming}}{\text{Number of staff approached (per service area)}} \times 100 = \underline{\hspace{1cm}} \%$$

$$\frac{\text{Number of staff courteous/polite}}{\text{Number of staff approached (per service area)}} \times 100 = \underline{\hspace{1cm}} \%$$

$$\frac{\text{Number of books reshelved within 24 hours after being removed from the shelves}}{\text{Number of books needing reshelving}} \times 100 = \underline{\hspace{1cm}} \%$$

$$\frac{\text{Number of current periodicals reshelved after being removed from the shelves}}{\text{Number of current periodicals needing reshelving}} \times 100 = \underline{\hspace{1cm}} \%$$

$$\frac{\text{Number of bound periodicals reshelved after being removed from the shelves}}{\text{Number of bound periodicals needing reshelving}} \times 100 = \underline{\hspace{1cm}} \%$$

$$\frac{\text{Number of microfiche filed after being removed from the cabinets}}{\text{Number of microfiche needing refiling}} \times 100 = \underline{\hspace{1cm}} \%$$

$$\frac{\text{Number of requests to digitize microfiche and e-mail the source}}{\text{Number of microfiche filed after being removed from the cabinets}} \times 100 = \underline{\hspace{1cm}} \%$$

$$\frac{\text{Number of computer printers in working order}}{\text{Number of computer printers in public service areas}} \times 100 = \underline{\hspace{1cm}} \%$$

community residents, especially those who use the government documents collections of libraries participating in the federal depository library program. In addition, as the student population becomes increasingly diverse, not only ethnically, but in terms of age, work history, and life experiences, and as the Internet becomes a common delivery system for credit courses to students far beyond the campus, library services may have to change to accommodate an expanded external customer base.

It is difficult to tell whether the people who place notes in the suggestion box, fill out forms on web pages, or make complaints reflect the views of the general customer population. To ascertain the expectations and perceptions of the customer base overall, it is necessary to take a formal survey. In some states and municipalities, government entities are required to conduct an annual customer opinion survey. Usually, these are short and the questions are general.

The more a library reaches out to its constituent groups, the less likely that customers participating in a formal data-collection activities survey will be regular or the most frequent users of the library. What incentive do noncustomers or infrequent customers have to participate? Because participation in a survey—however it is administered—involves an imposition, why should the noncustomer or infrequent customer be willing to accept that imposition? Traditionally, survey cover letters have stressed the value of participation to the organization and offered respondents a summary of the findings. Such a summary is a delayed reward for participation but it will not appeal to some individuals, especially if the data-collection instrument exceeds two pages and if respondents feel no loyalty to the library and the topic investigated. This type of reward may have limited appeal. Participants might expect or appreciate being included in a raffle or receiving a gift (a token remembrance or a gift card) or money.

Two critical questions are (1) Does the study need to produce findings generalizable to a population and, if so, how are those doing the research most likely to achieve an acceptable response rate—one much higher than 50 percent? and (2) From which customers do librarians want to compile findings that lead to improved service performance?

For various reasons, a library might prefer to survey a subpopulation (e.g., students, users of a particular library facility, or users of a particular collection). In such cases, the statements selected for customer response must be tailored to the interests and knowledge of the subpopulation surveyed. It is important to understand that the survey statements presented in this book can be answered only by customers. Do not assume that the staff knows what a broad range of respondents would say. Such an assumption might forestall customer input and simply continue the status quo.

A key question becomes: Does the library need to generalize the findings to the population, or can it study the perceptions of selected customers without having to make generalizations? Sometimes, government bodies are required to generalize survey results to a specified population—recipients of an agency's service. Thus, critical questions for library staff and evaluators to consider include

- Should we focus on a particular population or subpopulation? Why?
- Do we need to produce generalizable data?
- If so, is this for a certain time period?

Representativeness

Questions about where, when, and how to distribute surveys can influence the representativeness of the responses. Representativeness is the degree to which the characteristics of the respondents match the characteristics of the population under consideration. The population for purposes of the survey can be any group under study. For example, an academic library at a university offering night classes for working adults wants to sample its student customers. To obtain a cross section of student opinion, survey forms will have to be available on nights and weekends, when those adult students come to campus. Certain times during the school year can also influence the results; for example, surveys distributed right before final examination week or during any period of campus upheaval are likely to result in low responses and high levels of customer angst.

Distribution of surveys in public libraries having multiple branches with different hours of operation is more complicated. The distribution plan needs to take into account the customers who come at various times throughout the day and week.

The two basic types of sampling method are *probability sampling* (representativeness) and *nonprobability sampling* (lacking in representativeness). With nonprobability sampling, it is not possible to generalize from the sample because the sample may not be representative of the population. Such sampling may, however, be easier and cheaper to conduct, while still producing useful insights. Probability sampling might involve *random sampling*—the selection of cases or subjects so that each one has an equal and known chance of inclusion and the selection of one case or subject does not influence the selection of another —or *systematic sampling*, in which each member of the population is not chosen independently. With systematic sampling, once the first member of the population has been chosen, other members of the sample are automatically determined. For example, staff members might decide to select for participation every tenth person leaving the library.

Sampling extends to who will be surveyed and when (e.g., day, week, month, or school term). In a general survey of customers, evaluators might distribute the questionnaire to anyone entering the library. With this method, one needs to consider how the forms will be collected and how many will never be completed. (They may be found all over the building.) A variant of the door distribution method is to ask persons leaving the library to fill out a form. This method makes collection easier, but some people will claim the press of time as an excuse not to participate. As an alternative, evaluators might walk throughout the library and ask customers to complete the form. This method requires a decision about remaining with the person until the form has been completed, returning later to pick up the completed form and to answer any questions, or providing a centralized collection location. Of course, the person may leave, may only partially complete the form, or may decide against participation. If there is interest in a particular branch, service area, or location within the building, then only customers using that site should receive forms.

When library staff collects data for a so-called typical day or week, they are really using a type of nonprobability sample. How is *typical* defined, and how is that time period identified without the use of a probability sample to select from among various choices?

Number of Customers to Survey

Because customer participation is voluntary, the gap between the number of forms distributed and the number completed must be considered. Another major factor is the confidence that evaluators can place in the results; confidence is influenced by the size of the population to be surveyed and the number of forms completed.

In *Measuring Academic Library Performance*, Van House et al. recommend that "in most cases you will need at least 100 completed forms; closer to 400 is preferable."[30] One hundred forms corresponds to a sample size for a population of less than one hundred and forty at a 95 percent confidence level with a standard deviation of ±5, whereas four hundred pertains to a population of well over one hundred thousand (with a similar confidence level and standard deviation). Librarians wanting a more precisely determined sample size should consult figure 7.9, which is a general guide to determining sample size for a random sample.

Given the widespread use and acceptance of *Measuring Academic Library Performance* and similar manuals, we believe it legitimate to follow their advice. If the population served by the library is very small (fewer than one hundred), all of the customers might be surveyed. For small populations, a sample size of one hundred is viable; the larger the population, the more likely the sample should be between three and four hundred.

A note of caution should be inserted, however: if the larger organization expects the library to produce insights that accurately reflect a population's perceptions, it is best to consult with a statistician and draw a representative sample.

Formulating Survey Questions

The staff's statements labeled as highest priority—no more than twenty of them—become the basis for exploring customer expectations. (See figure 7.6.) The questionnaire should neither exceed two pages nor impose much of a burden on respondents for completion. The questionnaire might conclude with a few questions about respondent demographics. For college or university students, the survey designers might select questions regarding

- class level (e.g., graduate or undergraduate; freshman, sophomore, junior, or senior; lower division [freshman and sophomore] or upper division [junior and senior] undergraduate; master's or doctoral student)
- major
- gender
- residence (on-campus or commuter student)
- status (full- or part-time student)

In the case of faculty members, variables might include rank, department, areas of specialization, and status (full-time or adjunct).

In the case of public libraries, respondents might be asked about

- gender
- level of schooling completed (e.g., some or all of elementary school, some or all of junior high school, some or all of high school, vocational school, some or all of college, master's or doctoral degree)
- occupation (e.g., homemaker; manager or proprietor; operator, fabricator, laborer [machine operator, inspector, assembler; transportation and material moving; handlers, equipment cleaners, helpers, and laborers]; precision, production, craft, and repair; professional [teacher, doctor, accountant, etc.]; technical sales and administrative support [including technicians and related support, sales, and administrative support—clerical]; retired; student; unemployed; other [specify]).[31] As an alternative, staff might complete this category if respondents are unsure where their job falls in a list or if they have more than one occupation.

It is possible to add variables related to age, race, and ethnicity; language spoken at home; type of disability; or income, but these types of data may be technically complex and individuals may not answer these questions. Any list of variables, however, should be short and essential to know. Does the library want to distinguish among customers? If yes, the questions become "Why?" and "In what regard?"

From the sample questions depicted in figure 7.6, any variables relating to demographics might be added at the end. Again, the form should not exceed two printed pages and should be well-presented, using good quality paper and attractive layout of the statements on the pages. As an alternative, the investigator might use an online survey tool such as SurveyMonkey (www.surveymonkey.com)[32] to develop the questionnaire and then ask study participants to go to a particular website to complete it. The results could be inserted in Microsoft Excel or SPSS for statistical summarization.

Evaluators should pretest the instrument on library staff (both professional and nonprofessional), and on a few well-known customers. The pretest might involve a group discussion, a one-on-one discussion, or written responses to the wording and interpretation of questions, and to ways of enticing the survey population to respond.

FIGURE 7.9

SURVEY SAMPLE SIZE

Number	Sample Size	Number	Sample Size
50	44	850	264
75	62	900	269
100	79	950	273
150	107	1,000	277
200	131	1,500	305
250	151	2,000	322
300	168	2,500	332
350	183	3,000	340
400	195	3,500	346
450	207	4,000	350
500	217	4,500	353
550	226	5,000	356
600	234	6,000	361
650	241	7,000	364
700	248	9,000	368
750	254	10,000	369
800	259		

Note: Reflects 95 percent confidence level and ±5 standard deviation.

DISTRIBUTING THE SURVEY

Figure 7.1 assesses different methods of survey distribution and shows that each has strengths and limitations. Library staff members should review the options and make the choice that best meets their needs. Clearly, it is essential that customers understand why the library needs their comments and why they should accept the imposition. For this reason, the survey approach is probably best used for preexisting customers, rather than those labeled as lost or never gained. (Chapter 8 will address these other groups.) If the library does not want to target never-gained or lost customers specifically, it might survey a population of faculty, staff, students, or community residents and gain responses from some present, some lost, and some never-gained customers. The findings, however, might, be skewed in favor of actual customers because the other two groups might have little incentive to participate.

Response Rate

The response rate is the percentage of people who return completed and usable surveys:

$$\text{Response rate} = \frac{\text{Number completed and usable}}{\text{Number distributed}} \times 100 = \underline{\quad} \%$$

The number distributed includes the number of refusals.

Thus, if library staff distributes five hundred questionnaires and 410 are completed and usable, the response rate is 82 percent. If one hundred are returned, the response rate is 20 percent. In the latter instance, if the staff distributes another three hundred questionnaires and receives 250 in return, they might mistakenly define the response rate as 70 percent $[(100 + 250) \div 500]$; in fact, the response rate is 43.8 percent $[(100 + 250) \div (500 + 300)]$.

In an article published in 1999, Yehuda Baruch explored the response rate in 175 different social science studies published in five journals (*Academy of Management Journal, Human Relations, Journal of Applied Psychology, Organizational Behavior and Human Decision Processes,* and *Journal of International Business Studies*) for 1975, 1985, and 1995. The average response rate was 55.6 percent with a standard deviation of 19.7.[33] Tse-Hua Shih and Xita Fan, who conducted a meta-analysis of thirty-nine studies that compared web and snail-mail surveys, found that the former type of surveys, in general, have lower response rates.[34] College students are more responsive to web surveys, while some other groups (e.g., schoolteachers and general consumers) prefer traditional mail surveys. Follow-up reminders appear to be less effective for web survey respondents than for mail survey respondents.[35]

The lower the response rate, the greater the risk that the answers of respondents and nonrespondents differ, thereby inhibiting generalization to a population. For this reason, library evaluators should take great care to explain the value of participation and do all that they can to achieve response rates no lower than 60 percent. In the case of mailed and other questionnaires, library staff should consider a follow-up procedure(s), whereby they approach nonrespondents and invite their participation; again, they should offer compelling reasons for why they are asking a favor and why the individual should accept the imposition.[36]

Errors

Every survey has the possibility of error, which can invalidate the results. Examples include noncoverage (not surveying the right customers); nonresponse bias (customers' failure to participate); measurement bias (misinterpreting questions); response bias (failing to answer truthfully); and technical errors in recording, coding, tabulating, or analyzing data. Using the procedures discussed in this chapter and consulting sources on research methods can minimize nonsampling errors.

AN EXAMPLE: PREPARING A SERVICE QUALITY QUESTIONNAIRE FOR A LEARNING COMMONS

A number of academic libraries have created an information or learning commons that involves a partnership with other units on campus, perhaps information technology, the writing center, student advising, career and disability services, and so forth. Today, learning commons might not be limited to a fixed setting within the library. They might be more mobile and provide digital support to students wherever they meet in groups.

Figure 7.10 offers a generic survey form that includes an abbreviated segment on service quality. It is possible to add a section on satisfaction or replace coverage of service quality with satisfaction.

This instrument could be available in paper form or, more likely, as a digital instrument. Customers might be asked to respond for a particular time frame (this week or month) or they might be asked, "How much time do you usually spend in the learning commons per visit?" The subsequent questions then might look at use during that time frame. Depending on what the staff actually wants to know, it might also be useful to probe for any patterns regarding use by time of the day or day of the week. As discussed in chapter 10, the inclusion of the following questions adds a satisfaction component to the questionnaire:

- What do you like the MOST about the learning commons?
- What do you like the LEAST about the learning commons?
- If we could do one thing to improve, what would it be?

An additional question might ask if they want to see anything added to the learning commons and to rate their overall satisfaction with the learning commons (on a five-, seven-, or ten-point scale ranging from *very satisfied* to *very dissatisfied*). Furthermore, there might be a question about whether the commons delivers on its promises.

Demographic questions might ask for their class level and major. Respondents might even be asked about the equipment they own and bring into the library. They might also be asked if they are willing to participate in a focus group interview and, if they are, they might be asked to provide their e-mail address.

Before deploying a survey about use of, and expectations for, an information or learning commons, such as the abbreviated one associated with one's experiences for that day, library staff should decide if they can gather better evidence by observing use and conditions of the location. Chapter 11 suggests the possibility of an observational technique such as sweeping. On the other hand, if the staff wants to gauge satisfaction, they should adjust the abbreviated questionnaire and focus more on satisfaction.

Other considerations focus on research design, namely who will be studied (a population or a sample) and when will the study be conducted (how will the time frame be selected); will the instrument be distributed in paper form to those entering, using, or exiting the information commons, or will a survey be administered online; and what steps will be taken to assure an acceptable response rate.

CONTINUOUS EVALUATION

Evaluation within the context of customer-driven strategic planning should be an ongoing or continuous process. The staff should set internal benchmarks, meet those delivery expectations over time, and set more lofty benchmarks as the organization becomes more effective and efficient and as customers become completely satisfied. As any customer-focused pledge becomes more meaningful, staff aspires to meet or exceed it.

A FINAL WORD

A customer service plan should not be limited to existing customers. It should also address lost and never-gained customers. The purpose is to better serve existing customers while expanding the population of present customers. At the same time, because existing customers vary in their use, the goal is to make more of them delighted, regular customers.

Enterprise Rent-A-Car has developed a number of statements about customer service that it wants all its employees to internalize. These statements comprise the "Enterprise Way." Some of them are relevant to the issues raised in this chapter:

- The only way to know how you are really doing when it comes to taking care of your customers is to ask them
- It is essential to regularly survey customers about the various aspects of your business
- If you are going to conduct a survey make it targeted
- Ask customers three critical questions: How satisfied were you? What could we have done to improve our service? What do you think we do especially well?
- Hold everyone accountable for getting your customer satisfaction numbers higher
- Make pleasing customers a way of life and a daily habit that becomes part of the overall culture
- To better understand how your customers feel . . . put yourself in their shoes.[37]

Figure 7.11 highlights key steps discussed in this chapter. Within the context of figures 7.2 and 7.6, a library can determine which expectations are important for it to meet. Customers should play a key role in

FIGURE 7.10

LEARNING COMMONS SURVEY: SAMPLE QUESTIONS

1. How much time, on average, do you spend in the Learning Commons?

❏ Less than one hour   ❏ 4 to 6 hours

❏ 1 to 3 hours   ❏ More than 7 hours

2. How long did you have to wait for a computer?

❏ No wait   ❏ 21 to 30 minutes

❏ Less than 5 minutes   ❏ 31 to 45 minutes

❏ 6 to 10 minutes   ❏ More than 46 minutes

❏ 11 to 20 minutes

3. Are you studying alone ❏ or in a group ❏ ? If you are working in a group, how many people are in the group? ___

4. What type of computer do you prefer to use in the Learning Commons?

❏ PC

❏ Macintosh

❏ No preference

❏ Other: _____

5. What do you do in the Learning Commons and how often?

	Daily	Few times per week	Once a week	Few times per term	Not at all
E-mail					
Course website					
Ability to connect to classmates, TA, or professor					
Wire or edit paper					
Use databases, search engines, or other library resources					
Watch DVDs/videos					
Play games					
Surf the net					
Use spreadsheet (Excel)					
Scan images					

	Daily	Few times per week	Once a week	Few times per term	Not at all
Print course material					
Print papers/documents you create					
Create or edit images					
Edit movies					
Create or edit websites (Dreamweaver)					
Create or edit presentations (PowerPoint)					
Find help to get my computer fixed					
Other (please specify) _____					

6. What software not offered on a Learning Commons computer would help you with your coursework?
_____

7. Have you sought help from a staff member today   ❑ Yes   ❑ No

  If yes, what kind of help? _____

  How long did it take for you to receive that help? _____

  Did that help resolve the problem?   ❑ Yes   ❑ No

  Please explain: _____

  If you answered "no," is there a particular reason? _____

Please respond to the next set of questions using a five-point scale with 1 being strongly agree and 5 being strongly disagree.

	Strongly agree				Strongly disagree
8. Staff at the Learning Commons are friendly	1	2	3	4	5
9. The facility is					
Clean	1	2	3	4	5
Welcoming	1	2	3	4	5
10. Signs within the Learning Commons are clear	1	2	3	4	5

11. Any other comments (facilities, staff, or the service):

FIGURE 7.11

KEY STEPS TO CONDUCTING A SURVEY

PLAN

1. Conduct surveys for purposes that are clearly stated and designed to improve services to customers.
2. Assign responsible staff to conduct the survey.
3. Follow standard research methods, such as those explained in this chapter and the sources cited, to minimize errors and other potential problems.
4. Involve the staff in the process and in developing a commitment to customer service and the outcome of the survey.

IDENTIFY CUSTOMERS

5. Decide if the survey will focus on a particular population or subpopulation, and for what time period.
6. Determine when, where, and how the forms will be distributed.
7. Try to obtain responses from the greatest possible percentage of those selected and, if relevant, check to ensure that those who respond are representative of customers receiving the services being studied.

CONSTRUCT AND ASK QUESTIONS

8. Review the statements covered in figure 7.2, for instance, selecting, rewriting, and adding as necessary; or consider the use of SERVQUAL or another instrument.
9. Decide on any variables relating to individual customers (e.g., occupation).
10. Treat respondents respectfully and remember that you are imposing on them.
11. Be careful about the appearance of the survey form.
12. Conduct a pretest on some library staff and valued customers—bring six to ten individuals together and review each statement and variable with them, ensuring that the wording is clear and deals with what the library really wants to know.

STUDY LIMITATIONS

13. Review the limitations to be certain that they are acceptable. Limitations include a self-reporting method of data collection and the possibility of poor memory and misunderstood questions. (It is critical to conduct a pretest in which the staff gather individuals—perhaps six to ten—and ask them to review survey wording for clarity, accuracy, and the sequencing of the questions. Is it important to show respondents' "skip patterns," jumping to a specific question depending on how the present question is answered.)

RESPONSE RATE

14. Review the survey procedures and strategies for improving the response rate. Will respondents receive an incentive? What is it? Will it likely be effective? To this end, you should conduct a pretest in which you review the questions and probe issues related to nonresponse. You should also review sources such as Lokman I. Meho, "E-mail Interviewing in Qualitative Research: A Methodological Discussion," *Journal of the American Society for Information Science and Technology* 57, no. 10 (2006): 1284–1295; Michael D. Kaplowitz, Timothy D. Hadlock, and Ralph Levine, "A Comparison of Web and Mail Survey Response Rates," *Public Opinion Quarterly* 68, no. 1 (2004): 94–101; Stephen R. Porter and Michael E. Whitcomb, "The Impact of Contact Type on Web Survey Response Rates," *Public Opinion Quarterly* 64, no. 4 (2003): 579–588; Robert M. Groves, Don A. Dillman, John L. Eltinge, and Roderick J. A. Little, *Survey Nonresponse* (New York: Wiley, 2002).

EDIT AND ARCHIVE DATA

15. Make every attempt to ensure that the data are technically error-free.
16. Make it possible for others to confirm the results later.

ANALYZE DATA AND RESULTS

17. Objectively analyze all data.
18. Interpret results with the appropriate level of precision and express the proper degree of caution about conclusions that can be drawn from the results.
19. Use the data as input in outcome measures, where feasible.

the decision. As a first step, library staff should discuss service quality among themselves and with a few valued customers. The staff should not presume to know what customers expect, nor should they downplay the importance of letting customers voice their expectations and of customers seeing policies shaped around those expectations.

Development of a survey provides a rich opportunity for library staff to refine the list of priority expectations to meet now and in the near future—for the majority of customers. Once these have been met on a regular basis, library staff can move to meeting new (additional) expectations. Equally important, the staff enters a dialogue with customers, and both parties begin to know each other better.

Clear choices must be made regarding who is surveyed, when, and by what means. Whatever the decision, the staff should seek to obtain a respectable response rate—no lower than 60 percent. With the data obtained, the staff can continue the planning of customer-driven service (figure 7.7), become empowered, and achieve customer loyalty. These are worthy goals, but they require dedication and hard work to achieve and maintain on a broad scale.

[C]ustomer response must be rewarded, to be encouraged in the future.[38]

Notes

1. Phil Fragasso, *Marketing for Rainmakers: 52 Rules of Engagement to Attract and Retain Customers for Life* (New York: Wiley and Sons, 2008), 170.

2. Terry G. Vavra, *Improving Your Measurement of Customer Satisfaction: A Guide to Creating, Conducting, Analyzing, and Reporting Customer Satisfaction Measurement Programs* (Milwaukee, WI: ASQ Quality Press, 1997), 28.

3. Scott E. Sampson, "Ramifications of Monitoring Service Quality through Passively Solicited Customer Feedback," *Decision Sciences* 27, no. 4 (Fall 1996): 601.

4. Ibid.

5. Ibid.

6. Ibid.

7. Valarie A. Zeithaml, A. Parasuraman, and Leonard L. Berry, *Delivering Quality Service: Balancing Customer Perceptions and Expectations* (New York: The Free Press, 1990).

8. A. Parasuraman, Leonard L. Berry, and Valarie A. Zeithaml, "Refinement and Reassessment of the SERVQUAL Scale," *Journal of Retailing* 67, no. 4 (1991): 201–230.

9. Jeffrey E. Disend, *How to Provide Excellent Service in Any Organization: A Blueprint for Making All the Theories Work* (Radnor, PA: Chilton Book Company, 1991), 108.

10. Vavra, *Improving Your Measurement of Customer Satisfaction*, 42.

11. For copies of all three instruments, see Danuta A. Nitecki, "An Assessment of the Applicability of SERVQUAL Dimensions as Customer-based Criteria for Evaluating Quality of Services in an Academic Library," Ph.D. dissertation, University of Maryland, 1995.

12. See Danuta A. Nitecki, "Assessment of Service Quality in Academic Libraries: Focus on the Applicability of the SERVQUAL," in *Proceedings of the 2nd Northumbria International Conference on Performance Measurement in Libraries and Information Services* (Newcastle upon Tyne, England: Department of Information and Library Management, University of Northumbria at Newcastle, 1998), 193–196; Joan Stein, "Feedback from a Captive Audience: Reflections on the Results of a SERVQUAL Survey of Interlibrary Loan Services at Carnegie Mellon University Libraries," in *Proceedings of the 2nd Northumbria International Conference on Performance Measurement in Libraries and Information Services*, 217–222.

13. Peter Hernon and Philip Calvert, "Methods for Measuring Service Quality in University Libraries in New Zealand," *Journal of Academic Librarianship* 22, no, 5 (1996): 387–391; Philip Calvert and Peter Hernon, "Surveying Service Quality within University Libraries," *Journal of Academic Librarianship* 23, no, 5 (1997): 408–415.

14. Peter Hernon and Philip Calvert, "E-service Quality in Libraries: Exploring Its Features and Dimensions," *Library & Information Science Research* 27, no. 3 (2005): 377–404.

15. Danuta A. Nitecki and Peter Hernon, "Measuring Service Quality at Yale University Libraries," *Journal of Academic Librarianship* 26, no. 4 (2000): 257–273.

16. For information on the cost of participation see "LibQUAL+ Services and Fees," www.libqual.org/About/FeeSchedule/index.cfm. It merits mention that a shorter version of LibQUAL+ is currently under

development; everyone answers some questions and randomly selected subsets complete the rest of the instrument. See Association of Research Libraries, "News: ARL to Pilot LibQUAL Lite," www.arl.org/news/enews/enews-jan08.shtml#16; Bruce Thompson, Martha Kyrillidou, and Colleen Cook, "Item Sampling in Service Quality Assessment Surveys to Improve Response Rates and Reduce Respondent Burden," *Performance Measurement and Metrics* 10, no. 1 (2009): 6–16.

17. For an excellent analysis, see E. Stewart Saunders, "Meeting Academic Needs for Information: A Customer Service Approach," *portal: Libraries and the Academy* 8, no. 4 (October 2008): 357–371.

18. See, for instance, "LibQUAL+ Survey 2007: Timeline and Action Plan," http://library.queensu.ca/webir/libqual/timeline.htm.

19. See Association of Research Libraries, "StatsQUAL," www.digiqual.org.

20. See Peter Hernon and Philip Calvert, *Improving the Quality of Library Services for Students with Disabilities* (Westport, CT: Libraries Unlimited, 2006).

21. For the set of questions related to each dimension, see Jocelyn S. Duffy, Damon E. Jaggars, and Shanna E. Smith, "Getting Our Priorities in Order: Are Our Service Values in Line with the Communities We Serve?" *Performance Measurement and Metrics* 9, no. 3 (2008): 175.

22. Nitecki, "Changing the Concept and Measure of Service Quality in Academic Libraries," 188.

23. Nitecki and Hernon, "Measuring Service Quality at Yale University Libraries."

24. Zeithaml, Parasuraman, and Berry, *Delivering Quality Service*, 26.

25. Hernon and Calvert, "E-service Quality in Libraries," 401.

26. National Performance Review, *Serving the American Public: Best Practices in Customer-Driven Strategic Planning* (Washington, DC: Government Printing Office, 1997), 6.

27. Ibid., 7.

28. General Accounting Office [now the Government Accountability Office], The Government Performance and Results Act: 1997 Governmentwide Implementation Will Be Uneven, GAO/GGD-97-109 (Washington, DC GAO, 1997), 79.

29. The nominal group technique is a method for producing group consensus. See William P. Anthony, *Practical Strategic Planning* (Westport, CT: Quorum Books, 1985), 47.

30. Nancy Van House, Beth Weil, and Charles R. McClure, *Measuring Academic Library Performance: A Practical Approach* (Chicago: American Library Association, 1990), 44.

31. For guidance, consult the Department of Labor, Bureau of Labor Statistics, Occupational Classification System Manual, www.bls.gov/ncs/ocs/ocsm/commain.htm.

32. On the opening screen of SurveyMonkey, this note appears: "Using just your web browser, create your survey with our intuitive survey editor. Select from over a dozen types of questions (multiple choice, rating scales, drop-down menus, and more . . .). Powerful options allow you to require answers to any question, control the flow with custom skip logic, and even randomize answer choices to eliminate bias."

33. Yehuda Baruch, "Response Rate in Academic Studies: A Comparative Analysis," *Human Relations* 52, no. 4 (April 1999): 421–438. See also Yehuda Baruch and Brooks C. Holtom, "Survey Response Rate Levels and Trends in Organizational Research," *Human Relations* 61, no. 8 (August 2008): 1139–1160. This is an update of the previous stage and extends the research through 2005. They found that "the average response rate for studies that utilized data collected from individuals was 52.7 percent with a standard deviation of 20.4, while the average response rate for studies that utilized data collected from organizations was 35.7 percent with a standard deviation of 18.8" (p. 1139).

34. Tse-Hua Shih and Xita Fan, "Comparing Response Rates from Web and Mail Surveys: A Meta-Analysis," *Field Methods* 20, no. 3 (August 2008): 249–271.

35. See also Patrick D. Converse, Edward W. Wolfe, Xiaoting Huang, and Frederick L. Oswald, "Response Rates for Mixed-Mode Surveys Using Mail and E-mail/Web," *American Journal of Evaluation* 29, no. 1 (March 2008): 99–107; Martyn Denscombe, "The Length of Responses to Open-Ended Questions: A Comparison of Online and Paper Questionnaires in Terms of a Mode Effect," *Social Science Computer Review* 26, no. 3 (Fall 2008): 359–368; Dirk Heerwegh and Geert Loosveldt, "Personalizing E-Mail Contacts: Its Influence on Web Survey Response Rate and Social Desirability Response Bias," *International Journal of Public Opinion Research* 19, no. 2 (Summer 2007): 258–268; Benjamin Healey, "Drop Downs and Scroll Mice: The Effect of Response Option Format and Input Mechanism Employed on Data Quality in Web Surveys," *Social Science Computer Review* 25, no. 1 (Spring 2007): 111–128.

36. Why should the customer be motivated to respond? This question becomes even more important when library staff try to survey lost or never-gained customers.

37. Kirk Kazanjian, *Exceeding Customer Expectations: What Enterprise, America's #1 Car Rental Company, Can Teach You about Creating Lifetime Customers* (New York: Doubleday, 2007), 84–85.

38. Vavra, *Improving Your Measurement of Customer Satisfaction*, 84.

Chapter Eight

Listening to Customers through Focus Group Interviews

Focus-group interviews are becoming increasingly popular . . .
for exploring what individuals believe or feel as well as why they
behave in the way they do.[1]

For those libraries hesitant to undertake the expense of producing and tabulating the responses to multiquestion surveys distributed to many people, the focus group interview is a streamlined and inexpensive way to gather information about customers' perceptions of the library's service.

Public officials and candidates for public office have widely used such interviews to test voters' reactions to issues, and companies have used them to test and market their products. Group responses can also be used to develop survey questionnaires if the library decides that the study needs to produce findings generalizable to the library's entire population, which means that a high response rate is needed.

Focus group interviews have several advantages over surveys. The group or groups are usually small—no more than a dozen people—the participants' answers are open-ended, which may elicit statements and ideas new to library managers, and the whole session can be recorded for future reference. The library administration might also want to elicit opinions about the quality of service from the perspectives of different segments of the population of their service area. Customer groups include

- internal customers
    staff of other library departments
- external customers
    regular users of library services (present customers)
    infrequent users (present customers)
    nonusers
        former users (lost customers)
        never-gained customers

The purpose of this chapter is to present focus group interviews as a means of studying each customer group and for overcoming some of the inherent weaknesses of other types of surveys. Focus group interviewing is a powerful way to gather data on specific issues and problems. A focus group interview is a "carefully planned discussion designed to obtain perceptions in a defined area of interest in a permissive, nonthreatening environment."[2] For this qualitative data-gathering technique, a moderator guides the interaction and inquiry in a structured or unstructured manner, depending on the purpose of the session.

Figure 8.1 assesses the strengths and weaknesses of this data-collection technique.

CASE STUDIES

Case studies are useful both for exploratory research and for descriptive and explanatory purposes. There are three general bases for selecting instances applicable to case studies: convenience, purpose, and probability. "Each has its function and can be used to answer certain questions. . . . [A] good case study will use a basis for instance selection that is appropriate for the question to be answered. Using the wrong basis for selecting an instance is a fatal error in case

study designs, as in all designs."[3] These instances suggest choices for the selection of actual participants, and focus groups may consist of individuals selected by purpose, convenience, or probability sampling.

Figure 8.2 summarizes the three instances, when to use them, and what questions they address. Purposive selection requires a justification about how the site or participants fit one of the seven categories. For example, focusing on *typical* customers raises the question: What does *typical* mean and encompass? Expediency or convenience is an option, but evaluators likely will be unable to generalize responses to a population. Probability sampling is possible in academic institutions for faculty, students, and administrators, where the population and its characteristics are known. Public libraries may lack sufficient insights into the population, except one based on customers who visit during a particular time frame, or on a group such as public schoolteachers. Probability sampling, in comparison to convenience selection, may be too complex and time consuming to conduct. Clearly, libraries have choices depending on what question or questions are important to the development and maintenance of strategic planning or a customer service plan.

FIGURE 8.1

STRENGTHS AND WEAKNESSES OF FOCUS GROUP INTERVIEWS

Strengths	Weaknesses
Address a wide variety of issues, and anyone can participate	Limited generalizability to a large population
Provide data more quickly and cheaply than one-on-one interviewing	Dominating moderators inhibit discussion and may bias the discussion; they might fail to be objective.
Encourage interaction among participants; therefore, the findings reflect more than the cumulated responses of individuals	Some participants may be quiet and not feel comfortable about revealing their opinions in a group setting.
The comment of one individual may produce responses from others.	Summarization and interpretation of open-ended responses may be difficult.
Provide opportunity to clarify and probe responses, and to ask follow-up questions	
Produce data in respondents' own words	

FOCUS GROUP INTERVIEWS
Case Study Selection

In focus group interviews—a type of case study application—normally between six and twelve people participate in an interactive group discussion on highly focused issues or problems; open-ended questions enable subjects to comment, explain, and suggest notions that might differ from the answers they might give to highly structured questions. It is possible to base selection of participants—ones willing to donate approximately sixty to ninety minutes of their time—drawn from either a probability or nonprobability (convenience or purposive) sample. If the library wants to produce findings generalizable to a population (e.g., present customers who are students, faculty, teenagers, or the elderly), then the staff must select a probability sample. If library managers do not need to make broad generalizations, they can use a nonprobability sample, especially if the intent is to ascertain the views of lost or never-gained customers—groups for which a population is not easily identified (or possible to identify). Lost and never-gained customers, especially a sufficient portion, are unlikely to respond to a written or telephone survey, or participate in a detailed interview, especially if they, a friend, or a colleague experienced unsatisfactory service.

Increasingly, the population studied might not be knowable. This is especially true if a study examines the uses of library home pages and resources for which access is not password-protected. Even if a library is part of a private institution, some resources—even those in digital archives—may not have restricted

---

FIGURE 8.2

INSTANCE SELECTION IN CASE STUDIES

Selection Basis	When to Use and What Questions It Can Answer
Convenience sampling	Is this site selected because it was expedient for data-collection purposes, what is happening, and why?
Purposive sampling	
Bracketing	What is happening at extremes? What explains such differences?
Best cases	What accounts for an effective program?
Worst cases	Why is the program not working?
Cluster	How do different types of programs compare with each other?
Representative	In instances chosen to represent important variations, what is the program like, and why?
Typical	In a typical site, what is happening and why?
Special interest	In this particular circumstance, what is happening, and why?
Probability sampling	What is happening in the program as a whole, and why?

Source: U.S. General Accounting Office [now the Government Accountability Office], Program Evaluation and Methodology Division, *Case Study Evaluations* (Washington, DC: GAO, 1990), 23.

access. In such instances, a nonprobability sample may be required.

As more libraries want to expand their customer base and penetrate the noncustomer segment of the population, convenience selection becomes more attractive. It affords an opportunity to listen to some individuals who share a certain characteristic—lost or never-gained status—without having to mount a large, time-consuming data-collection effort.

An area to probe with present customers, especially students, relates to the extent to which they expect (and the library can provide) technology and software (e.g., Internet use) that is on a par with what they have at home or can find elsewhere. This is a topic of concern to a number of librarians. The students might be selected by a nonprobability sample. As well, librarians want to maintain a service relationship with those comprising Generation Y (born between 1977 and 1994). Such individuals have been portrayed as confident and social, and they rely on the Internet, mobile telephones (including text messaging), and perhaps e-mail. They often associate libraries with books and may be unaware that the digital resources they use come from the library.[4]

Libraries might have an interest in studying the opinions of different segments of their customer base, such as parents of preschoolers, teens, and homeschoolers. These people can be easily identified by their circulation preferences. Even if circulation records are expunged after several days, the data could be collected for a few people the day after the borrowed items are returned. E-mail is an effective way to contact these borrowers to ascertain their willingness to participate in a focus group interview.

Another area to examine is internal customers. Libraries today might have a workforce that consists of four generations: Veterans (1922–1945), baby boomers (1946–1964), Generation X (1965–1980), and Generation Y. Depending on the size and complexity of the organization, a sample might involve either probability or nonprobability sampling. The study might focus on the effectiveness of the workforce, especially the work that occurs within teams or groups. Organizational psychologist J. Richard Hackman and management scholar Richard E. Walton view such effectiveness as the degree to which "a group's productive output (i.e., product or service) meets the standard of quantity, quality, and timeliness of the people who receive, review, and/or use that output (*results*)"; the "process of carrying out the work enhances the capability of members to work together interdependently in the

future (*socialization*)"; and how a "group's experience contributes to the growth and personal well-being of team members (*professional growth*)."[5]

As they explain, determining how well a team performs is much more complicated than quantifying performance measures. Team effectiveness, which is multidimensional, includes the continued socialization of team members and their growth as individuals. Personal, social, and systems conditions within the organization must also be addressed to gauge team effectiveness.

Purpose of the Interview

Library staff might use a focus group interview as a pretest for reviewing and refining the list of statements to include on a survey. A focus group interview, however, might be the primary (perhaps only) means or a secondary means (used in conjunction with another method to reinforce or enrich the findings) of data collection. In the latter instance, participants might even be asked to complete a brief questionnaire after the session or to review a subsequent transcript of the session; researchers would thus elicit additional quantifiable data, or receive further validation of the findings. Combining different methods of data collection can produce a more in-depth picture. Such research is known as *triangulation* or *multimethod* research, if it integrates qualitative and quantitative methods.

In another instance, customers might complete a questionnaire distributed in the library or by snail mail or e-mail. From among the respondents—those willing to supply their names and participate in a follow-up study—the library staff could select a subset for participation in one or more focus group interviews. The findings from a survey might shape the questions asked in focus group interviews and enable participants to clarify and expand on general findings.

It is possible to take a group such as incoming freshmen and invite them to participate in a focus group interview. That focus group might convene on a regular basis as a panel, one in which the same individuals participate throughout their program of study. The results might have multiple benefits, including demonstrating the library's contribution to student outcomes such as the retention rate.

When using focus group interviews as either a primary or secondary means of data collection, researchers must validate that the research presented is a balanced, realistic, and authentic reflection of participants' views and beliefs. After all, the criteria for good case study research of a qualitative nature are trustworthiness, credibility, transferability, confirmability of the data, and consistency or dependability of the data.[6]

The Group

The mixture of participants for a focus group interview should be carefully considered so that they complement one another and can provide the library with the desired feedback. The staff should ask: Why do we want this individual in a focus group? If the library anticipates holding more than one group interview, then a second question is: Why do we want that person in this particular session? Behind the second question is the need to determine how many focus group interviews are convenient, realistic, and necessary to conduct. Will there be one? If more than one, how many? The answer to this question depends on the amount of time that the staff has to engage in data collection, what they want to know, what they intend to do with the findings, and how far they want to generalize the findings.

Even one focus group in which the participants were selected by convenience represents a type of generalizability of findings: generalizable to the one group. The inclusion of additional groups expands the generalizability of the findings, but it merits noting that the purpose is not to show consensus within, between, and among groups; rather, it is to obtain varied and in-depth perceptions on a defined area of interest in a permissive, nonthreatening environment. Even when the moderator, near the conclusion of a focus group session, shares the findings of previous sessions, conclusions about the extent of similarity and dissimilarity across groups are tenuous. Nevertheless, they can provide additional insights as a group has more information to consider.

Another potentially difficult issue revolves around getting customers, potential or actual, to participate. Why should they accept the invitation and agree to participate? In brainstorming sessions, the staff can review rationales for attracting people and letting them know the value of their contribution and how the information obtained will be related to improving service performance. This does not mean that the library will accept all the suggestions offered.

The meeting area should be inviting, some refreshments provided, and participants given an opportunity to visit briefly and get acquainted if they do not know one another. An informal setting may help the participants relax. Arranging the furniture so that participants face one another reinforces a positive, friendly atmosphere.

The Moderator

The moderator conducts the session, explains the purpose of the session, helps participants to feel at ease and willing to contribute, asks the questions, and maintains the constant flow of the conversation. A good moderator, however, blends into the background and lets the dialogue develop among the participants. For many libraries, it may be difficult to find an impartial moderator who can elicit the desired information and ensure that participants leave the session feeling positive about the experience and believing that they benefited personally from the discussion. In several well-conducted focus group interviews that we have witnessed, many participants thanked the moderator for being invited; they enjoyed the experience and did not regret the imposition on their time!

The moderator must not become defensive if customers criticize library policies or services. A key question is: Can someone on the staff perform this function impartially? If the answer is no, the library might draw on staff from another library, the community, or, in the case of academic institutions where such an office exists, on institutional researchers. These individuals often know how to conduct focus group interviews, but they would need training to ensure that they understand the library's needs and the intent behind each question being asked.

NON-FACE-TO-FACE FOCUS GROUP INTERVIEWS

Instead of holding focus group interviews in a physical setting, librarians might explore their use online. Lynne Chase and Jaquelina Alvarez compare both types of interviews and acknowledge that the online version is still in its infancy.[7] However, it might appeal to certain constituent groups who are comfortable with the online environment, are not intimidated by the technology, and are neither shy nor reserved in sharing their thoughts and ideas. Such interviews might be conducted as online discussions and involve other information professionals. The purpose might be to ascertain what they are doing and to see what might be adaptable to other environments.

LOST AND NEVER-GAINED CUSTOMERS

In addition to gathering the opinions of present customers, a library may want to explore the attitudes of lost or never-gained customers, ascertaining their needs and expectations and seeing what role to play in converting them to actual customers. Given the complexity of and, more than likely, the limited time available for data collection, the groups should be limited to *either* lost customers *or* never-gained ones. Lost customers can be identified by inactive borrowers' cards or by asking student workers to suggest friends who fit this category. Since a focus group has such a small number of individuals, it is possible to pull a sample for lost customers. Furthermore, participants might be asked to suggest individuals similar to themselves for a subsequent focus group interview; this technique is called snowball sampling (a type of nonprobability sampling).

In a brainstorming session, library staff members—both professional and nonprofessional—should be able to identify a sufficient number of lost or never-gained customers to ensure enough participants for at least one focus group interview. Of course, those individuals asked to participate will be selected based on convenience. Some people will refuse to participate and others might require some persuasion.

Careful consideration must be given to the five to seven open-ended questions to be discussed (see figure 8.3), the welcome, and the beginning of the session. The moderator (or someone else) might demonstrate or explain a document delivery service, for example, and then question the participants about its potential value to them. The moderator must be careful that the session does not exceed ninety minutes. (We have had participants tell us that they can only give us thirty minutes; sixty minutes into the session, they are still enjoying the interaction! Still, their time should not be abused. Remember that one purpose, albeit a secondary one, is to gain and retain their goodwill. Part of that goodwill might be to let others know about the experience and to encourage them to participate in a future session.)

Other than for a brief demonstration, no library staff (except the moderator and perhaps a note taker) should be present. The session might be taped, if the participants agree and if the library wants to pay for transcription. The moderator might take brief notes, but cannot be expected to pace discussion while simultaneously recording responses. The moderator can, however, periodically recap the key points mentioned by participants to ensure that their views are represented correctly. (After the session, the moderator should develop a more complete written record of the interview.) If there is a note taker, this person should meet with the moderator to compare notes.

At the end of the session, the moderator might ask participants to identify peers who might be willing to participate in a subsequent focus group. This snowball technique represents an effort to go beyond the initial pool of people known to the library staff. Perhaps the original participants will be willing to let the library staff say that, "James Miller suggested your name. If you have any questions, please contact James."

FIGURE 8.3

SAMPLE QUESTIONS FOR LOST AND NEVER-GAINED CUSTOMERS

LOST CUSTOMERS

1. What types of information do you need? Where do you turn to meet these needs?
2. What was your experience with the library?
3. Did you tell friends and colleagues about that experience? What did you say?
4. What might this library do to regain your business?
5. How can you tell whether service employees are truly interested in providing you with outstanding service? Do you think they know what customers expect?

NEVER-GAINED CUSTOMERS

1. What types of information do you need? Where do you turn to meet these needs?
2. Do you use a library? Which one? Why? When did you last use a library? For what purpose(s)?
3. What might this library do to gain your business?

For lost and never-gained customers, it may be important to conduct some type of follow-up (on a regular basis, at irregular intervals, or just once, say, six months later) to see if their information-seeking patterns changed, and why or why not. The typical focus group interview discussed in the literature of library and information science occurs once with no follow-up session; however, for monitoring perceptions of customer expectations about service, follow-up produces useful comparative insights.

INTERNAL CUSTOMERS

The literature on service quality agrees that the staff must be satisfied, trained, able to cope with customers, and empowered to resolve problems. Clearly, they must think like a customer and realize that they are customers themselves: library staff members provide service to one another. Thus, focus group interviews should not be confined to external customers. Library staff should participate, and their participation need not be confined to development of an external customer service plan or survey. The questions depicted in figure 8.4 would provide an excellent basis of discussion as the staff prepares to be more responsive to one another and to the expectations of external customers.

It may be that the library need not conduct many surveys of external customers, especially at first. Discussions among internal customers, such as new staff, provide a rich opportunity to put staff in the shoes of customers, anticipating expectations, and trying to resolve matters before they become problems.

A FINAL WORD

Busy librarians who want to listen to customers but are unable to invest in a survey because of time and financial constraints, or who are questioning the application of a survey to lost or never-gained customers, might consider focus group interviewing. (See figure 8.5.) Marketing researchers have used this technique most effectively to ascertain purchasing patterns of the public and subpopulations and to target products to teenagers and others. A cynical person might even suggest that many politicians decide their position on an issue based on what focus groups reveal. Clearly, the success of focus groups in other contexts suggests their usefulness to libraries wanting to listen to customers.

Still, librarians should not forgo communicating with customers through blogs, wikis, and social networks such as Facebook. They can analyze the messages posted on a regular basis as well as how those messages are framed. Valuable insights can also be gathered from the use of usability testing to determine how customers navigate a library's home page. Data collection can go beyond self-reporting to suggest

---

FIGURE 8.4

SAMPLE QUESTIONS FOR INTERNAL CUSTOMERS

1. Do you see working here as a privilege? Are you proud to represent the library to its customers?
2. What image does the library project?
3. Overall, how satisfied are you with the service provided by the library?
4. How do you arrive at this sense of overall satisfaction? What aspects or dimensions of library services and operations are you basing your satisfaction on? (Examples might be staff helpfulness, convenient hours, and attractiveness of the environment.)
5. How can you tell whether or not library staff members are truly interested in providing outstanding service? Do you know what customers expect? Is there a gap between those expectations and the services actually provided? Does public service staff provide prompt answers to questions, without making the customer feel like an intruder? Do you sense that the library is an impersonal organization? Does the staff treat customers with interest and respect?
6. Do you see competitors for the library? How does the library compare to them?
7. Would you recommend [name of the library or service] to others? Why or why not?
8. Do you feel comfortable telling those administratively higher than you about any problems? Is it easy to do so, or would you just not bother?

FIGURE 8.5

FOCUS GROUP INTERVIEWS: A SUMMARY

DEFINITION
Interactive group discussion on a specific topic. Not a freewheeling or unfocused discussion. Qualitative method of data collection. (Not lip-service consultation; rather, sincere listening and learning.)

USES
1. Obtaining background for a survey; deciding on questions and response options
2. Exploring something not well understood
3. Confirming and testing a hypothesis
4. Engaging those not often asked for their opinions (e.g., lost or internal customers) to motivate them to become coproducers of service quality.

PARTICIPANTS
Six to ten internal or external customers, such as students, administrators, faculty, or individuals from city government, local businesses, public schools, religious organizations, local heritage agencies, or Friends of the library. They are selected through probability or nonprobability sampling, such as convenience and snowball. It is best not to mix participant groups; for example, there should not be a mix of students, faculty, and administrators.

NUMBER OF GROUPS
Depends on what staff wants to know, funding, etc.

PERSUADING EXTERNAL CUSTOMERS TO PARTICIPATE
Remember that an invitation is an imposition—you are asking a favor. Why should they accept it?

LENGTH OF SESSION
No longer than ninety minutes

NUMBER OF QUESTIONS
Maximum of seven. Note that figure 8.4 includes eight questions; however, only seven of the questions should be included. It is possible for staff to substitute questions in figure 8.4.

SINGLE OR MULTIPLE INTERVIEWS
Depending on the needs of the staff, participants might or might not be invited back for follow-up group interviewing. Do not abuse the privilege of having them participate.

ATMOSPHERE OF THE SESSION
Should be warm and inviting. Make participants feel comfortable.

POTENTIAL PROBLEMS
1. Getting enough people together who are willing to participate (donate their time)
2. Attracting a high-quality, neutral moderator

MODERATOR
Should be carefully selected. Not everyone can be neutral, maintain a conducive atmosphere, and be knowledgeable enough to facilitate meaningful discussion.

TRANSCRIPTION

Will the session be taped? Does taping affect the nature of comments? Does the moderator take selected notes, and is there a person present solely to take notes? Who is that person? Has that person been trained?

RELIABILITY AND VALIDITY

For qualitative data collection, the issues are confirmability, dependability, trustworthiness, and credibility. For instance, periodic summarization of the major points brought out in the discussion by the moderator; sharing of key findings among different focus groups; and later asking participants to verify copies of a written summary will help demonstrate confirmability, dependability, and trustworthiness. Also, participants might receive a demonstration of a technological application and respond to the value of what they observed; such an example seeks credibility in that participants have a common base of fact around which to respond.

COSTS

Refreshments, moderator (perhaps), transcription, and any supplies or handouts

COMPLEMENTARY DATA COLLECTION

1. Ask participants to complete a written survey about key issues raised and to provide information about themselves
2. Share a written summary of the session for verification and additional comment.
3. Examine posting on the library's bogs, wikis, and social networks

Note: See also Richard A. Krueger, "Designing and Conducting Focus Group Interviews," http://mentalmodels.mitre.org/cog_eng/reference_documents/conducting%20focus%20group%20interviews.pdf.

how customers actually use online resources and what makes them delighted or unhappy.

Surveys, focus groups, and complaint and compliment systems become ways to listen directly. Chapter 10 discusses other ways to gain insights into matters of importance to customers. Again, our intent is to identify choices from which individual libraries can select those most meaningful to them.

Customer satisfaction starts deep in your . . . [organization's] culture.[8]

Listen well.[9]

Notes

1. Fatemeh Rabiee, "Focus-Group Interview and Data Analysis," *Proceedings of the Nutrition Society* 63 (2004): 655, http://journals.cambridge.org/action/displayFulltext?type=6&fid=902304&jid=&volumeId=&issueId=&aid=902300.

2. Richard A. Krueger, *Focus Groups: A Practical Guide for Applied Research* (London: Sage, 1988), 18.

3. General Accounting Office [now the Government Accountability Office], Program Evaluation and Methodology Division, *Case Study Evaluations*, Transfer Paper 9 (Washington, DC: GAO, 1990), 22.

4. See Lynn Silipigni Connaway, Marie L. Radford, and Jocelyn DeAngelis Williams, "Engaging Net Gen Students in Virtual Reference: Reinventing Services to Meet Their Information Behaviors and Communication Preferences," in *Pushing the Edge: Explore, Engage, Extend; Proceedings of the Fourteenth National Conference of the Association of College and Research Libraries*, ed. Dawn M. Mueller (Chicago: Association of College and Research Libraries, 2009), 10–27.

5. J. Richard Hackman and Richard E. Walton, "Leading Groups in Organizations," in *Designing Effective Work Groups*, ed. Paul S. Goodman and Associates (San Francisco: Jossey-Bass, 1986), 72–119.

6. General Accounting Office, *Case Study Evaluations*, 53, 76.

7. Lynne Chase and Jaquelina Alvarez, "Internet Research: The Role of the Focus Group," *Library & Information Science Research* 22, no. 4 (Winter 2000): 357–369.

8. SurveyMethods, "Is Your Business Really Customer-focused?" www.surveymethods.com/glossary/article_business_seg_l.aspx.

9. Jeff Jarvis, *What Would Google Do?* (New York: Collins Business, 2009), 128.

Chapter Nine

Customer-Related Indicators and Requirements

Customers are not all alike.[1]

Traditional library statistics and measures, whether for academic or public libraries, do not adequately describe the library's contributions or productivity. Nor do they reflect the significant changes that have occurred and continue to occur in library operations and services. Furthermore, a number of academic administrators and local government officials, under pressure to contain or reduce costs, now want proof—or at least reasonable indications—that each unit gives "value for money." The cost of higher education particularly is being scrutinized. Peter Drucker notes that, "The cost of higher education has risen as fast as the cost of health care."[2] Because of the financial squeeze on middle-class families, he predicts a bleak future for universities.

As resources shrink, statistical reports that emphasize budget, staff, and collection size reinforce the notion that the library serves mainly as a warehouse. Although rankings among peer institutions by specific types of resources might still exert some influence on academic administrators, they tend to carry little weight with local government officials. In a world of electronically delivered information, size no longer matters. A student using a computer in a dormitory room can access the same information as one sitting at a terminal in the library—and both can be using another library at the same time.

Figures showing staff workloads, such as the number of items cataloged, may raise disquieting (and enlightening) questions about productivity. The continuous improvement philosophy, now prevalent in many businesses, can easily be applied to various library processes. Shrewd administrators in academe and local government are likely to track workload statistics reported from year to year, looking for productivity increases equal to the increase in the annual budget. Alternatively, they may question why certain processes are still being done after the acquisition of new technology. Traditional statistics do not reflect how people now gain access to information that libraries provide. The number and diversity of electronic resources will continue to multiply, and—as the five-part manual of the Association of Research Libraries (ARL) indicates—e-metrics have an impact on traditional measures, what vendors and publishers compile, and how input and output measures are defined.[3]

The most serious problem with traditional statistics is that they do not indicate either how well libraries serve customers or how libraries might change or improve their service. Also, except for its relationship to the operating budget, each measure is isolated from the others. Common sense indicates that not all measures are equally important, yet current statistical systems do not distinguish among measures, except to note the importance of the overall budget and its percentage increase or decrease.

We propose a more comprehensive system of indicators that fall into two different, but interrelated, areas: (1) customer-related indicators and (2) customer requirements, which focus on the internal workings and processes of the library. Customer-related indicators report on service. They are based on customer actions and expressed preferences, surely more reliable indicators than checkmarks on a survey purporting to measure customer satisfaction.

Libraries, like many other organizations, have surveyed customers about their satisfaction. Questions about overall satisfaction, or satisfaction with specific aspects of the service, might be "measured" on a five-point scale, ranging from *very dissatisfied* (1) through *satisfied* (3) to *very satisfied* (5). Common practice has been to interpret all responses of three or higher as *satisfied* and, thus, to arrive at rather elevated levels of customer satisfaction. Unrecognized bias is built in by summing responses to three categories as indicating *satisfaction* but summing responses to only two categories as indicating *dissatisfaction*. (A four-point scale that allots only one category to express dissatisfaction is even more biased.)

Research has shown that "satisfaction is an inadequate, incomplete, and maybe even inaccurate measure of customer loyalty."[4] A report from the Conference Board of Canada cites studies done for BancOne, Xerox, and AT&T Universal Card Services that indicate that scores of three and four rankings on a five-point scale are relatively meaningless.[5] Some marketing experts have characterized these scores as a *zone of tolerance*—the difference "between customers' ideal or desired level of service and the level of service they would find minimally acceptable."[6] Figure 9.1, adapted from a chart created by Xerox, Inc., illustrates the tracking of customer responses. Customers rating their satisfaction as three or four on a five-point scale are quite likely to take their business elsewhere, whereas customers who rate satisfaction as five tend to remain. Xerox's research characterized customers who are merely satisfied with a company or a service as being in a zone of indifference toward a continuing relationship with that company or service.[7]

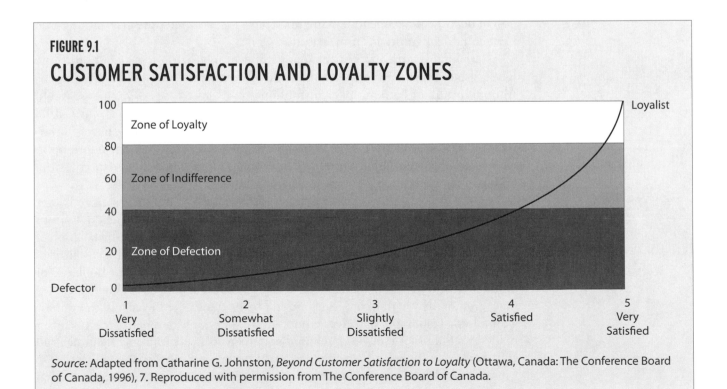

FIGURE 9.1

CUSTOMER SATISFACTION AND LOYALTY ZONES

Source: Adapted from Catharine G. Johnston, *Beyond Customer Satisfaction to Loyalty* (Ottawa, Canada: The Conference Board of Canada, 1996), 7. Reproduced with permission from The Conference Board of Canada.

Libraries might collect information about customer behaviors, thereby going beyond the collection of self-reported opinions. The customer-related indicators proposed here allow library managers to evaluate not only market penetration of the library among its community, but also such important things as the length and strength of customer relationships as measured by the frequency and intensity of library use. Such indicators are considered loyalty ratios.[8] They include the following:

maintenance ratio—the number of current customers retained to the number who defect within a year

retention ratio—the number of customers retained per dollar of investment

amount/continuity ratio—comparison of the length and intensity of the relationship between core customers and all customers (Core customers are those who buy heavily, refer other customers, or have a long-standing relationship with a firm.)

Businesses rely on sales revenue to evaluate intensity. Libraries, on the other hand, can analyze borrowing, uses, and calls for service (e.g., reference queries, entries to the building, and access to electronic files) as surrogates for sales because they, in effect, represent sales to the library. Data reflecting customer behaviors can be obtained from those integrated automated systems that capture the information gathered. It may be possible to compare the borrower file to the circulation and use files.

MINING THE AUTOMATED SYSTEM

The computerization of library records gives staff a tremendous opportunity to learn more about customers and their uses in order to improve the service. Yet, as Stephen Atkins complains, "It is almost a crime how little this capacity has been utilized by the library community."[9] He was writing before the enactment of both USA PATRIOT Acts (2001 and 2006) and the government's use of national security letters to compel libraries and others to release records for investigative purposes. Geographic information systems (GISs), through the array of commercial data that can be geocoded to specific streets and addresses on those streets, provide detailed data for preparing a community analysis. With the inclusion of information about

households in which family members have library cards and those who do not, libraries could relate the data more to household use. They might also use GIS data for reviewing where to place or remove a branch library. Still, libraries should have a policy about computerization involving relational databases that if released to the government would reveal household reading habits.

The automated system might be part of a management information system (MIS) in which the various metrics discussed in this book could be stored, organized, retrieved, and prepared for delivery in reports and presentations. An MIS is useful for planning purposes (e.g., creating obtainable objectives); assessment and evaluation, including determining the current status of services and progress toward improvement (e.g., identifying weaknesses, applying a solution, and measuring change); managerial decision making (e.g., fund allocations or a change in hours open); responding to surveys from the institution, other libraries, library consortia, organizations, and the federal government; and communicating conclusions, results, and information through reports and presentations with an emphasis on improving accountability to meet stakeholder information needs.[10]

PRIVACY ISSUES

Many organizations, including libraries, need certain information about individuals in order to conduct business. Libraries, for instance, collect information about who owes fines, who has placed reserves, and how those with library cards can be contacted. Some libraries ask for Social Security numbers and dates of birth from people wanting cards; providing such information, however, is usually voluntary. Some libraries do not delete the identity of the two previous borrowers of an item so that, in case damage is detected, these individuals can be contacted for payment. When libraries turn over to collection agencies the names, addresses, telephone numbers, and fine amounts owed by borrowers with titles long overdue, they justify that action as necessary for the conduct of library business.

The data used for statistical reporting purposes in the customer-related indicators proposed here need not identify any individual borrower or any item borrowed. It is, however, not unusual for registration applications to state that data about cardholders may be used for administrative purposes, which would cover use in some of the indicators proposed in the following sections of this chapter.

Respecting privacy means that the people who work in the organization do not share information about customers to those who do not need to know it for legitimate library purposes. The pharmacist does not discuss what medicines an individual takes. The bank teller who cashes a check is required to look at the person's account balance to see whether the amount can be recovered in case the check is bad; that teller does not, however, discuss the account balance with other customers (internal or external).[11]

TRACKING TRENDS

Most library surveys are snapshots of a situation at one particular point in time. They are seldom compared with earlier surveys, and the wording of questions may vary over time. Similarly, the current statistical reports of both academic and public libraries are essentially glimpses of the current reporting year. The data obtained from the customer-related indicators outlined here can be compared to a report card in that they give a picture of the current situation. These same data can also be tracked over a period of years to indicate whether the strength of the relationship between the library and its customers is increasing or diminishing.

Such information might give senior managers an indication that something is wrong in the system, but not specifically what has gone wrong. Gaining insight into problems that need to be addressed requires using *operational indicators,* which analyze where the system is malfunctioning. (Indicators relating to operations will be described later in this chapter.) Because of the differences in the operation of academic and public libraries, and in the needs of their customers, the sections on customer-related indicators are specific to each type.

The figures presented in this chapter are illustrative rather than prescriptive. The intent is to show how the data recommended could be categorized and presented. All data, whether daily, monthly, quarterly, or annual tallies, should be entered on whatever spreadsheet program is available. Many libraries already collect some of the data recommended in the indicators, such as number of new borrower registrations and number of visitors. If the current methods of collecting and tabulating these data are satisfactory, libraries should keep on using them. The summaries

should, however, be entered into the spreadsheets for updating, tabulation, and analysis.

VIEWING LIBRARY USE

Figure 9.2 characterizes library use, a multidimensional concept that applies to visits to physical space as well as use of digital resources remotely or in the library. Individual libraries may add additional components or delete some of the choices, as well as examine different uses by format, time, and demographics (e.g., faculty or student, occupation, and geographical location within the city). The critical issue is that library use is not simply defined in terms of circulation statistics and the number of visitors to the physical premises.

For any of the components, a public or academic library can develop a set of customer-related indicators that depict use, market penetration, and loyalty. Market penetration focuses on the percentage of a population or subpopulation that uses one or more of the components. Loyalty concentrates on repeat use and those making the most use of the library and its services. If a library has a survey question probing the extent of satisfaction with it and respondents answer on a ten-point scale (with ten being *completely satisfied*), only those marking a ten are considered loyal customers. Does this percentage increase over time?

CUSTOMER-RELATED INDICATORS FOR PUBLIC LIBRARIES

The first edition of this book was written at a time when use tended to focus more on a physical setting and the lending of material. That environment was captured by figures 9.3 to 9.20. Today, that environment is more complex, as figure 9.2 of this edition emphasizes. As a result, the remaining figures will be based on the content of this figure, and they will cover an aspect of library use.

Time Periods Covered

Most public libraries will want to tally records by month and then by year. Daily counts will need to be recorded and totaled for the monthly reports. Figures 9.3 and 9.4 concentrate on a given year, whereas figure 9.5 need not do the same.

Market Penetration

Public libraries are supported on the basis of their being available to all residents of a community. Both the library management and local officials have an interest in knowing whether or not a large proportion of the population uses the library. (See figure 9.5.)

The indicators for market penetration might include registered borrowers and visitors to the library, both in-person and virtual through electronic transport. It is important for libraries to keep registration information current by annual re-registrations. Many libraries already have such a policy. Claims that registered borrowers exceed the service area's population invite distrust. Registration files that are years out of date need to be updated to make the following indicators useful.

Libraries can monitor market penetration by day, month, year, or year-to-date. Many libraries already collect these data. To identify trends in market penetration, comparisons with the same point in time (e.g., the previous year, month by month, quarter by quarter, and year by year) are encouraged. Libraries with multiple outlets should keep data for each branch and then transfer branch information to a systemwide database for comparisons. (Again, many libraries already do this.) Consequently for each month and year, libraries and their branches can record the number of

- in-person visits
- virtual visits (perhaps defined in terms of home page hits)
- new registrants

Registrants

New borrowers are those who have registered during the past twelve months. For them, library measures might focus on the following:

- Number of new borrowers registered for the year-to-date for each outlet and for the whole system.
- Number of new borrowers registered during the preceding year. If data are available by outlet for each month, so much the better for comparison. If not, the staff should use whatever data categories match those of the current year.
- Percentage of this year's new registrants to previous years. Are numbers of new registrations increasing or decreasing?

Envision a table that for a given year or set of years, each month is depicted. At the end of the year, the total and the percentage of change should be calculated. In other words, for each month of the year,

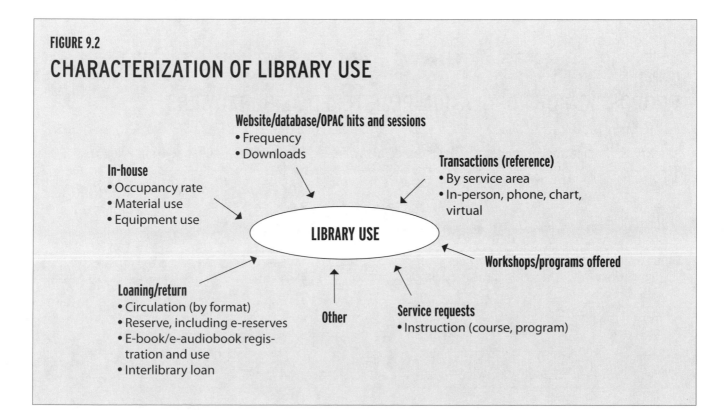

FIGURE 9.2

CHARACTERIZATION OF LIBRARY USE

Website/database/OPAC hits and sessions
- Frequency
- Downloads

In-house
- Occupancy rate
- Material use
- Equipment use

Transactions (reference)
- By service area
- In-person, phone, chart, virtual

LIBRARY USE

Workshops/programs offered

Loaning/return
- Circulation (by format)
- Reserve, including e-reserves
- E-book/e-audiobook registration and use
- Interlibrary loan

Other

Service requests
- Instruction (course, program)

record the number of newly registered persons. After the first year, compute the percentage change for each month and for the entire year. The calculation is as follows: Subtract the prior year's count from this year's count. Divide the result by the prior year's count and multiply by one hundred. The result is the percentage change between the two months of the different years. For example, suppose the January 2010 count is fifty, and the January 2011 count is fifty-five, Subtracting the first value (fifty) from the second one (fifty-five) gives five more registrants in January 2011 than January 2010. Divide by the January 2010 count (fifty), giving 5/50, or 0.10. Multiply by one hundred, resulting in 10 percent. Even if the subtraction yields a negative number, the process is the same, but represents a decline. Suppose the January 2010 count was fifty-five, and the January 2011 count was fifty. The subtraction gives negative five. Again divide by the earlier year's count (55): −5/55 = −.0909. Multiply by one hundred to give negative 9.09 percent, a decline.

The changes in the registration rates over time indicate how well the library attracts new customers. If the *new customer* rate falls off, steps should be taken to remedy this. However, although registration may be growing, the service area population may also be increasing, so a further measure is needed to account for this. Population estimates can be gathered from several sources. Though the official census is taken only every ten years, annual estimates are available from the *American Community Survey* (www.census .gov/acs/www/), local and state government agencies, the Chamber of Commerce, and other sources.

For all registrants, the staff might focus on the number and percentage of the population in the legal service area over *x* years of age registered as cardholders over the past five years. Are the numbers increasing or decreasing out of proportion to the general change in the population? (When comparing to demographic data, be sure to subtract the subpopulation too young to qualify as cardholders from the population total so that only those meeting borrower requirements are compared with actual cardholders.) Figure 9.3 illustrates how such data can be presented.

In-Person Visitors

The following measures apply only if the library has an automatic door counter:

- the number of visitors for the year to date, for each outlet and systemwide
- the number of visitors for the previous four years and the percentage change by year, for each outlet and systemwide

A configuration similar to what was discussed in the preceding section can be used for both the indicators.

FIGURE 9.3

PROPORTION OF POPULATION REGISTERED AS BORROWERS

Year	Population Estimate	Registered Borrowers	Percentage	Change from Prior Year
2010				////////////////////////////////
2011				
2012				
2013				
2014				
2015				

Virtual Visitors

Returning to figure 9.2, for customers who use library resources remotely, libraries might track the

- number of visits to the library's home page for the year to date
- number and percentage of home page visits comparing current year with previous years
- number and percentage of OPAC visits comparing current year with previous year

In addition, there are various options for data reporting within the context of the COUNTER Codes of Practice for Journals and Databases.[12] (See chapter 4.) COUNTER statistics, among other things, cover total searches and sessions (month and journal):

- name of the service
- platform
- total searches run
- searches—federated and automated
- total sessions

The data collected could be inserted into a table that reports data by month (or quarter) and the percentage of change as discussed above. In addition, the ARL manual, especially part five, offers excellent coverage of remote use and the types of measures to gather and report.[13]

Loyalty Indicators

Identifying and serving loyal customers—those who are very frequent users—are an important part of the success of any organization. It is far easier and cheaper to keep a current customer than it is to get a new one. Current customers who frequently use the library have already demonstrated their support.

FIGURE 9.4

LOYALTY INDICATORS: DISTRIBUTION OF CUSTOMERS BY YEARS OF CONTINUOUS REGISTRATION AND ACTIVITY

Year of Registration	Number of Registered Customers	Number of Active Borrowers
< 1		
1		
2		
3		
4		
5		
N		
Total		

Many businesses identify and reward customer loyalty. The frequent flyer programs of airlines are a conspicuous example. Libraries could adopt programs to encourage frequent use, but at present, many of them cannot identify, much less encourage, the array of frequent-use customers.

Any determination of loyalty must address figure 9.2 and the purpose for library use. The purpose might relate to use of the facilities, technology, staff, or collections. Collections include

Journal articles and their electronic counterpart (increasingly the electronic form may have no paper counterpart).

Books (fiction, nonfiction, and reference) and their electronic counterpart (again, e-books may lack a print counterpart). Books also appear through Google, Google Scholar, and institutional repositories (perhaps only one chapter is accessible without charge).

They might also comprise e-audiobooks, e-books, and playaways, in which the digital content is preloaded and the "book" includes a battery to make it play and a place to plug in earbuds. E-books might also appear in digital form through the Internet and free of charge.

Newspapers. As the print form decreases in popularity, the form available through the Internet is gaining popularity. Newspapers, even historical back runs, appear through the Internet, and microfiche copies in libraries might be scanned and available in digital form.

Government documents. As libraries downsize their print collection, they are expanding access to those in digital form from government agencies and commercial vendors.

FIGURE 9.5

MARKET PENETRATION BY AGE AND GENDER

AGE	NUMBER OF REGISTERED CARDHOLDERS		SERVICE AREA POPULATION		PERCENT SERVED BY LIBRARY	
	Female	Male	Female	Male	Female	Male
10 and younger						
11–15						
16–21						
22–35						
36–50						
51–65						
66+						
Undetermined						
Total						

Other sources. This category includes, among other things, the digitization projects of major research libraries and the placement of these materials on the Internet. Some of those sources are restricted to the clientele of a particular institution.

Collection use statistics need to address types of sources, although it is becoming more difficult to identify and characterize certain types of loyal customers. A number of students who rely on databases may be unaware that their favorites are available through the library. They may perceive themselves as loyal to the university databases or a particular one, but they may not translate their loyalty to the library. Still, circulation records comprise one means of determining the library's holding power—both retention and the intensity of the relationship with its cardholders. Among the data that can be gathered from nearly any automated circulation system are the following:

Number of customers who have been continuously registered as borrowers for three, five, ten, or *n* years (the number can be tracked from figure 9.4).

Number of customers who have been continuously active borrowers for three, five, ten, or *n* years. In essence, how long has the most loyal customer used the library? With that person's consent, is the time sufficiently long to honor formally his years of loyalty?

Age and gender of cardholders in relation to the service area population. Figure 9.5 indicates the distribution of cardholders by age and gender.

Demographic profile of loyal customers, using such data as gender, age, and ZIP code. Which groups in the community are underrepresented? For example, what is the representation of teenage boys among loyal customers? Figure 9.5 is an example of how the data can be formatted for spreadsheet analysis. Data may be broken down to study customer patterns by library branch. As well, the figure can depict registered borrowers.

Loyalty Demographics

Figures such as 9.5 increase in relevance when they include variables such as race and ethnicity. The 2010 Census of Population and Housing adheres to the categories as defined by the Office of Management and Budget (OMB), Office of Information and Regulatory Affairs, in its Revisions to the Standards for the Classification of Federal Data on Race and Ethnicity in 1997:

OMB is accepting the recommendations of the Interagency Committee for the Review of the Racial and Ethnic Standards with the following two modifications: (1) the Asian or Pacific Islander category will be separated into two categories—"Asian" and "Native Hawaiian or Other Pacific Islander," and (2) the term "Hispanic" will be changed to "Hispanic or Latino."

The revised standards will have five minimum categories for data on race: American Indian or Alaska Native, Asian, Black or African American, Native Hawaiian or Other Pacific Islander, and White. There will be two categories for data on ethnicity: "Hispanic or Latino" and "Not Hispanic or Latino."[14]

Another possibility is that the institution or the city may have categories that they prefer to use. Whatever the categories used, it is important to develop market penetration and loyalty throughout the community served.

Before asking about someone's race and ethnicity, it is important to remember that such information may be sensitive; furthermore, it may be illegal for staff to ask borrowers at registration. Some customers resent being asked about their race and ethnicity. If the person registering them gets to decide, the possibility for error is great. As a result, it is important to discuss the matter with key stakeholders in the various communities and decide how to proceed.

Declining Loyalty?

People cease to be customers for predictable reasons, most notably relocation out of the area or death. Thus, a certain percentage of customer loss (about 25 percent) is both expected and natural. This section, however, emphasizes cardholders who have not borrowed any materials during the past year. Relevant measures become the following:

- Number and percentage of cardholders to the total of registered customers who neither borrowed any items nor contacted the library electronically during the past year.
- Number and percentage of cardholders compared to the total number of registered customers who have had no recorded

contact with the library in each of the preceding four years. Such information, over time, can depict trends.

- Percentage of this year's number of customers with no recorded contact to that for the previous year. Is the number of these persons increasing, decreasing, or remaining constant? (Figure 9.3 can be adapted for this type of data.)

It is also possible to create a demographic profile of the cardholders who have no recorded contact with the library during the past year, using such data as race and ethnicity, gender, age, and ZIP code. Data might be subdivided to study use patterns by branch.

Comparisons of distributions and percentages over a few years will provide valuable insights into the library's customer base and the ability of the library to retain customers over time. Emerging patterns regarding heavy-use, lost, and longtime customers can indicate areas for target marketing of library services. Such an identification of customers could allow the library to establish focus groups. (See chapter 8.) With heavy-use customers, library staff can use focus groups to discuss what they like about the service and what improvements they would like. Groups of former customers might disclose their reasons for leaving the library and suggest changes that might result in regaining them as customers. The identification of longtime loyal customers is an opportunity to let them know that the library appreciates their patronage. Formal appreciation of longtime customers is also an excellent public relations opportunity for the library.

Information about Customer Preferences

There is an extensive literature on the public's reading preferences and the shifting emphasis to reading and browsing the Internet by using online newspapers, blogs, and social networks. A number of people, especially within Generation Y, like to communicate with their friends but like less to communicate with individuals they do not know. A question becomes, to what extent will they communicate directly with library reference staff online such as through text referencing? It is not our intent to enter the long-standing controversy over *meeting the demand* versus *trying to uplift preferences*. Nevertheless, two questions raised by Charlie Robinson, longtime director of the Baltimore County Public Library, seem pertinent:

- Should I buy what they don't want?
- Or, should I buy what they should want?[15]

The information recommended to be gathered about collection use is intended to make library managers more aware of customer preferences and how those preferences change over time. Data for the types of indicators listed here can be compiled monthly and cumulated annually. Data should be reported by branch for in-depth analysis.

Library staff might examine the following:

Distribution of circulations by type of material; for example, video, adult fiction, adult nonfiction, picture books, juvenile nonfiction, and audio (including talking books). Complicating matters, as discussed above, some of the types might appear in electronic form. What is the ratio of circulations to holdings for these various types of material? The answer should factor in the format of the material. What do we learn from facts such as that adult fiction represents 62 percent of circulations, but only 50 percent of holdings? Should the library consider acquiring more adult fiction, and in print form?

Which areas of the collection are used most intensely; for example, what is the percentage of videos borrowed to videos owned? This is also called the *turnover rate*.

Distribution of circulations for this year by call number groupings representing specific subjects or time periods. Generally, this means groupings by the tens for Dewey systems. The call number groupings can be expanded or contracted based on collection size (e.g., medical titles by topic or U.S. history by time period). Clearly, e-books should not be ignored in producing any count.

As the staff gathers the type of data discussed above, they should not forget to investigate patterns of e-resources used, including e-books and e-audiobooks. Downloads may reveal more about use patterns than do circulation records. At any rate, both types of statistics should be gathered. Vendors may be able to provide statistics about use patterns for their online databases; the problem is that the results may not be comparable among vendors and different products.

CUSTOMER-RELATED INDICATORS FOR ACADEMIC LIBRARIES

Figure 9.2 has definite implications for academic libraries, especially when the population served is not neatly characterized as faculty, students, staff, and administration. Some libraries might allow city or area residents to use the collections or the home page; they might be willing to serve even a broader geographical area. In such instances, ratios and percentages cannot be meaningfully calculated. As a result, this section is merely suggestive.

Market Penetration

College and university officials who authorize library funding expect the library to serve most if not all the departments on campus, not just a handful. Therefore, the issue of widespread usage of the library, its market penetration of the campus, is a critical issue.

Turning to figure 9.2 and the section on loaning/returns, it is possible to calculate the percentage of the student or faculty populations that have registered with a vendor for e-books. It is also possible to talk with faculty and ascertain what percentage of them per department have provided links from their syllabi, as included in course management software, to library resources. Further, what percentage place material on reserve or take advantage of e-reserves? An important indicator of market penetration is the percentage of academic departments that use the library either by loans, reserves, interlibrary loans, or requests for instruction for their students. Market penetration by departments is heavily influenced by subject matter. Those departments whose content is heavily verbal should use the library much more than departments whose content relies on symbols. Extreme examples are history and mathematics. Another indicator of market penetration might be the number of faculty requests by department to the library to identify websites useful to their subject matter. Art or photography collections at distant museums are an example. Student usage by department can also be tracked by OPAC and Web usage, as well as loans and reserves. However, the status of the students—undergraduate or graduate—should influence market penetration, with graduate students making broader and more intense use of library facilities and offerings. When the data collection goes into frequency of use, the findings have implications for customer loyalty.

Loyalty Indicators

Because graduates leave and new students enroll at regular intervals, academic library managers may not have given much thought or attention to the retention of student customers. Most students are perceived as being in flux, as they move through the system, so to speak. This characterization overlooks, however, the importance of turning first-year students into customers for their remaining years on campus, and the value of building loyalty beyond graduation. Students tell one another about their experiences, both positive and negative, in selecting courses, dealing with faculty, using the library, eating in campus facilities, and so forth.

Faculty turnover is much lower than that of students, and faculty can be customers of high value in that the types of assignments they set strongly influence student use of the library. An example of a loyalty indicator—expressed in terms of repeat users—is use of Google Analytics (www.google.com/analytics/) to determine the number of repeat users from monthly log-ins. Multiplying that number by one hundred yields a percentage.

Comparisons of distributions and percentages over a few years will provide valuable insights into the customer base. (Any such comparisons should not, however, assume that all departments and faculty have a similar level of need for library use.) Noncustomers will be identified, and, perhaps, their reasons for not using the library can be addressed. Knowing faculty usage by department allows library staff to discuss library-faculty cooperation more knowledgeably and to elicit suggestions for changes from faculty that might increase their usage and/or that of their students. However, as figure 9.2 indicates, use is not a concept that is simply captured.

CUSTOMER REQUIREMENTS FOR BOTH ACADEMIC AND PUBLIC LIBRARIES

Process measures relate to work units completed. For example, traditional statistics include the number of items purchased or cataloged, questions answered, and so forth. Productivity has long been a measure of performance, but productivity merely in terms of the number of units processed is not of much interest to customers. They have other standards by which to measure the quality of an organization's service.

Most people have a lot of experience as customers and, as a result, hold some rather definite ideas about how service organizations should treat them. Some service elements cut across all types of service organizations, although the details differ from organization to organization. Regarding safety, for instance, expectations for an amusement park are rather different from those for a bank. Yet, customers expect both organizations to protect them.

Although most people might prioritize service elements differently depending on the service and organization used as well as on their particular needs, they would all agree about the importance of service quality and being satisfied with the service and its delivery. We refer to these attributes as *customer requirements*. Requirements important to customers, including internal ones, should replace process measures as indicators of performance. Library managers have some power to change operations that affect the quality of the requirements proposed here. A variety of service organizations, ranging from appliance repair shops to zoos, recognize the importance of these requirements. Let us see how they might apply to libraries.

Acceptable Physical Facility

Just as there are different standards of housekeeping, any group has different levels of acceptability. *Acceptability*, as used here, means that, for most customers, satisfaction focuses on personal safety, the safety of their belongings, physical comfort in terms of temperature and noise, and the cleanliness of the facility. These are all factors over which the library has some control. Safety concerns will drive customers away faster than any other problem, as few people will place themselves or their possessions in jeopardy to use the library.

The library might establish a safety log to record incidents and reports from customers and staff. These can then be analyzed for ways to reduce problems.

Although noise tolerance varies among any group of customers, the degree of tolerance can be a significant factor in whether or not customers continue to use the facility. Concerns about cleanliness, or at least the appearance of cleanliness, are growing in importance as the media report more stories about bacteria and viruses identified as intractable to antibiotics. Even though janitorial services may be provided by another unit, the library has to monitor the acceptability of custodians' work, and also take responsibility for the cleanliness of its own equipment, such as OPAC keyboards and screens—items too often neglected.

Timeliness

Timeliness encompasses on-time delivery, short cycle times, and speedy handling of problems. Basically, timeliness means that what customers want is available when or soon after they request it. From retail establishments, customers expect fresh food, current news, and the latest fashions, just as they want the latest books, videos, and journal issues from the library. When customers make a request, pose a reference question, or file a complaint, they appreciate a quick response.

Timeliness is affected by

- process routines that are either streamlined or cumbersome
- due dates, or the lack of them, for the completion of tasks
- anticipating or ignoring customer requests based on past behaviors

Delays can be predicted when imbalances occur in a unit that produces work on which other units depend. Such imbalances can be caused by lack of staff, work overloads, or failure to smooth out predictable peaks and valleys in work flow.

Convenience

Convenience relates to hours, locations, and amenities, and to such questions as

- Is the library open to accommodate people who work different shifts?
- Is the library open on weekends?
- Are service desks staffed so that people can obtain help?
- Are public restrooms, drinking fountains, and places to eat available, or must customers leave the building for these amenities?

Convenience also means saving customers' time. Saving time means making the system so transparent that customers new to libraries can figure out what to do with minimal frustration. Both public and academic libraries have embraced self-service. Customers are now expected to use the OPAC, check out their own materials, pick up their own reserves and do their own Internet and periodical searches. All of these activities, however, can be confusing for new customers and those unfamiliar with library procedures. Therefore, to make using the library convenient for unsophisticated customers, the library needs to ensure that directions and signage are placed so that people can navigate the system.

Accuracy

Accuracy, or doing things right the first time, is much more important than most managers realize. Things done incorrectly make the organization look inept and cause customer frustration and anger. Accuracy in the library means that

- items returned are discharged properly so that customers are not charged fines
- fines paid are credited
- materials are properly shelved the first time
- shelves are regularly read for misplaced and hidden books
- answers to reference questions are correct and complete, which means the library must ensure that information about current situations is kept up to date. Staff must remember that information contained in any source can become outdated.

Reliability and Dependability

Reliability and dependability mean that the organization provides what it purports to offer. Customers expect to be able to get a can of peaches in the supermarket, cough syrup in the drugstore, and bedrooms at the hotel. They also expect to get materials and answers to reference questions at the library. When an organization offers a new service, customers expect to be able to obtain it. For example, one public library offers lessons from Rosetta Stone in a number of foreign languages via a remote service. An English tutor wanted to demonstrate to her student the usefulness of the program and how to access it in the library. However, they could not access the program even though the tutor had accessed it successfully a number of times from her home via the library computer system. Frustrated, the tutor asked a library staff member for help. The staff member could not access the Rosetta Stone program either. The tutor and her student left frustrated. Offering the Rosetta Stone lessons is perceived as a valuable service; however, the library neglected to ensure that staff was adequately trained to facilitate its use. The library lost credibility in the eyes of those users because the service was unreliable and undependable.

Competent, Professional, and Knowledgeable Staff

Competent, professional, and *knowledgeable* are terms that apply to the ability of the staff to satisfy customers' information inquiries. Tests of reference accuracy from the early 1970s to the present have reaffirmed that customers are quite likely to be given incorrect answers or have their questions turned away as not answerable. Despite a rather low percentage of accuracy in answering questions, many libraries, both academic and public, on the grounds of economy, regularly staff reference desks, especially on evenings and weekends, with students and library assistants. When they do so, they should not assume an acceptable level of service. They should monitor the situation and take corrective action as needed. Such action means implementation of an effective staff training program.

Courtesy

Customer interactions with staff in any service organization are crucial for producing repeat business. The professional literature is replete with articles describing both wonderful and woeful examples of such interactions, and indicating that many staff members decide individually what levels of service or courtesy they will extend. By establishing standards of observable behaviors for staff, the library can make explicit what behaviors are expected. In June 2004, the Reference and User Services Association, a division of the American Library Association, approved a document titled, "Guidelines for Behavioral Performance of Reference and Information Service Providers,"[16] which is a major revision of the 1996 guidelines. The guidelines offer excellent examples of desired behaviors designed to produce service of high quality. Any library seriously interested in achieving, maintaining, and monitoring the quality of public service should implement these guidelines.

Librarians are customers every day in various service organizations. They have clear ideas about what constitutes quality service and how they want to be treated. Customers in the library have the same ideas and want the same treatment.

A FINAL WORD

The indicators and customer requirements presented here offer insights into and knowledge about the library's customer base and its reputation among the library's service community. Knowledge of who the customers are and the kinds of materials they prefer allows the staff to base service on evidence rather than on opinions, beliefs, or hopes. The evidence may or may not be pleasing, but, at the least, it provides a foundation on which to build, especially as it indicates segments of the population that could be targets of marketing.

These indicators allow us to think about service quality or library "goodness" in a different way. Resources no longer constitute the highest criterion of quality, nor is productivity of staff an independent standard. Instead, quality and goodness are understood as abstractions that exist in the minds of the people who interact with the library and react based on their experiences. We hope that data obtained from monitoring and analyzing these interactions will assist librarians to adjust service priorities to better meet customer expectations.

Some will resist these indicators for philosophical reasons or because of procedural difficulties in implementing them. We recognize that tradition is honored and that change is difficult and usually slow. Yet, the information environment is experiencing rapid and unexpected changes—changes beyond the control of any library or the profession at large. If libraries fail to retain, maintain, and expand the customer base, they are likely to be in trouble. Getting and keeping customers are what it is all about, and all the platitudes about service, education, or imparting of knowledge will not change the need for customers.

The efficient collection of relevant statistics and their effective use
. . . [are] more important today than ever before.[17]

Notes

1. Arthur M. Hughes, *The Customer Loyalty Solution: What Works (and What Doesn't) in Customer Loyalty Programs* (New York: McGraw-Hill, 2003), 251.

2. Robert Lenzer and Stephen S. Johnson, "Seeing Things as They Really Are: An Interview with Peter Drucker," *Forbes* 159 (March 10, 1997): 127.

3. Association of Research Libraries, *Measures for Electronic Resources (E-Metrics)*, 5 parts, www.arl.org/resources/pubs/monographs/index.shtml.

4. Catharine G. Johnston, *Beyond Customer Satisfaction to Loyalty* (Ottawa: The Conference Board of Canada, 1996), 20.

5. Ibid., 20–21.

6. Benjamin Schneider and David E. Bowen, *Winning the Service Game* (Boston: Harvard Business School Press, 1995), 262.

7. Johnston, *Beyond Customer Satisfaction*, 6.

8. Ibid., 21–22.

9. Stephen Atkins, "Mining Automated Systems for Collection Management," *Library Administration & Management* 10, no. 1 (Winter 1996): 16.

10. For a fuller treatment, see Robert E. Dugan, Peter Hernon, and Danuta A. Nitecki, *Viewing Library Metrics from Different Perspectives* (Westport, CT: Libraries Unlimited, 2009), chapter 10.

11. See Daniel J. Solove, *The Future of Reputation: Gossip, Rumor, and Privacy on the Internet* (New Haven, CT: Yale University Press, 2007).

12. COUNTER (Counting Online Usage of Networked Electronic Resources), "The COUNTER Code of Practice, Journals and Databases, Release 3" August 2008, www.projectcounter.org/r3/Release3D9.pdf.

13. See Association of Research Libraries, *Measures for Electronic Resources (E-Metrics)*.

14. Office of Management and Budget, Office of Information and Regulatory Affairs, "Revisions to the Standards for the Classification of Federal Data on Race and Ethnicity," www.whitehouse.gov/omb/fedreg/1997standards.html. See the website of the U.S. Census Bureau (www.census.gov) for further clarification. For instance, "The racial categories included in the census questionnaire generally reflect a social definition of race recognized in this country, and not an attempt to define race biologically, anthropologically, or genetically. In addition, it is recognized that the categories of the race item include racial and national origin or sociocultural groups. People may choose to report more than one race to indicate their racial mixture, such as 'American Indian and White.' People who identify their origin as Hispanic, Latino, or Spanish may be of any race" (https://ask.census.gov/cgi-bin/askcensus.cfg/php/enduser/std_adp.php?p_faqid=7375&p_created=1219235812&p_sid=IoTrCuvj&p_accessibility=&p_lva=&p_sp=cF9zcmNoPSZwX3NvcnRfYnk9JnBfZ3JpZHNvcnQ9JnBfcm93X2NudD0mcF9wcm9kcz0mcF9jYXRzPSZwX3B2PSZwX2N2PSZwX3BhZ2U9MQ**&p_li=&p_topview=1&p_search_text=race%20defined%202010%20census).

15. Baltimore County Public Library's Blue Ribbon Committee, *Give 'Em What They Want! Managing the Public's Library* (Chicago: American Library Association, 1992), 3.

16. American Library Association, Reference and User Services Association, *Guidelines for Behavioral Performance of Reference and Information Service Providers* (Chicago: American Library Association, 2004), www .ala.org/ala/mgrps/divs/rusa/resources/guidelines/ guidelinesbehavioral.cfm.

17. Patricia M. Larsen, "Mining Your Automated System for Better Management," *Library Administration & Management* 10, no. 1 (Winter 1996): 10.

Satisfaction and Service Quality: Separate but Intertwined

Providing awesome customer experiences shouldn't be hard.[1]

*Actively encouraging customer contacts means, quite simply,
that you want customers to contact you whenever and however
they need to do so.*[2]

How many customers leave the library in a state exemplified by the Rolling Stones song, "I Can't Get No Satisfaction"? But they tried, but they tried. Satisfaction is a complicated phenomenon. It has a number of facets, any one of which can influence the feeling of satisfaction either positively or negatively: how they were treated by the staff; how much time was expended; and whether they obtained what they sought, or left frustrated. If one were to ask customers about their satisfaction after a single library visit, the validity of the responses would be shaky. Yet elected officials who want a grade for the library like a report card often use this method.

Frequently, a satisfaction question is part of a customer survey that the local government requires the library to do periodically. High levels of overall satisfaction are usually considered good and a positive reflection on the library. Yet, the councilors in one city had a rather surprising reaction to a 95 percent satisfaction response. They decided that a lower percentage—perhaps something above 75 percent—would be quite acceptable, and cut the library's budget accordingly.

A college or university president, in an informal session, might ask students about their educational experience and be told that they are satisfied with library collections and services. That president would be concerned only if the students mentioned a problem. A problem might occur when parents or others question the accessibility of so-called pornography from the library's Internet terminals, and complain to central administration.

As the preceding examples indicate, the polling of satisfaction might be very general and not very revealing. Imagine, however, that one night a local television station runs one of its call-in surveys. The commentator asks, "Are you satisfied with the public library? If so, call this number. If not, call this other number." Either way, the phone company collects sixty-five cents per call, and the station reports to city officials the results of the survey. A negative response might be embarrassing for the library, but it reveals little about specific problems or even who the respondents are. To what extent do they represent the taxpayers or others living in the community?

As an alternative to a general survey about city services, or those of an academic institution, the staff might want to probe customer satisfaction with library collections and services. The survey questions might ask about expectations, thereby equating expectations with satisfaction. In fact, determining expectations and comparing the perceptions about those expectations to any gap with the actual services delivered comprises service quality, not satisfaction. Complicating matters more, libraries might ascertain the percentage of satisfaction with various services (e.g., interlibrary loan service, reference desk service, and dial-in to the library's home page) and compute various comparisons. Library A achieves a 57 percent rating on reference desk service, whereas Library B has a 72 percent rating and Library C has a 74 percent rating. When compared, what do these statistics indicate?

Another library might produce a laundry list of services and ask customers to rate their level of satisfaction with each service, or that library might concentrate on a specific service. The results might be translated into percentages that indicate, for instance, the number of respondents expressing any degree of satisfaction, or the ratio of satisfied to dissatisfied customers.

As these examples indicate, there is some confusion about the concept of satisfaction, and the results obtained may not be meaningful for library planning and decision making. All librarians can hope for is that the library comes out better—or at least no worse—than other city or academic institution services and achieves, overall, a positive rating. The purpose of this chapter is to clarify the differences and interrelationships between service quality and satisfaction, and include ways that librarians can evaluate customer satisfaction for the purposes of planning and informed decision making. Satisfaction, as used in this book, is a reflection of the "customer's mind," but also as a driving force for "customer retention and future choice" about the use of a product, a service, or an organization.[3]

WHAT IS SATISFACTION?

The word *satisfaction* is derived from the Latin *satis* (enough) and *facere* (to do or make).[4] As Roland T. Rust and Richard L. Oliver explain, "satiation," a related word, "loosely means 'enough' or 'enough to excess.' These terms illustrate the point that satisfaction implies a filling or fulfillment. Thus, consumer satisfaction can be viewed as the consumer's fulfillment response."[5] Consumer researchers writing in the late 1980s and the 1990s "have moved away from the *literal* meaning of fulfillment or satisfaction and now pursue this concept as the consumer experiences and describes it."[6]

Satisfaction is subjective and deals with expectations;[7] it is a sense of contentment that results from an actual experience or set of experiences in relation to an expected experience. Similar to service quality, satisfaction addresses expectations in terms of the confirmation and disconfirmation process. (See chapter 7.) It might also involve the same type of gap analysis used in service quality; that is, if the organization wants to compare satisfaction with an ideal or other service providers. Because satisfaction contains multiple facets and because there are many ways to judge it, it is more likely that libraries will approach it from one of two perspectives. The first is *service encounter satisfaction*—customer satisfaction or dissatisfaction with a specific service encounter—and the second is *overall service satisfaction*—customer satisfaction or dissatisfaction with an organization based on multiple encounters or experiences.[8] As discussed in the next section, perusal of various satisfaction surveys from the retail trade and hotel industries, and from libraries in the United States and elsewhere, reveals that *attribute satisfaction*, which examines views toward staff and the information provided, might be a subset of either service encounter or overall service satisfaction.

Figure 10.1, adapted from the work of Mary Jo Bitner and Amy R. Hubbert, illustrates items indicative of service encounter satisfaction and overall service satisfaction. For service encounter satisfaction, customers reflect on a particular incident, and their satisfaction might be measured using a seven-point scale indicating that (1) the service experience ranged from delightful to terrible, (2) they were satisfied with the service, (3) they were satisfied with the decision to use the service, (4) they would do the same thing again, (5) it was a wise decision to use the service, (6) they feel bad about the decision, and (7) they were dissatisfied or not happy about having used the service.

With overall service satisfaction, customers are asked to "step back" from the one encounter and to think about *all experiences* with that specific service provider.[9] Using a five-point scale this time, satisfaction might be gauged in terms of overall satisfaction (not limited to the one library or service provider), their level of dissatisfaction (with the one library), comparison satisfaction (compared with other libraries), and general satisfaction. "Following the scaled items, an open-ended question . . . [might ask] respondents to describe what led them to rate their overall service satisfaction/dissatisfaction as they [did]."[10]

SURVEY CHOICES

It is important to remember that choices exist. Those choices involve more than external customers visiting the library in person or using its resources online. Instead of asking them to comment on an overall or a specific experience, they might be asked about a particular service used or workshop attended. Another choice is to survey staff or ask them to participate in focus group interviews.

WAYS TO MEASURE SATISFACTION

Any customer survey must limit the number of questions and dimensions on which customers comment. The more points probed through the survey, the fewer people will respond and do so with careful consideration. Thus, as with service quality, library staff must review the list of possible points and determine the subset of priority ones. In this case, however, they may include open-ended questions, giving customers an opportunity to elaborate with specific comments. (Service quality surveys avoid the use of open-ended questions because the intention is to probe only selected expectations, ones most relevant to service priorities.)

Figure 10.1 offers sample questions that examine satisfaction; figure 10.2, which is a composite of questions from a number of library surveys and from surveys used in the retail industry that we have modified

---

FIGURE 10.1

CONSTRUCT INDICATORS FOR SERVICE ENCOUNTER SATISFACTION AND OVERALL SERVICE SATISFACTION

SERVICE ENCOUNTER SATISFACTION
1. How did you feel about the service you received today?[a]
2. I was satisfied with the service received.[b]
3. I was satisfied with my decision to obtain service from the library today.[b]
4. If I had it to do over again, I would *not* have gone to the library.[b]
5. My decision to use the library today was a wise one.[b]
6. I feel badly about my decision to go to the library.[b]
7. I was dissatisfied with my experience in using the library today.[b]
8. I think I did the right thing by going to the library today.[b]
9. I am *not* happy that I patronized the library today.[b*]

OVERALL SERVICE SATISFACTION
1. Based on *all of your experiences,* how satisfied overall are you with the library's service?[c]
2. Based on all of *my own experience* with the library, I am:[d*]
3. Compared to other libraries that you have used, how would you rate your satisfaction with this one?[c]
4. In general, I am satisfied with this library.[b]

Source: Adapted from Mary Jo Bitner and Amy R. Hubbert, "Encounter Satisfaction versus Overall Satisfaction versus Quality," in *Service Quality: New Directions in Theory and Practice,* ed. Roland T. Rust and Richard L. Oliver (Thousand Oaks, CA: Sage, 1994), 81. Copyright © 1994 (Sage Publications). Reproduced by permission of Sage Publications, Inc.

[a]Fully anchored; end points: Delighted/Terrible
[b]Anchored at end points: Strongly agree/Strongly disagree
[c]Fully anchored; end points: Very satisfied/Very dissatisfied
[d]Anchored at end points: Very dissatisfied/Not at all dissatisfied
*Reverse scored

for possible application in libraries, suggests other potential survey items. The questions might be general, or they might focus on specific services. A number of the questions tend to be open-ended, meaning that respondents must write something. Customers may not want to write much, however, and the more open-ended questions asked, the less likely that customers will respond and do so with care. As well, someone will have to review completed forms and develop categories representing the responses given. Data entry and analysis thus become labor-intensive activities, but, on the positive side, customers have the option of discussing whatever they want. The central question becomes: Which questions will provide the library with the most useful information for planning and decision making? Each library will have to answer this question for itself.

In reaching an answer, the staff might ascertain whether customers recommend library services to others (word of mouth) and whether they display loyalty to the library. Clearly, figures 10.1 and 10.2 are suggestive rather than comprehensive.

Because a number of library and other satisfaction surveys that we have examined include items about the attributes of staff and the information provided or received, figure 10.3 offers additional choices for libraries wanting to measure customer satisfaction. Such attributes might be dealt with through questions such as, "How satisfied are you with . . ." and the respondents might select from a five-point scale (*very satisfied, somewhat satisfied, neither satisfied nor dissatisfied, somewhat dissatisfied, very dissatisfied*). Because attribute satisfaction is viewed within the context of service encounter satisfaction or overall service satisfaction, some examples are in order:

- In using the library today, I found the staff to be courteous (service encounter satisfaction).
- In using the library today, I found the circulation desk staff to be courteous (service encounter satisfaction).

FIGURE 10.2

SATISFACTION: A POOL OF QUESTIONS

SERVICE ENCOUNTER SATISFACTION

1. Overall, how satisfied are you with today's library visit? (Highly dissatisfied/Highly satisfied)
2. (Name specific services, facilities, and staff [by service points or location].) Ask respondents about which ones they used and how satisfied they are with the service provided. (Highly dissatisfied/Highly satisfied)
3. How would you rate the *value* of your visit? (Poor/Outstanding)
4. Did you find what you were looking for? Yes ___ No ___. If not, why?
5. If "yes," how satisfied were you with what you found? (four-point scale: very satisfied, satisfied, unsatisfied, very dissatisfied)
6. Did you experience any problems in the use of the library? If "yes," what was the problem or problems? How did the staff deal with the problem? Please assess the course of action they took to resolve the problem. Will you use the library again?

OVERALL SERVICE SATISFACTION

1. Based on all of your experiences in using the library, what are we doing that you particularly like?
2. Based on all of your experiences in using the library, what are we doing that you really don't like?
3. Based on all of your experiences in using the library, what are we doing that you really don't care about?
4. Based on all of your experiences in using the library, what aren't we doing that you would like us to do?
5. Based on all of your experiences in using the library, how and where could we most improve to provide high-quality service and guarantee 100 percent satisfaction?
6. Based on all of your experiences in using the library, what do you like *best* about us?
7. Based on all of your experiences in using the library, what do you like *least* about us?
8. If we could do ONE thing to improve, what should it be?

- Based on all of my experiences in using this library, I found the staff to be courteous (overall service satisfaction).
- Based on all of my experiences in using this library, I found the circulation desk staff to be courteous (overall service satisfaction).

In this instance, the five-point scale ranges from *strongly agree* to *strongly disagree*. Clearly, the categories for any scale must match the question asked.

In any survey, staff members should give careful thought to the measurement scale selected, and they should avoid alternating among five-point, seven-point, or other types of point scale. When librarians set goals and try to meet service targets to attain those goals, they might consider the use of a ten-point scale. Such a scale reflects incremental change over time when used repeatedly, and it reflects the extent of progress in reaching service targets.[11]

FIGURE 10.3

ATTRIBUTE SATISFACTION: SAMPLE ELEMENTS FOR CREATING SURVEY QUESTIONS

Staff	Information Provided
Courteous	Accurate
Enthusiastic	Complete
Friendly	Cost-effective
Giving of their time	Helpful
Helpful	Relevant
Interested	Sufficient (no overload)
Knowledgeable	Timely
Patient	Understandable
Self-confident	

EXAMPLES

Taking a specific area, staff might probe satisfaction with the library's home page by asking such questions as

1. How satisfied are you with the library's home page? (*completely satisfied, satisfied, don't know, dissatisfied, completely dissatisfied*)

   - ease of use/able to navigate it to find what you want
   - appearance/layout
   - your ability to find what you are seeking
   - your ability to download and/or e-mail to yourself full-text articles

2. Do you experience any problems? Yes__ No__. If yes, what problems?

3. Do you use any of the self-help guides available on the home page? Yes__ No__. If yes, how satisfied are you with them? If not, why not?

4. What are some improvements that would make it easier for you find and retrieve online resources?

Library evaluators have a choice: They can approach such questions from a specific use (e.g., today or this week) or globally—all of the customer's uses of the network. They might even include a question such as "Would you recommend the library's home page to a friend or colleague?" (yes/no; discuss), "Have you recommended the library's home page to a friend or colleague?" (yes/no; discuss), or "Would you use the service again?" (yes/no; discuss). Willingness to recommend a service or return to use it again are important indicators of satisfaction. The open-ended questions represent a variation of one of the questions in figure 10.2.

Evaluators should ask meaningful questions, ones that do not produce "simple and misleading answers." Rachel Applegate advocates that staff establish "a real dialogue in which a user's needs, expectations, knowledge, and emotions will be communicated."[12] Thus, she appears to favor the use of in-person interviewing to provide in-depth insights applicable to a few customers. Libraries needing more information that is more cheaply gathered and that applies to a specific population should use a survey—preferably one distributed in person. There is no reason why in-person interviewing might not be used on a selective basis, perhaps with some of the respondents and/or nonrespondents to the general survey, to generate a richer or more in-depth array of data.

Applegate emphasizes that there are different aspects of satisfaction that a study might explore. Furthermore, that study might focus on a material satisfaction model or on an emotional satisfaction model (simple path or multiple path). In the simple path model, customers "are 'happy' or emotionally satisfied when their questions have been answered," whereas with the multiple path model their "happiness depends not only on questions answered (material satisfaction) but also on factors such as setting and expectations."[13] The choice of a model has implications for library services. One of these models might be combined with either service encounter satisfaction or overall service satisfaction.

Figure 10.4, which draws upon chapter 7 and figure 7.6, illustrates that library staff can combine questions about service quality with those about satisfaction. With the inclusion of three open-ended questions about satisfaction, it is extremely important that the survey form be short and easy to complete. The staff should have a rationale for the inclusion of each question; why do they want to know about this point over all the other choices they could have made? It is possible that they might tailor separate survey forms to specific services, such as using the online public access catalog, borrowing material, asking an information or reference question, or using the Internet.

COUNTING OPINIONS

As of fall 2009, all public libraries in the state of California began using the Counting Opinions satisfaction survey. Having access to the data set for the San Francisco Public Library, the authors are delighted with the visual display of the data collected. That display includes quadrant charts (quadrant analysis), bar charts, dashboards, and other visuals that can be shared with library stakeholders and library managers.

Incorporated in June 2004, Counting Opinions (CO) provides comprehensive, evidence-based management solutions for libraries (public, academic, and special) and library-related organizations. These solutions can be integrated vertically and horizontally across organizations, be they local, regional, state, national, international, or any combination thereof.

CO's mission is the provision of continuous "actionable insight." The company delivers upon this mission through a range of services that includes core measures, both qualitative and quantitative, for customer satisfaction, summer reading programs, and other key statistical measures for library services; self-managed custom forms and surveys; integrated location mapping and directory services; performance data capture; integrated peer-benchmarking; simplified data integration and custom reporting services; as well as the ability to implement and deploy low-cost, custom solutions for its library customers and related organizations using the underlying platform.

Their services provide secure, real-time, on-demand access for data collection, management, and reporting. In the development and implementation of library solutions, the company follows a collaborative model. As such, it strives to deliver solutions that address (and solve) real-world library issues while providing enhanced insight for improved planning, operational excellence, identification and tracking of priorities, measurement of outcomes, and enhanced advocacy efforts.

CO solutions

- are web-based, easily customized, and ready to deploy
- do not require any hardware or software purchases nor require dedicated IT resources
- allow for the capture and analysis of qualitative and quantitative data
- eliminate the problems typical of multiple separate data silos (e.g., ILS, gate counters, and financial) that do not communicate with one another
- provide real-time, comprehensive, and on-demand data reporting functionality—text and graphic
- are accessible 24-7, with no limitation on the number of data access users or uses (All library data access is managed and controlled by the subscriber.)
- include full, ongoing on-demand support (toll-free phone, e-mail, webcast)

CO also takes an innovative approach regarding applications architecture. Often with technology-based solutions, users need to adapt their procedures to accommodate the limitations of the application. Not so with Counting Opinions, whose solutions are designed to fit any organizational structure.

FIGURE 10.4

LIBRARY CUSTOMERS: A SURVEY OF EXPECTATIONS AND SATISFACTION

We ask you to spare about _____ minutes of your time to identify what you think are the most important indicators of high-quality service that you expect a [college, university, public] library to provide. Some indicators are probably more important to you than others. The information that you provide will enable us to understand your service needs and priorities.

For questions 1–6, please circle the number that indicates how important each of the following points is for the *high-quality service* you expect a [college, university, public] library to provide.

If you don't use a particular service, please DO NOT circle a number for that statement.	No Importance						Highest Importance
1. I do not have to wait in line more than three minutes when I ask for assistance at a reference or information desk.	1	2	3	4	5	6	7
2. I do not have to wait in line more than three minutes when I borrow material.	1	2	3	4	5	6	7
3. Library staff is							
a. approachable and welcoming.	1	2	3	4	5	6	7
b. available when I need them.	1	2	3	4	5	6	7
c. courteous and polite.	1	2	3	4	5	6	7
d. friendly and easy to talk to.	1	2	3	4	5	6	7
4. Library staff							
a. communicates with me using terms I understand.	1	2	3	4	5	6	7
b. encourages me to come back to ask for more assistance if I need it.	1	2	3	4	5	6	7
c. demonstrates cultural sensitivity.	1	2	3	4	5	6	7
5. Materials are reshelved promptly.	1	2	3	4	5	6	7
6. Equipment is in good working order:							
a. computer printers	1	2	3	4	5	6	7
b. microfilm and microfiche readers	1	2	3	4	5	6	7
c. photocopiers	1	2	3	4	5	6	7

The final three questions are open-ended and provide an opportunity for you to comment on library service in general or an aspect of it.

7. Based on all of your experiences in using the library, what are we doing that you particularly like?

8. Based on all of your experiences in using the library, what are we doing that you really don't like?

9. Based on all of your experiences in using the library, if we could do ONE thing to improve, what should it be?

Thank you for your participation.

Note: For other sample questionnaires, see Peter Hernon and John R. Whitman, *Delivering Satisfaction and Service Quality: A Customer-Based Approach for Libraries* (Chicago: American Library Association, 2001), 101–104, 109–110.

For an example of a Counting Opinions product, visit the home page of the San Francisco Public Library (http://sfpl.lib.ca.us). The upper right portion of the page will start to peel back, revealing "Please Take Our Survey: Customer Satisfaction Survey," which was developed through Counting Opinions. Figure 10.5 reprints the well-thought-out survey.

Library staff might also turn the questionnaire into an active means of data collection. In other words, they might formally invite a subpopulation of a sample, either probability or nonprobability generated, to complete the survey. Respondents might do so by going to a special web page or completing a print copy distributed within the library, perhaps on randomly selected days or hours.

CRITICAL INCIDENTS

Critical incidents are a type of interview in which either groups or individuals who are customers relate their experiences. The number of such interviews ranges from ten to twenty; the goal is to have a sufficient number so that deficient information from one is offset by sufficient information from others. During the interview, each participant is asked to describe five to ten positive, and the same number of negative, instances or one-sentence statements that characterize their experience. The description of the service should avoid the use of general terms such as *good* or *nice*. It is important to determine what made that incident good or nice.

The ten to twenty instances constitute the critical incidents that define good and poor service. If twenty people are interviewed, there is a list of between two hundred (one hundred positive and one hundred negative) and four hundred (two hundred positive and two hundred negative) critical incidents.[14] The list likely includes similar incidents that can be grouped together. In producing the categorization, the focus is on the adjective or verb they share. Once the incidents have been grouped into clusters, library staff can develop a phrase that categorizes the content of each cluster. A cluster, known as a satisfaction item, can include both positive and negative incidents.

Let us say that a number of participants commented on reference desk service thus:

Participant 1: "I waited a long time before I was helped."

Participant 2: "I waited a long time but had to leave before someone helped me."

Participant 3: "I did not have to wait at all."

Participant 4: "I was in a hurry, but had to wait in line while the person answered phone calls."

Participant 5: "I was in a hurry but waited a long time before I was helped."

The satisfaction item obviously addresses the verb *wait*.

Once the list of satisfaction items has been compiled, the staff should look for patterns. Perhaps some items form subsets of some overarching themes. Those themes should be labeled; they reflect specific service quality dimensions. (See chapter 7 and the dimensions for either SERVQUAL or LibQUAL+.) In the case of the above example, "wait" is recast as *service responsiveness*, and this dimension actually expresses customer requirements.[15]

RECOMMENDATIONS

A survey such as the ones shown in figures 10.4 and 10.5 should adhere to the data-collection procedures discussed in chapter 7. Some public libraries might find themselves in the same situation as a number of other government bodies, having to produce valid survey research in which responses come from reasonably representative subsets of given populations. They, as well as any library, should work toward service improvement and

- state clearly what is being measured and how the measure is derived or calculated;

- explain why the measure is relevant to the program or service being provided;

- identify the data source(s) used to calculate the measure and indicate how the data are updated, including basic information on how and when the data were collected and where the data can be obtained;

- include a supplemental attachment with information and explanation of data sources, . . . methodology, and other information required to evaluate . . . data for . . . audit purposes; and

- develop systematic data retention schedules, which will allow interested parties to verify and further analyze customer satisfaction data.[16]

FIGURE 10.5

CUSTOMER SATISFACTION SURVEY: SAN FRANCISCO PUBLIC LIBRARY

San Francisco Public Library

	< not important					very important >			
	1	2	3	4	5	6	7	8	9	10
Overall, how important is this library to you?	O	O	O	O	O	O	O	O	O	O

	< not satisfied					very satisfied >			
	1	2	3	4	5	6	7	8	9	10
Overall, how satisfied are you with the services of this library?	O	O	O	O	O	O	O	O	O	O

	< fall short					exceed >			
	1	2	3	4	5	6	7	8	9	10
How well do these services compare to your expectations?	O	O	O	O	O	O	O	O	O	O

	< low quality					high quality >			
	1	2	3	4	5	6	7	8	9	10
Overall, how do you rate the quality of these services?	O	O	O	O	O	O	O	O	O	O

	< unlikely					very likely >			
	1	2	3	4	5	6	7	8	9	10
Would you recommend the services of this library to others?	O	O	O	O	O	O	O	O	O	O
How likely are you to reuse the services of this library?	O	O	O	O	O	O	O	O	O	O

Compared with other Library Systems...	Select A Choice
This library provides	--Select A Choice--
In the past year, you have ...	--Select A Choice--
You ...	--Select A Choice--

When dealing with our library staff ...	< disagree					agree >			
	1	2	3	4	5	6	7	8	9	10
Overall, you are satisfied with your experiences	O	O	O	O	O	O	O	O	O	O
Considering the services used, you are supportive of the library staff	O	O	O	O	O	O	O	O	O	O
When called upon, staff provide useful assistance	O	O	O	O	O	O	O	O	O	O
Staff respond in a professional manner	O	O	O	O	O	O	O	O	O	O
Your inquiries are routed to the appropriate person	O	O	O	O	O	O	O	O	O	O
Your inquiries are answered in a timely manner	O	O	O	O	O	O	O	O	O	O
The overall quality of services is excellent	O	O	O	O	O	O	O	O	O	O
Materials describing available services are excellent	O	O	O	O	O	O	O	O	O	O
It is easy to submit suggestions and comments	O	O	O	O	O	O	O	O	O	O

Please indicate how long you have been using the services of this library

less than 1 year	1 - 5 years	6 - 10 years	more than 10 years
O	O	O	O

Please indicate how often you have used the services of this library, in the past year

first time	2-5 times	6-9 times	10-20 times	more than 20 times	more than 50 times
O	O	O	O	O	O

Please indicate how often you expect to use the services of this library in the future

less often	about the same	more often
O	O	O

(cont.)

FIGURE 10.5 (cont.)

Please indicate your overall satisfaction with this library compared with the following information sources ...	< much less					much more >				
	1	2	3	4	5	6	7	8	9	10
Bookstore	○	○	○	○	○	○	○	○	○	○
Information available across the Internet (not from the library)	○	○	○	○	○	○	○	○	○	○
A person (other than a Librarian)	○	○	○	○	○	○	○	○	○	○
Media (Television, Radio, Newspapers, etc.)	○	○	○	○	○	○	○	○	○	○
Other Libraries	○	○	○	○	○	○	○	○	○	○
Other sources (not listed above)	○	○	○	○	○	○	○	○	○	○

You use the services provided by this library for ... (choose all that apply)

education related	self improvement	leisure activities	work related	other reasons
☐	☐	☐	☐	☐

To find information in this library, in the past year you have ... (check all that apply)

☐ Located information on your own, without assistance

☐ Received help from a library staff member

☐ Found information using a library workstation (computer, Internet, CD-ROM, public access terminal, ...)

☐ Found information using the library's posted signs and browsing the library's collections

☐ Found information by accessing one of the library's online information systems from a location other than the library

☐ Found information from other sources

You are ... (select the best fit)

a student	in the workforce (not an educator)	a homemaker	an educator	retired	other
○	○	○	○	○	○

The primary reason for using the services of this library relates to ... (select the best fit)

education	self improvement	leisure	work	other
○	○	○	○	○

Please indicate all services of this library, used in the past year ... (choose all that apply)

☐ Borrowed items (books and/or other materials)

☐ Used materials while in the library (read, view, listen to, browse)

☐ Used the library's equipment (computers, workstations, audio/video equipment, printers, copiers, ...)

☐ Attended events, programs or meetings

☐ Used the library's facilities (chairs, tables, rooms, washrooms, parking lot, ...)

☐ Accessed library services from a location other than the library (online or over-the-phone)

☐ Accessed the Internet while at the library

☐ Accessed an online database at the library

With respect to this library, in the past year...	< totally disagree					totally agree >				
	1	2	3	4	5	6	7	8	9	10
Locating information is simple and easy	○	○	○	○	○	○	○	○	○	○
You often have success in finding the information you are seeking	○	○	○	○	○	○	○	○	○	○

We appreciate your feedback, comments and suggestions

You have a current library membership card for ...	Yes	No
This library	○	○
Another library (or libraries)	○	○

Please indicate your satisfaction, the importance to you and the likelihood of recommending to others, the following services of this library.	Importance	Satisfaction	Recommendation
Accessing an online database from someplace other than the library	--Importance--	--Satisfaction--	--Recommendation--

Your interests include services for ... (choose all that apply)

Pre-schoolers	Children	Teens	Young Adults (18-25 years)	Adults (26-64 years)	Seniors (65+ years)
☐	☐	☐	☐	☐	☐

Please indicate your level of satisfaction with and the importance of the following facilities of this library ...	Satisfaction	Importance
Hours of access and operation	--Satisfaction--	--Importance--
Accessibility (Transportation to/from and access within and into building)	--Satisfaction--	--Importance--
Seating/Workspace	--Satisfaction--	--Importance--
Personal safety and security	--Satisfaction--	--Importance--
Maintenance and cleanliness: Building interior	--Satisfaction--	--Importance--
Building exterior	--Satisfaction--	--Importance--
Exterior grounds and spaces	--Satisfaction--	--Importance--
Restrooms	--Satisfaction--	--Importance--
Dedicated spaces for: Children	--Satisfaction--	--Importance--
Teens	--Satisfaction--	--Importance--
Adults	--Satisfaction--	--Importance--
Meeting space/Program room	--Satisfaction--	--Importance--
Exterior courtyard or garden	--Satisfaction--	--Importance--

Please Indicate your level of satisfaction with and the importance of the following equipment at this library ...	Satisfaction	Importance
Printers	--Satisfaction--	--Importance--
Copiers	--Satisfaction--	--Importance--
Catalogue Terminals	--Satisfaction--	--Importance--
Catalogue/Database stations	--Satisfaction--	--Importance--
Self Check-out stations	--Satisfaction--	--Importance--

The following information is strictly optional	
Zip/Postal Code: [ ]	This information will help us identify response coverage throughout our community
Email Address: [ ]	If you wish to receive an Email reminder for an annual survey follow-up

Source: SFPL survey copyright © Counting Opinions (SQUIRE) Ltd. Reprinted with permission of Counting Opinions (SQUIRE) Ltd. and the San Francisco Public Library.

Note: See also Jacksonville Public Library, "Customer Satisfaction Survey," www.countingopinions.com/jpl/; Orange County Library System, "Customer Satisfaction Survey," http://ocls.countingopinions.com.

And, "in creating performance measures from customer satisfaction surveys, . . . agencies should adhere to guidelines for valid survey research."[17]

Staff should consider standardizing some of the items asked so that there is some consistency from year to year about what a library evaluates and reports pertaining to customer satisfaction. Some customers might be tracked on a regular basis to ascertain their views on problems and review the impact of corrective actions on resolving the problems.

As noted earlier, the information gathered might be important as part of an audit trail. When libraries, like other organizations, must produce performance reports,

> a certain rigor [collecting data generalizable to some population] is necessary since they [the reports] are designed to help improve important public programs, provide accountability to the public and information to policymakers who must decide how to allocate scarce resources. Also, only rigorous methods can provide the quality of information that agencies need to support their claims of good performance. . . . [Nonetheless,] when the best methods are followed some error is inevitable. However, if surveys are properly conducted, they can produce valid, appropriate measures of performance. Otherwise . . . agencies should use customer feedback cautiously, since the results could be misleading.[18]

Figure 10.6 offers an excellent summary of twenty-nine points to address in conducting customer satisfaction surveys. It is important to remember that completely satisfied customers are much more likely to repeat their business than customers who are merely satisfied. As a result, those analyzing and reporting the data might generate an average (mean and/or median), but they should also concentrate on the *very satisfied* or *completely satisfied* category and compare all other responses to it. After all, the question is not, "How many customers are satisfied?"; rather, it is, "What proportion of the respondents is completely satisfied?"

Research conducted by Enterprise Rent-A-Car found a major difference between completely satisfied customers and those who were satisfied. More than 70 percent of the *completely satisfied* promised to use Enterprise for their next car rental. Only 22 percent of the *satisfied* said they would come back. The company followed up these intentions against actual behavior and found that those who were *completely satisfied* really did come back in higher numbers than the merely *satisfied*.[19]

CUSTOMER-RELATED MEASURES

As presented in chapters 4 and 7, customer-related measures provide insights into questions of "How well?" "How valuable?" "How reliable?" "How responsive?" and "How satisfied?" The last one, "How satisfied?" is an output and not an outcome; it might contribute indirectly to an outcome, but that correlation has yet to be established and accepted by a number of stakeholders such as regional accreditation organizations. Because satisfaction is often measured on a point scale (five-, seven-, or ten-point scale), it is possible to compute the following percentage:

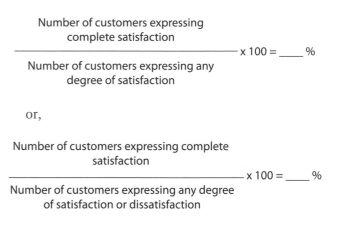

When libraries strive to keep and build their pool of present customers, and aspire to achieve customer loyalty, it becomes essential to seek complete satisfaction for priority services.[20] (See figure 9.1.) A relevant measure would be as follows:

For any percentage that emerges, managers need some framework for its interpretation and some plan to raise the percentage over coming years. For instance, they might determine that in the year 2010, at least 60 percent of the faculty members using interlibrary loan should be completely satisfied with that service. At the same time, the managers should set targets, such as to increase the percentage of completely satisfied faculty by 3 percent per year for the next five years (beginning in the year 2011). The intended result becomes, for instance, that by the year 2015, at least 75 percent of the faculty will be completely satisfied (60 + 15 = 75). Examples of other areas for setting goals and intended results might be

FIGURE 10.6

GUIDELINES FOR CUSTOMER SATISFACTION SURVEYS

PLAN

1. Conduct customer satisfaction surveys for purposes that are clearly stated and designed to improve services.
2. Decide the frequency for repeating data collection—use of repeated measures.
3. Decide if focus group interviews will be a follow-up method to expand on the findings.
4. Seek approval from a human subjects committee or other appropriate body.
5. Assign and supervise trained staff to be responsible for the survey.
6. Follow standard, scientifically valid methods to minimize errors and other potential problems.

IDENTIFY CUSTOMERS

7. Decide whether or not to generalize the findings to a population.
8. If generalization is required, develop a list of those who have received services that are the subject of the survey or devise a sampling strategy (e.g., based on time periods). Select customers, perhaps all of them, from the list or select a random sample of customers large enough to provide accurate estimates of satisfaction.
9. Try to obtain responses from the greatest possible percentage of those selected and check to ensure that those who respond are representative of customers receiving services being studied.

CONSTRUCT AND ASK QUESTIONS[a]

10. Write clear questions or statements and response options.
11. Allow for various degrees of satisfaction/ dissatisfaction, or agreement/disagreement.
12. Be neutral throughout.
13. Ask about several aspects of customer satisfaction during a specific time period.
14. Expect only moderate knowledge and recall of specific services as time goes by.
15. Use efficient, well-established data-collection methods.
16. Treat respondents respectfully.
17. Encourage voluntary participation and remember that you are imposing on the respondents.
18. Confirm that respondents are customers. (Some libraries might house academic departments or other government services. Thus, individuals within the building may not necessarily be library customers.)

RESPONSE RATE

19. It is important to design the questionnaire and the cover letter to invite a high response. Staff should also consider inviting participation more than once and in different ways. For discussions of response rate see, for instance, J. Sitzia and N. Wood, "Response Rate in Patient Satisfaction Research: An Analysis of 210 Published Studies," *International Journal for Quality in Health Care* 10, no. 4 (1998): 311–317; Colleen Cook, Fred Heath, and Russell L. Thompson, "A Meta-analysis of Response Rates in Web- or Internet-Based Surveys," *Educational and Psychological Measurement* 60, no. 6 (2000): 821–836; Don A. Dillman, Glenn Phelps, Robert Tortora, Karen Swift, Julie Kohrell, Jodie Berck, and Benjamin L. Messer, "Response Rate and Measurement Differences in Mixed-Mode Surveys Using Mail, Telephone, Interactive Voice Response (IRV), and the Internet," *Social Science Research* 38, no. 1 (March 2009): 1–18. Available from ScienceDirect.

EDIT AND ARCHIVE DATA

20. Make every attempt to ensure that the data are technically error-free.
21. Justify any changes to original data.
22. Make it possible for others to independently confirm the results later.

ANALYZE DATA AND RESULTS

23. Objectively analyze all relevant, usable customer satisfaction data.
24. Attempt to explain unexpected or unusual results.

(cont.)

FIGURE 10.6 (cont.)

25. Ensure that published data are consistent with survey results.
26. Interpret results with the appropriate level of precision and express the proper degree of caution about conclusions that can be drawn from the results.
27. Make note of possibly significant problems and limitations.
28. Provide basic descriptive information about how the survey was done.

OTHER (EMPLOYEE SURVEYS)
29. Ensure respondent anonymity, secure management approval for the survey, keep the survey brief, explain the benefits of participation realistically, keep any promises made, and see that employees are informed of the findings and how they are used—linked to strategic planning.

Note: See also Terry G. Vavra, *Improving Your Measurement of Customer Satisfaction: A Guide to Creating, Conducting, Analyzing, and Reporting Customer Satisfaction Measurement Programs* (Milwaukee, WI: ASQ Quality Press, 1997).

[a]If the survey is web-based, introduce it with a welcome screen that is motivational, emphasizes the ease of responding and the appropriate length of time to complete the survey, and instructs respondents on the action needed for proceeding to the next screen. Begin with a question that is fully visible on the first screen of the questionnaire, one that is easily comprehended and answered by all respondents. Keep the question short. Pilot test the survey with different people using different browsers.

The receipt and resolution of complaints (e.g., by the year _____, no more than _____ percent of the people who complain about a particular service will do so again)

Out-of-service conditions (e.g., all equipment needing repair will be reported to the repair shop within twenty-four hours of breakdown)

In-service conditions (e.g., no photocopier will be out of operation more than _____ days per month).

Measures relating to conditions involve the review and renegotiation of service contracts, and the quality (e.g., durability) of equipment purchased or leased.

Setting targets and intended results ensures that the library engages in regular evaluation, consistently uses the same questions or statements, and commits the resources necessary to meet its goals. Failure to meet a target places increased pressure on the organization to analyze and overcome problems. For instance, regarding the complete satisfaction of faculty with interlibrary loan, managers might identify why the library was unable to meet one of the 3 percent targets, and they would have to take corrective action to meet or exceed the next target and to achieve the ultimate result: 15 percent increase after five years. Needless to say, the library needs to use rigorous methods of data collection to ensure that failure to meet a target is not due to mistakes made in conducting the research.

THE CUSTOMER'S VOICE

Libraries have options concerning what they investigate regarding customer satisfaction and what types of customer-related measures and research questions they address. They can examine "satisfaction with access, facilities, communications, personnel, types of services provided, service outcomes, and overall satisfaction."[21] They can focus, for example, on content or context, while examining a specific service encounter or encounters in general. Whichever one they choose, it appears that service encounter satisfaction is distinct from overall service satisfaction and service quality.[22] Each provides valuable information; together, they provide a more complete picture of library service. Nonetheless, overall service satisfaction may not provide sufficient in-depth information about problem areas, while the time frame for service encounter satisfaction could be so loosely set that memory or recall presents a problem.

To gain more complete knowledge about customer satisfaction with library services, managers might gauge overall service satisfaction, and then, depending on the findings (where problems are suggested), explore specific services and service encounter satisfaction. When managers determine that such data collection is too costly and time consuming, and that they must settle for less than the complete picture, they need to determine which part of a smaller picture is most important to them and how much time they can devote to data collection.

A FINAL WORD

This chapter further develops material presented in chapter 7, in that the steps in conducting a satisfaction survey mirror those for ascertaining service quality. The emphasis, however, differs. Service quality tends to focus on expectations, those precise statements to which libraries are willing to give high priority if customers find them important. Satisfaction, on the other hand, is less focused on specific statements and tries to gauge how content customers are with the library or a specific service. It might even be transaction-specific. Still, it should be remembered that, without consistent wording of questions and continual data collection at regular intervals, it is impossible to monitor satisfaction over time. With both service quality and satisfaction, the key issue is less the score that a library attains; rather, the important point is how does the library or those providing the service use the results for improvement.

Traditional accounting leaves customer relationships off the balance sheet.[23]

Too often, customer satisfaction is approached as a report card rather than as a source of information about services where improvement and further analysis and thinking are required.[24]

Notes

1. Bill Price and David Jaffe, *The Best Service Is No Service: How to Liberate Your Customers from Customer Service, Keep Them, Happy, and Control Costs* (San Francisco: Jossey-Bass, 2008), x.

2. Ibid., 152.

3. Roland T. Rust and Richard L. Oliver, "Service Quality: Insights and Managerial Implications from the Frontier," in *Service Quality: New Directions in Theory and Practice*, ed. Roland T. Rust and Richard L. Oliver (Thousand Oaks, CA: Sage, 1994), 3.

4. Richard L. Oliver, "A Conceptual Model of Service Quality and Service Satisfaction: Compatible Goals, Different Concepts," in *Advances in Services Marketing and Management: Research and Practice*, vol. 2, ed. T. A. Swartz, D. E. Bowen, and S. W. Brown (Greenwich, CT: JAI Press, 1993), 65–85.

5. Rust and Oliver, "Service Quality," 4.

6. Ibid.

7. Expectations can be divided into three groups: core expectations, which are elements of service assumed to be common to everyone (e.g., courtesy and respect); learned expectations, which are developed from experience and a widening exposure to the world; and anticipated expectations, which are an aspect or element of service that is not currently offered. Peter Hernon and John R. Whitman, *Delivering Satisfaction and Service Quality: A Customer-Based Approach for Libraries* (Chicago: American Library Association, 2001).

8. Mary Jo Bitner and Amy R. Hubbert, "Encounter Satisfaction versus Overall Satisfaction versus Quality," in Rust and Oliver, *Service Quality*, 76–77.

9. Ibid., 80.

10. Ibid.

11. For a discussion of the differences among scales and examples of each, see Hernon and Whitman, *Delivering Satisfaction and Service Quality*, 129–132.

12. Rachel Applegate, "Models of User Satisfaction: Understanding False Positives," *RQ* 32, no. 4 (Summer 1993): 526.

13. Ibid., 525.

14. As long as the activity probed is simple, fifty to one hundred incidents is sufficient. For more complex activities, several thousand incidents might be collected. See John C. Flanagan, "The Critical Incident Technique," *Psychological Bulletin* 51, no. 4 (July 1954): 327–358.

15. For more on critical incidents see Mary Jo Bitner, Bernard H. Booms, and Mary Stanfield Tetreault, "The Service Encounter: Diagnosing Favorable and Unfavorable Incidents," *Journal of Marketing* 52, no. 1 (January 1990): 71–84.

16. Minnesota Office of the Legislative Auditor, *State Agency Use of Customer Satisfaction Surveys: A Program Evaluation Report* (St. Paul, MN: Minnesota Office of the Legislative Auditor, 1995), 91.

17. Ibid., xv.

18. Ibid., x.

19. Kirk Kazanjian, *Exceeding Customer Expectations: What Enterprise, America's #1 Car Rental Company, Can Teach You about Creating Lifetime Customers* (New York: Doubleday, 2007), 64.

20. Please note that we prefer the scale for figure 9.1 to range from *completely dissatisfied* to *completely satisfied.*

21. Minnesota Office of the Legislative Auditor, *State Agency Use of Customer Satisfaction Surveys,* 17.

22. Bitner and Hubbert, "Encounter Satisfaction," 92.

23. Emily Yellin, *Your Call Is (Not That) Important to Us: Customer Service and What It Reveals about Our World and Our Lives* (New York: Free Press, 2009), 12.

24. Joseph R. Matthews, *The Evaluation and Measurement of Library Services* (Westport, CT: Libraries Unlimited, 2007), 254.

Chapter Eleven

Interpreting Findings to Improve Customer Service

The library is our home away from home — a place to eat, sleep, study, and socialize. It's our anchor during our busiest weeks — a place to relax while still in a learning environment. . . . The library is our campus commune.
— student at Georgia Institute of Technology[1]

One of the authors of *Performance Measures for Public Libraries* ruefully admitted that the use and effect of these measures on library operations and decision making had been limited and that the fault lay mostly with the developers of the measures. A major reason hindering widespread impact: "We greatly overestimated staff ability to tabulate and analyze the data," and as a consequence, "the most formidable problem to the practitioners was interpreting the results."[2]

The purpose of this chapter is to identify some general ways to analyze and present study results; the chapter is not intended as an introduction to statistics. Rather, it presents ways to link data collection to broader strategies and to capture the interest of customers and stakeholders. Library managers can decide what they want to know and collect the pertinent data. Next the data need to be analyzed by number crunching, and library managers interpret the data for their own institution. The information collected can give them a powerful source of sound arguments to support decisions. This information can also be effective in appealing for funds and demonstrating accountability.

Chapters 7 and 10 discuss ways to collect data using quantitative methods, and chapter 8 explores the use of a qualitative method. As was noted in these chapters, library staff has choices regarding which method of data collection to use and which statements or questions to include. There are also choices related to the method of data analysis. Which method to use is influenced by several considerations, especially the following:

1. **Level of measurement for the variables studied.** There are four levels of measurement: nominal, ordinal, interval, and ratio. Persons, things, and events characterized by a *nominal* variable are not ranked or ordered by the variable; for example, being female is neither better nor worse than being male. Nominal variables such as gender, therefore, have no inherent order. With an *ordinal* variable, the attributes are ordered. For instance, observations about the frequency with which customers ask for the assistance of reference librarians might be arrayed into four classifications: *never, sometimes, frequently,* and *always.* Although the ordinal level of measurement yields a ranking of attributes, no assumptions are

made about the distance between the classifications. In this example, we do not assume that the difference between the number of persons who say they always request assistance and the number who say they frequently request assistance is the same as the number who sometimes do so.

The attributes of an *interval* variable are assumed to be equally spaced, whereas the attributes of a *ratio* variable have equal intervals as well as a true zero point. An interval scale is a seven-point scale for measuring service quality or satisfaction in which the end points (e.g., *completely satisfied* and *completely dissatisfied*) are equally anchored, and each number in between (i.e., two, three, four, five, and six) has an equal interval from the other numbers. An example of a ratio variable would be the actual dollar amount for the library's budget; with this number, researchers can create their own categories.

Depending on the specific variable and the wording of the question, demographic variables might be nominal, ordinal, or interval scale. Frequency of library use might be expressed at the ordinal level, assuming that there are not equal intervals among the response options. Thus, data-collection instruments represent statements and questions involving more than one level of measurement scale.

2. **Unit of analysis or the entity about which we want to say something.** Possible units might be customers, never-gained or lost customers, classroom, school, business, city government, residential area, student major, faculty in the humanities, and the institution.

3. **Shape of the distribution.** A distribution is an association between different values of a variable and another measurement. This association can be depicted as a table or a graph. When the associated measurement is the number of cases, the result is a frequency distribution, which might be portrayed in graphic form as a histogram. A normal distribution is a family of distributions that forms a symmetrical bell shape. This bell-shaped curve extends infinitely in both directions on a continuum close to the horizontal axis or baseline, but never touching it. The fact that the tails of the curve do not actually touch the baseline is not important because the area under the extreme ends or tails is negligible. The most important feature of the curve is that it is symmetrical about its mean or central point. This signifies that if a normal curve were folded along its central line, the two halves of the curve would coincide.

Normal curves can have different shapes depending on the mean. However, there is only one normal distribution per mean and standard deviation, In a normal curve, all three measures of central tendency are identical: half of the case fall above the central point and half fall below it. If the measures of central tendency are not equal, the distribution is distorted. The tail of the curve might be either top or bottom heavy: the largest part of the tail goes to the right (top heavy) or the left (negatively skewed). Kurtosis is another type of distortion for the distribution. In this instance, the curve may be flat (platykurtic) or very peaked (leptokurtic).

The advantage of displaying the normal curve graphically, either hand or computer calculated, is that, for a symmetrical normal distribution, the approximate percentage of cases that fall within a certain range is visualized. The fact that the areas under the curve are given in standard deviation units associated with a percentage of the population that fall within that range enables researchers to place a random value obtained from a normal distribution in context of the population.

4. **Study design used to produce the data from populations or probability samples.** A population might be depicted in numbers, percentages, and descriptive statistics (e.g., range and average), and findings from a probability sample might be shown in numbers, percentages, descriptive statistics, or inferential statistics—which make inferences back to the population.

5. **Completeness of the data.** For instance, in a survey, some people may decline to participate and others may not answer certain questionnaire items.

BASIC CONCEPTS
Frequencies and Percentages

One way of summarizing data is to calculate the frequency of occurrence of a specific value, or how often that given value occurs in the data set. To calculate frequencies, investigators often use software such as Excel or SPSS, which rank the scores from lowest to highest and then determines the frequency of occurrence of each value.

Another way of examining the frequency of values is through the use of percentages. A percentage reflects the proportion of scores of a particular value. The percentage for a particular value is calculated by dividing the frequency of a given value by the total number of scores in the data set and by multiplying the number by one hundred.

Presenting Averages

There are two general approaches to describe the average, or measure of central tendency, of a distribution: (1) presenting data through a table or figure, and (2) finding a descriptive statistic that best summarizes the distribution. A descriptive statistic is a number that, in some way, describes the group of cases. Measures of central tendency (mode, mean, and median) form a class of descriptive statistics, each member of which characterizes the typical value of a variable: the central location of a distribution. The mode is the most frequently occurring number; although it can be used as a measure of central tendency for any level of measurement, the mode is most commonly used with nominal variables. A distribution can have more than one mode, when two or more attributes tie for the highest frequency.

The mean, or arithmetic average, is calculated by summing the observations and dividing the sum by the number of observations. It is used only with interval and ratio-level data. The mean may not, however, be a good indicator if several cases are outliers—extreme values—or if the distribution is notably asymmetric. The reason is that the mean is strongly influenced by the presence of a few extreme values at either end of the distribution, which may give a distorted view of the average. The median—calculated by determining the midpoint of rank-ordered cases—can be used with ordinal, interval, and ratio-level data, and no assumptions need to be made about the shape of the distribution. Because the median is not greatly affected by changes in a few cases, outliers have less influence on it than on the mean.

Variability

While averages indicate the middle of the distribution, variability shows the spread of the data. Measures of variability indicate the extent to which the scores are tightly packed together versus spread out. Both the variance and standard deviation are measures of variability, and they report the spread of the data around the mean.

Variance is the sum of the squared deviations about the mean, whereas the standard deviation, which is often used with interval or ratio data, comprises a measure of the spread of scores around the mean,

or the extent of variation among cases, when those cases approximate a normal distribution. The greater the scatter of scores, the larger is the standard deviation. For a normal distribution, researchers interpret the standard deviation as the distance measured from the midpoint (the center of the curve) to a point along the baseline. The baseline is divided into standard deviation units. Plus or minus one standard deviation from the center of the curve includes approximately 68 percent of the cases in a sample, and plus or minus two standard deviations accounts for 95 percent of the cases. Thus, studies engaging in gap analysis to measure service quality and using interval-level data might report both the mean and the standard deviation.

Pearson Product-Moment Correlation

The Pearson Product-Moment Correlation, commonly called Pearson's *r*, is a measure of linear correlation between two interval-ratio variables; in other words, it indicates the extent to which a straight line best depicts the relationship between the variables. A correlation examines the extent of the relationship between two random variables within specified limits; these limits are stated as correlation coefficients. A correlation coefficient, a number that indicates the degree of relationship between two variables, reflects the extent to which variations in one variable accompany variations in the other variable. For example, there are news stories that a down economy brings more people to the library. If a library wanted to verify that with some data, it might correlate the changing unemployment rate over each of the past six or more quarters with library use, as indicated either by door counts or circulation records.

Correlation coefficients range from minus one to plus one, with zero indicating no linear association. Plus one indicates that the relationship is a perfect positive one: As one variable changes, the other variable goes through equivalent changes in the same direction. Minus one is a perfect negative correlation. A negative (or minus) correlation indicates that changes in one variable are accompanied by equivalent changes in the other variable. The change, however, is in the opposite direction. Consequently, as one variable diminishes, the other increases.

By squaring the *r* value, it is possible to examine the strength of the overall relationship. The squared value can be converted into a percentage, for instance, when *r* equals .9, $r^2 \times 100 = 81$ percent.

It is possible to calculate measures of central tendency; the actual one selected depends on the measurement scale and the extent to which the mean or median best depicts the distribution. If the measurement scale is interval or ratio, the standard deviation and perhaps Pearson's r become relevant statistics. Thus, it is possible to display findings in a list ranging from the highest to lowest number of occurrences and percentages, averages, standard deviations, and Pearson's r. Such information becomes useful for interpreting the results. In some instances, library staff might use quadrant analysis, which is covered below.

Presenting Descriptive Data

Survey results might be viewed as numbers and percentages, perhaps displayed in tabular or graphic form. In *Improving Your Measurement of Customer Satisfaction*, Terry G. Vavra presents different types of tables and graphs and discusses which is best for a given circumstance. For instance, in the case of displaying "growth, trends, and change," he recommends and illustrates line or area graphs, or scattergrams. A Pareto diagram, which "is a special form of a vertical bar chart," he points out, is an excellent way to illustrate progress or present "the possible causes of a problem or general dissatisfaction."[3]

Factor Analysis

Factor analysis is mentioned here as it might be used in the context of studying the dimensions used with service quality—especially e-service quality, where little research has occurred. (See chapter 7.) Generally, factor analysis is used when there is a large number of variables in the data set and the investigator wants to reduce the number to a manageable size.[4] Expressed another way, factor analysis tends to examine the relationship between the large set of variables and tries to explain any correlations using a smaller number of variables. Initially, factor analysis uses the overall correlation matrix of the variables and determines which items share an underlying dimension. Factor analysis mathematically identifies the number of factors or underlying dimensions that best represent the observed correlations between the initial set of items. Generally, in the set of existing items, those that are highly correlated with each other are represented by a single factor or dimension.

After the number of factors or dimensions has been identified, the next step is to determine which items fall within their respective dimensions. This is accomplished by a procedure known as rotation, which indicates which dimensions represent a given set of items.

Quadrant Analysis

Quadrant analysis, a graphic correlation technique, may involve the use of data related to customer expectations to produce "pictorial results that are easy to communicate, understand, and interpret";[5] those results have value for strategic planning and decision making. As James Lynch, Robert Carver Jr., and John M. Virgo note, quadrant analysis is useful for "administrators whose skills have progressed beyond simple frequency distributions but who do not have the time, need, nor opportunity to master the intricacies and nuances of advanced statistical methodologies."[6]

Figure 11.1 reflects two dimensions commonly used in quadrant analysis: One dimension (*ideal expectation*) indicates the importance of an expectation to customers, and the other dimension (*actual service*) records the degree to which customers perceive a service as fulfilling the expectation. Quadrant analysis indicates what customers expect from a service (i.e., their ideal) and how they perceive a particular service in relation to the ideal. Quadrant analysis is *not* appropriate for use in comparing perceived expectations to indicators of the actual service provided, which was discussed in chapter 7. Rather, it applies to analysis of the gaps between customers' expectations and their perceptions of service (the type of data obtained through the use of SERVQUAL).

A number of expectations can be plotted within the four quadrants if the average responses on both dimensions are known. Customers might be asked to rate the importance of certain service expectations on a five-, seven-, or ten-point scale. The averages (i.e., means) for the importance of customer expectations are used to locate each expectation's position along the vertical axis. The mean of the perceived service actually provided is subtracted from the mean of the perceived expected measure. In other words, the gap is computed for each expectation. Using both averages as coordinates, the average location of each expectation and perception within the four quadrants can be determined.

The expectations falling into quadrant one are very important to the customers, and they perceive the library as trying to meet those expectations. Librarians would want present and potential customers to be aware that the library places a high value on meeting these fundamental expectations. Over-delivery of services in this quadrant (perceptions of actual service provision exceed expectations) might "represent areas where resources could be saved and reallocated."[7] The expectations that fall into quadrant two are also very important to customers, but are not perceived as being prominent features of the service. If the customers' perceptions are correct and services in these areas are not meeting expectations, service changes may be called for. It may be, however, that the services do in fact meet expectations and the customers need to be made aware of this.

Any expectations shown in quadrant three are relatively unimportant to customers, but customers associate those expectations with the service. By trying to elevate the importance of these expectations, library staff seeks to enhance the image of a given service. Alternatively, the staff might refocus the service so that its image matches the expectations shown in quadrants one or two, not those depicted in quadrant three.

Chapter 12 suggests competitors for libraries. By contrasting libraries with their competitors, librarians can view quadrant four as an opportunity to see what expectations their competitors are not meeting that might have some potential to cultivate. Alternatively,

because the expectations are unimportant to customers and are not met by either libraries or their competitors, the expectations might be ignored and resources reallocated.

Quadrant analysis contains other elements: solid and dashed lines. Thus, quadrants become subdivided. The solid lines, which represent the midpoints on the original ideal and actual scales, indicate the thresholds that separate whether or not an expectation describes the ideal or perceived expectation. The dashed lines are based on averages computed across measurement scales. This approach

> produces quadrants defined by the survey results rather than by question design. This should produce a quadrant configuration that is more reflective of the preferences . . . [of those studied]. It also makes it easier to discuss individual . . . [expectations] since they can be described as being "above average" or "below average."[8]

The solid and dashed lines provide two different ways to view survey results. Most typically, the results fall within midpoint lines—in either quadrant one or two, since statements of expectation "are only likely to be included in a questionnaire if, *a priori*, there is reason to believe that they are important to the target segment being studied."[9] In contrast, the dashed lines,

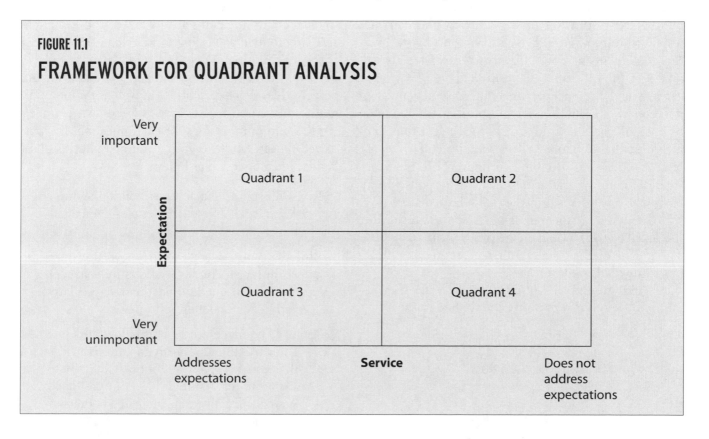

FIGURE 11.1

FRAMEWORK FOR QUADRANT ANALYSIS

based on scale averages, provide more "discriminating information."[10] That is, in the idealized version, the four squares are of equal size. In reality, once the expectations and gaps are factored in, the quadrants differ in size.

Nicola Harwood and Jillene Bydder examined student expectations and compared the results with perceptions about the service provided. Although their terminology differs from that used here, it is possible to adapt their work to illustrate the use of quadrant analysis.[11]

Harwood and Bydder studied gap analysis at the University of Waikato in Hamilton, New Zealand. One interesting table depicts the gap for eleven statements having a discrepancy of greater than one point between expected and actual perceptions. (See figure 11.2.) They also note that five questions had the largest gap:

1. Materials in their proper place

2. OPAC accurate and extensive

3. Range of materials in the library

4. Seven-day recall

5. Good order copiers

Figure 11.3 depicts quadrant analysis. Before interpreting the results, let us explain how the data are displayed in the figure. First, drawing on figure 11.2, the eleven mean scores for *expected* service (based on a seven-point scale) are positioned along the vertical axis and the gaps between these scores and the perception of actual service are positioned along the horizontal axis. The midpoint of the scale is four, and is represented in figure 11.1 by solid lines. This represents an idealized situation. In figure 11.3, however, we plot the means of the *actual* survey responses from figure 11.2, representing them by dashed lines. We add the eleven "expected service" scores and divide the result (69.98) by eleven, getting a mean of 6.3618. The mean of the "actual service" scores is 5.0218 (55.24 divided by eleven).

Six statements fall within the newly drawn quadrant one, which is now above the dashed lines:

1. Materials in their proper place

2. Range of materials in library

3. Good order copiers

4. Staff available when needed

5. OPAC accurate and extensive

6. Hours open

As such, these statements are important to customers, and they perceive the library as doing these things. The statements tend to focus on and reinforce customer self-sufficiency.

The five other statements collapse into quadrant three, as now reconfigured with the dashed lines. They are associated with libraries but are less important to the customers surveyed. Because "knowledgeable staff always available" and "staff on desks knowledgeable" were among the less-important statements, the library staff might use focus group interviews to determine the reasons for this placement and to mount a marketing campaign about the value of knowledgeable staff and their approachability. Clearly, at this university, students and the library staff have some differences of opinion about the role of, and necessity for, knowledgeable staff.

LIBQUAL DATA PRESENTATION

Typical reports from the libraries using LibQUAL+ include tables and graphs (including line graphs). The library reports use radar charts to display the responses to the twenty-two paired statements. (See chapter 7.) In radar charts, the items are arranged around a circle and are grouped according to three categories: affect of service, information control, and library as a place. For each item, the mean rating is indicated for the perceived level of expectations as well as for the minimum and desired levels. Circles are drawn connecting the minimum ratings for each question, the perceived ratings, and the desired rating. The resultant bands are color-coded as follows:

Red: The perceived level is below the minimum level. These deficiencies need attention.

Blue: The perceived level is above the minimum level. The level of quality is acceptable and is called the adequacy gap. A large gap indicates better performance.

Yellow: The perceived level is below the ideal. Known as the superiority gap, this is an area that can be given attention if the library wishes to reach a high level of excellence. A small negative gap indicates better performance.

Green: The perceived level is greater than the desired. The library exceeds desired maximum performance.

Figure 11.4, which the Association of Research Libraries supplied, illustrates a radar chart. Such a graph is useful for displaying gap scores in a clear and logical way.

DASHBOARDS

The balanced scorecard (see chapter 1) recognizes that an organization's strategic directions evolve more from perspectives than cost efficiencies and the customer. In its truest form, the balanced scorecard links performance information to the organization's strategic directions. It includes explicit information about perspectives (the high level strategic areas), objectives, measures (sometimes called key performance indicators), and stoplight indicators. The balanced scorecard presentation includes four strategic perspectives:

1. The customer (How do customers see us?)
2. Internal (What must we excel at?)
3. Innovation and learning (Can we continue to improve and create value?)
4. Financial (How do we look to shareholders?)

As more libraries embrace service quality and customer service, their strategic perspectives might place

---

FIGURE 11.2
GAP BETWEEN EXPECTATIONS AND ACTUAL SERVICE PROVIDED

Questions	MEAN SCORE		Gap between the Means
	Expected	Actual	
Materials in proper place	6.68	4.79	1.89
Range of materials in library	6.65	5.16	1.49
Good order copiers	6.59	5.19	1.40
Staff available when needed	6.52	5.28	1.24
OPAC accurate and extensive	6.45	4.92	1.53
Hours open match your schedule and needs	6.33	5.05	1.28
Staff on desks knowledgeable	6.28	5.23	1.06
Seven-day recall	6.28	4.80	1.48
Desk copy available	6.18	5.18	1.00
Knowledgeable staff always available	6.15	4.88	1.27
24 hours from storage	5.87	4.76	1.11

Source: Nicola Harwood and Jillene Bydder, "Student Expectations of, and Satisfaction with, the University Library," *Journal of Academic Librarianship* 24, no. 2 (March 1998), 162.

the customer perspective more central to the depiction of their scorecard.

The balanced scorecard is analogous to an airplane pilot's dashboard, where information for a variety of sources, all timely, are available at a glance for making decisions to fly the aircraft. Dashboards have developed as more than a metaphor for presentation. Organizations use them to communicate complex and extensive information about performance. In contrast to the prescriptive and formal character of balanced scorecards, dashboards are designed to be more open to interpretation. They present a series of graphs, charts, and various visual indicators, leaving to the viewer to select what is of interest, whether or not linked to strategic directions.

With simple dashboards becoming more relevant and conveying measures and ordinal data in the form of pie chart, line graph, bar chart, simple table, and so forth, it is easy to see insights into the four perspectives without having to read narrative text. More precisely, dashboard indicators might cover teaching/learning, scholarship/research, service/outreach, workplace satisfaction, and financial. As an alternative, the system of Minnesota state colleges and universities has created

an accountability dashboard for the board of trustees, policymakers, and other stakeholders that display key measures applicable to all thirty-two institutions. (See www.mnscu.edu/board/accountability/index.html.) The board and system institutions use the data to improve their services to students and to citizens of the state.

Texas Tech University has created a dashboard that highlights academic excellence, access and diversity, engagement (gate count), and technology (number of public workstations and the percentage of computer uptime). The dashboard presents numbers in terms of "progress," defined as "toward [the] target," "minimal change," "away from target," and "target reached." For each metric—inputs and some general outputs— the library is actually working "toward target" or experiencing "minimal change." (See www.irs.ttu.edu/ dashboardareas/Dashboard.aspx?collid=35&year=20 07&deptid=0.) A symbol reflects the change from the previous year. What makes this dashboard most interesting is that it is linked to strategic planning for the university's colleges and academic and support areas and then to their individual dashboards. Another link is to "state accountability measures" and another set

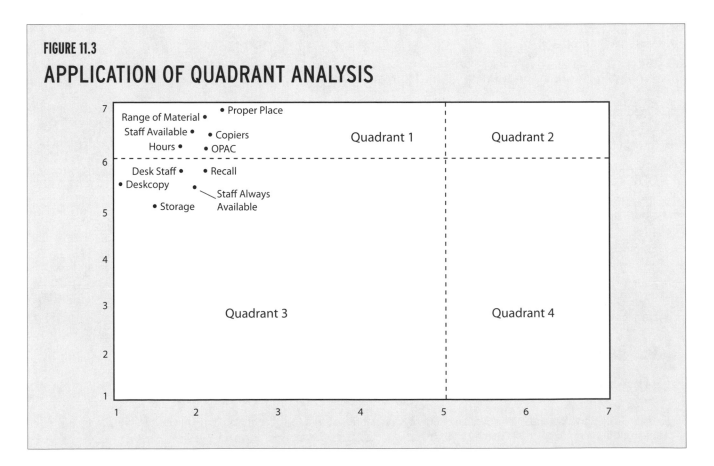

FIGURE 11.3

APPLICATION OF QUADRANT ANALYSIS

FIGURE 11.4

THE RADAR CHART

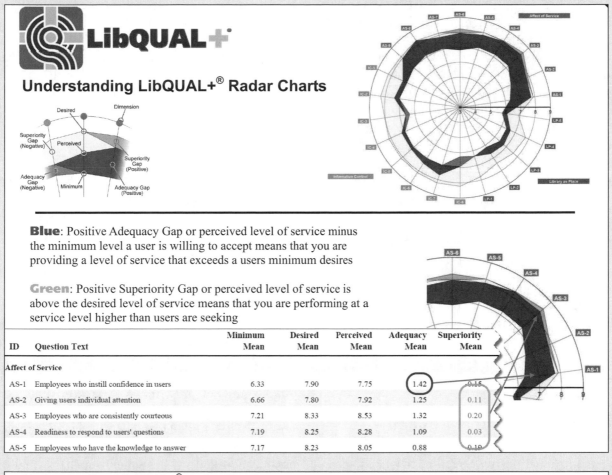

LibQUAL+

Understanding LibQUAL+® Radar Charts

Blue: Positive Adequacy Gap or perceived level of service minus the minimum level a user is willing to accept means that you are providing a level of service that exceeds a users minimum desires

Green: Positive Superiority Gap or perceived level of service is above the desired level of service means that you are performing at a service level higher than users are seeking

ID	Question Text	Minimum Mean	Desired Mean	Perceived Mean	Adequacy Mean	Superiority Mean
Affect of Service						
AS-1	Employees who instill confidence in users	6.33	7.90	7.75	1.42	0.15
AS-2	Giving users individual attention	6.66	7.80	7.92	1.25	0.11
AS-3	Employees who are consistently courteous	7.21	8.33	8.53	1.32	0.20
AS-4	Readiness to respond to users' questions	7.19	8.25	8.28	1.09	0.03
AS-5	Employees who have the knowledge to answer	7.17	8.23	8.05	0.88	0.19

Understanding LibQUAL+® Radar Charts

ID	Question Text					
IC-6	Easy-to-use access tools that allow me to find things on my own	7.02	8.16	7.43	0.40	-0.73
IC-7	Making information easily accessible for independent use	7.00	8.23	7.68	0.68	-0.55
IC-8	Print and/or electronic journal collections I require for my work	6.92	8.23	6.27	-0.65	-1.96

Red: Negative Adequacy Gap or perceived level of service is below their minimum level of service means that your level of service does not even meet the minimum level that users would usually accept

Yellow: Negative Superiority Gap or perceived level of service is not as great as their desired level of service, but your level of service is above users minimum level of acceptable service

of dashboards. The goal is to help the university measure its progress in becoming "a national leader in higher education—manifesting excellence, embracing diversity, inspiring confidence, and engaging society. The university aspires to national recognition of excellence and performance in scholarship through teaching, research, and service."[12]

In summary, the gauges, perhaps similar to those found in a car, are used to display the status of achieving goals and objectives, or of a static measure within a range. Results might be displayed for one organization, an institution, an entire college or university system, and so on. Given these developments, four key questions become

1. What story is the library trying to tell through a set of dashboards?

2. Is that story limited to input measures, perhaps mixed with a few output measures?

3. Will a dashboard enhance strategic planning and library decision making?

4. How might the library relate its activities to the dashboard indicators that colleges and universities compile?

STRATEGY MAP AND REPORT CARD

From its introduction in 1992, the balanced scorecard provides a comprehensive framework to communicate an organization's strategy in terms of a set of strategic objectives and performance measures. The strategy map, developed by Robert S. Kaplan and David P. Norton, provides a visual framework that logically integrates the objectives across the different perspectives of the balanced scorecard.[13] The scorecard presentation is in the form of a quadrant grid, with objectives and metrics organized by each perspective, and it is used for communicating the measurement of the organization's performance. The strategy map, by comparison, illustrates the cause and effect relationship among and across the objectives and perspectives outlined in the scorecard. The map, together with the performance measurement presentation of the balanced scorecard, "describes how the organization works and what is critical to its success."[14]

Paul R. Niven, who discusses the application of the balanced scorecard in government and nonprofit organizations, favors a strategy map, "a clear and concise one-page document" that presents a strategy for what an organization finds most critical.[15] "An effective map," he points out, "should tell the story of your strategy, with the objectives chosen helping to make your story leap from the page."[16] He offers an example of a strategy map developed by the Finance and Administrative Services division of Cal State San Marcos University.[17] The cause and effect arrangement of the ovals graphically relate the objectives and specific drivers within each of the four perspectives from the balanced scorecard to highlight the organization's strategy to achieve the outcomes that characterize its mission.

Some organizations might view the balanced scorecard and strategy map as too complex to produce and use. For them, a report card simplifies the presentation of data. A report card reports on effectiveness, looking at the organization or a service from the customers' perspective. The use of the report card to check progress and overall performance, as well as communicate the resulting *health* of an organization to stakeholders, managers, and customers, is based on the educational practice of using this tool to highlight strengths and weaknesses of primary, middle, and secondary school students and to identify areas for personal improvement. The grading rubric for each of the four perspectives combines multiple metrics and sources of data. Grades are not prescriptive (scores do not identify what caused poor performance) but are excellent diagnostic devices. Pulled together, the overall report card, compiled on a regular basis, reflects the health of the organization and, with frequent feedback, highlights problem areas as a way to foster improvement.

For a library, a customer service report card might focus on key services and offer a grade composed of delivery of service (availability, speed, and accuracy) and the extent of use and customer satisfaction. Using these criteria, Martin Klubeck and Michael Langthorne note that:

Each component is worth a portion of the final grade for the service or product. The values can be weighted for each key service, and the aggregate of the grades becomes the organization's GPA for the term. The organization might be failing at one facet of effectiveness while excelling in others. Even with a decent overall grade, we would know which areas needed attention. The weak area might require working harder, getting additional help, or dropping that service/product completely.[18]

Examples of use of the report card can also be found in libraries. Although sometimes used to solicit customer feedback, the report card also appears as a summary format for presenting metrics about a library's success from multiple perspectives. For each month in 2002, for instance, the Cunningham Memorial Library, Indiana State University (see figure 11.5), analyzed, published, and circulated "all our customer ratings and comments to all Library staff. We take these ratings and comments seriously and act on them in the best way we can to meet the needs of the greatest number of Library customers."[19] It is possible to convert the responses to a report card. However, libraries would need to review what elements to include in the report card and select a passing grade. Should a grade of C be considered passing? Might the individual grades be compiled into an overall service grade?

SATISFACTION INDICES

When the topic of a satisfaction index arises, *The American Customer Satisfaction Index* (ACSI) comes to mind. Reporting "scores on a 0–100 scale at the national level," the ACSI also produces indexes for ten economic sectors, forty-three industries (including e-commerce and e-business), and more than two hundred companies and federal or local government agencies. The measured companies, industries, and sectors are broadly representative of the U.S. economy serving American households. Smaller companies are grouped together in an "all others" category for each industry.[20] As well, *The ACSI E-Government Satisfaction Index*, a quarterly report of the American customer, is produced by the University of Michigan in partnership with the American Society for Quality. Anne Martensen and Lars Grønholdt developed and applied a model that enables "librarians to quantitatively measure library users' perceived quality, satisfaction and loyalty with a library as well as the degree to which specific elements of a library's services, collections and environment contribute to those perceptions."[21]

SURVEY OF EXPECTATIONS

Figure 11.6 depicts high and low service ratings; the goal is to achieve a high rating for doing something of high importance to customers and, by extension, to meet the mission and goals of the organization. The decision about which statements to include in a survey, as well as the interpretation of study findings, should be viewed within the context of the figure, strategic planning, and the customer service plan.

Librarians might compare external customer perceptions about expectations to staff perceptions about either service expectations or the actual service provided. In both instances, quadrant analysis is appropriate. On the other hand, if staff only elicits perceptions of expectations, then there is no horizontal axis for quadrant analysis. In such instances, there are alternatives for presenting and interpreting the data.

Options include

1. Calculating both the mean and median, and arraying the statements in descending order for both averages

2. Generating the mean and standard deviation, and arraying the statements in descending order for both values

3. Presenting Pearson's *r*, and arranging the statements in descending order for both values

The third option assumes that the staff will survey customers about a vast number of expectations and employ factor analysis to determine groupings among the various statements. Unless the intention is to develop and reorder a far-reaching set of statements (e.g., figure 7.2), this is the least appropriate option.

The decision about which of the other two options to use might depend on the software available. A number of packages determine an average, but they might not produce the standard deviation. As a result, the second option might not be available. Furthermore, if the staff doubts that their measurement scale is interval-level, they would not need the standard deviation. Instead, they would array the data in descending order of median values. On the other hand, if they are dealing with interval-level measurement and the assumptions of the mean are met, the second option is most appropriate.

FOCUS GROUP INTERVIEWS

As discussed in chapter 8, focus group interviews produce qualitative, as opposed to quantitative, data. In other words, the results cannot be reduced to numbers. Rather, the write-up is in narrative form and emphasizes the key points of discussion—probably organized around the research questions discussed.

There might, however, be a section comparing general trends among different focus groups. If the participants complete an exit survey eliciting their perceptions, the results (depending on what is asked and as long as there are horizontal and vertical axes) might be summarized by quadrant analysis.

ONE-ON-ONE INTERVIEWS

Although more time-consuming to arrange and conduct than a focus group interview, one-on-one interviews provide greater depth to the responses given to open-ended questions. Participants should be selected

---

FIGURE 11.5

CONTENTS OF A REPORT CARD

Help the Library improve its services to YOU! Please take a moment to fill out this survey.

Once a month, we analyze, publish, and circulate all our customer ratings and comments to all Library staff. We take these ratings and comments seriously and act on them in the best way we can to meet the needs of the greatest number of Library customers. If you want a reply or need assistance, be sure to include your e-mail or phone number.

For reference questions use RefLive[a]

View comments with replies[b]

Scale: A (Excellent); B (Good); C (Average); D (Below Average); F (Failing); N (Not Sure)

1. W[ere] the Library staff friendly and courteous in their interactions with you?
   A　　B　　C　　D　　F　　N　　　Comment on this
2. Did the Library staff have the knowledge and expertise to help you?
   A　　B　　C　　D　　F　　N　　　Comment on this
3. Were the Library's collections (books, journals, videos, etc.) useful to you?
   A　　B　　C　　D　　F　　N　　　Comment on this
4. Was it easy for you to find and use the materials (books, journals, videos, etc.) you needed?
   A　　B　　C　　D　　F　　N　　　Comment on this
5. Were the Library's electronic resources easy to find and use?
   A　　B　　C　　D　　F　　N　　　Comment on this
6. Did these electronic resources provide the information you were seeking?
   A　　B　　C　　D　　F　　N　　　Comment on this
7. Was the equipment (copiers, printers, computers) functioning to your satisfaction?
   A　　B　　C　　D　　F　　N　　　Comment on this
8. Did the environment in the Library facilitate your work?
   A　　B　　C　　D　　F　　N　　　Comment on this

Your comments/suggestions will help the library. What can we do to improve? What new services would be useful?

If you would like a reply to your comments, please give us your name, e-mail address, status, dept/major and/or phone number (optional)

Name: _____

Status: ❑ Undergrad Student　❑ Grad Student　❑ Faculty/Staff　❑ Other

Dept/Major: _____

E-mail: _____　Phone: _____

Source: Indiana State University, "Cunningham Memorial Library Report Card," http://panther.indstate.edu/cml/reportcard.asp. Report Card questions used with the permission of University of Arizona Library. Copyright 2002 Indiana State University. Reprinted with permission of Indiana State University and the University of Arizona Library.

[a]Indiana State University, Cunningham Memorial Library, "Reference Live! Chat Online with Your Reference Question," http://lib.indstate.edu/tools/reflive.html.
[b]Here is an opportunity for the person to review what was entered.

based on the problem statement and research questions that guide the data-collection process. The interviewer should accurately communicate the questions to the participant, maximize the respondent's ability and willingness to answer questions, and listen, probe, and respond to what the participant says. The interviewer encourages the flow of relevant information, while maintaining a good interpersonal relationship with the respondent. Before serving as an interviewer, any candidate should be trained and asked to engage in role-playing.

OBSERVING PEOPLE USING THE LIBRARY AND ITS SERVICES

Usability Testing

There are numerous ways to study the usability of a library—particularly the library's website. Some of the choices include an analysis of server logs, which reflect actual user behavior, and survey and focus group interviews, which offer user perceptions about a site and the extent of their satisfaction. It is now increasingly common for librarians to select some users and ask them to answer some location or "find-type" of questions. These questions focus on navigation of a site and how or if one finds, for instance, the name of the library director, the hours open, a particular journal, and so forth. Using a verbal protocol, the participants might explain where they search and why they sequence their search in a particular way.[22]

Sweeping the Library

A sweeping study provides a way to see what people actually do in the library. At predetermined times (e.g., hours selected by random sampling), investigators sweep all or some library floors. They have floor

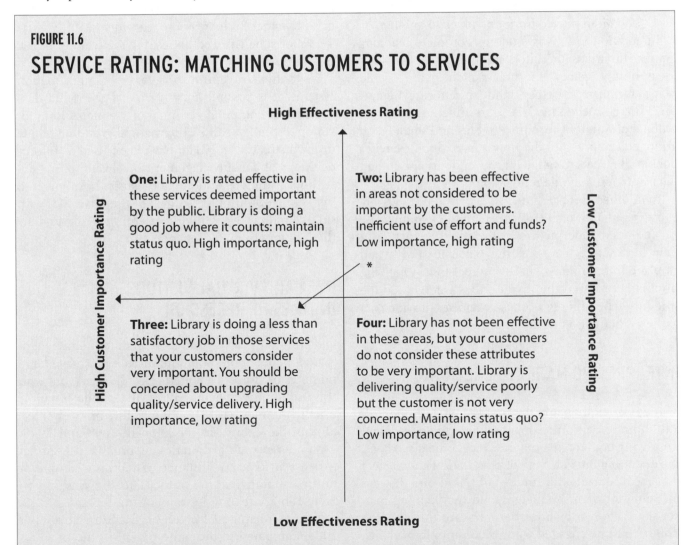

FIGURE 11.6

SERVICE RATING: MATCHING CUSTOMERS TO SERVICES

High Effectiveness Rating

One: Library is rated effective in these services deemed important by the public. Library is doing a good job where it counts: maintain status quo. High importance, high rating

Two: Library has been effective in areas not considered to be important by the customers. Inefficient use of effort and funds? Low importance, high rating

Three: Library is doing a less than satisfactory job in those services that your customers consider very important. You should be concerned about upgrading quality/service delivery. High importance, low rating

Four: Library has not been effective in these areas, but your customers do not consider these attributes to be very important. Library is delivering quality/service poorly but the customer is not very concerned. Maintains status quo? Low importance, low rating

High Customer Importance Rating

Low Customer Importance Rating

Low Effectiveness Rating

*This arrow shows the direction in which to shift resources.

plans and mark how people use public spaces: are they using a laptop (perhaps one loaned by the library), reading, and so on? The findings have implications, like the study at the University of Rochester, for facilities redesign or planning to accommodate information behaviors and use patterns. The goal is to make the library "a vibrant and vital public space."[23]

Other Methods

The University of Rochester Libraries has gained a better understanding of how students use the library, its services and physical spaces, as well as student lifestyles. They hired an anthropologist to work with library staff, engage in assorted data collection, and use the findings to improve the services and space.[24] To see what students actually do all day, librarians gave some of them campus maps and asked them to plot what they did. They found that the students have core designations (e.g., dorm rooms, classes, and dining halls) and often moved from one place to another.

In addition to having students complete mapping diaries, librarians recruited students to design their ideal library spaces. In their sketches, they could place furniture, services, and resources wherever they thought necessary. Next, the students took paper cutouts of different furniture (tables and chairs) and arranged them within the floor space. Such exercises enable librarians to talk with the students about their decisions and to guide renovation.[25]

In another exercise, students received a disposable camera and a list of twenty things to photograph. The list included "one picture of the libraries to show a new freshman," "your favorite place to study," and "a place in the library where you feel lost." Once the librarians reviewed the images, they interviewed the students. The findings of these exercises provide data gathered both visually and orally.

INTERPRETING MARKET PENETRATION

Market penetration and the building of customer loyalty should be priorities for the library, and, perhaps, improving both might convince local officials to boost the operating budget. Market penetration is a concept that local officials can understand, and one that has meaning for them. Achieving and maintaining market share are worthwhile goals. Toward this end, the library must be engaged with its community and seek to retain existing customers, while expanding its cus-

tomer base and the value of the services offered to customers and taxpayers. Market penetration therefore is more than merely expanding the number of cardholders. At the same time, Joseph R. Matthews asserts, but does not provide supporting documentation, that "on average, a public library will lose from 25 to 30 percent of its customers every three years."[26] Consequently, market penetration must be accompanied with a retention strategy.

In *The Engaged Library*, the Urban Libraries Council provides a questionnaire about relationships with local associations which libraries can use to assess these relationships on a five-point scale from *none* to *a great deal* along with a community asset map, which challenges public libraries to move beyond serving as "a passive repository of book and information or an outpost of culture." Instead, the library should be "an active and responsible part of the community and an agent of change."[27] Figure 11.7 reproduces the community asset map, which enables public libraries to identify areas to target for increased engagement, while figure 11.8 shows the engaged library and the relationships it has nurtured.

With the availability of geographic information systems, it is possible to study social-economic data linked to a computerized map of a congressional or voting district, or some other natural grouping of city or town streets. Such data have been used to inform decisions about the placement or closing of a public library branch. Another application is for targeted marketing; for instance, knowing where families with small children live would be useful in trying to draw them in for children's services.[28]

REAL AND VIRTUAL VISITORS IN TIMES OF RECESSION

Data on numbers of visitors present another aspect of market penetration. Some public libraries have large numbers of visitors who are not cardholders, but who still use library services. In fact, the public library is usually the most visited public facility in most cities. During the economic recession of 2008 and 2009, a number of public libraries reported a substantial increase in use. For instance, based on a sample of thirty-six public libraries in the state, the Washington State Library reported the following increases in six categories measured from June 2008 to November 2008, compared to the same period in the previous year:

- attendance (patron visits): 7.5 percent
- circulation (material checkouts): 11.2 percent
- virtual visits (such as to a library web page): 20.2 percent
- reference transactions: 4.4 percent
- percent of time public Internet computers are in use: 9.7 percent
- number of public Internet computer users: 13.8 percent.[29]

Various stories in the press reinforce this trend. CNN, for instance, reports that

> An unemployed woman sits at a computer in a public library in New York. She's not an avid reader, but because it's a way to research job openings and use the Internet for free, she goes to the library. . . . In times of recession, people take advantage of free services, and the library is among the most popular.[30]

On the other hand, some public libraries in the state of Massachusetts have seen severe cuts in their libraries' budgets and as a result have lost their state accreditation. Other libraries in the state cannot offset the loss of services.

SOME SOURCES OF DATA TRENDS

The Association of College and Research Libraries released the 2007 *Academic Library Trends and Statistics*, which is part of an annual series that describes the collections, staffing, expenditures, and service activities of 1,311 academic libraries in the following categories:

- collections (including volumes, serials, and multimedia)
- expenditures (library materials, wages and salaries, and other operating costs)
- electronic resources (including expenditures, collections, services, and usage)
- personnel and public services (staff and services)
- Ph.D.s granted, faculty, and student enrollment

The data can be used for self-studies, budgeting, strategic planning, annual reports, grant applications, and benchmarking.

Similarly, the National Center for Education Statistics, Department of Education, collects data from institutions of postsecondary education relating to enrollments, program completions, graduation rates, faculty, staff, finances, institutional prices, and student financial aid. Known as IPEDS, the Integrated Postsecondary Education Data System contains a wealth of data about those institutions and their libraries (http://nces.ed.gov/IPEDS/). The College Navigator (http://nces.ed.gov/collegenavigator/) has a number of search options so that parents and others can investigate and compare institutions and programs.

The Association of Research Libraries (ARL) has several relevant data sets. Dating from 1907 to 1908, ARL Statistics is a series of annual publications that describe the collections, expenditures, staffing, and service activities for ARL member libraries. Also,

> Starting with 2005–06 data, ARL is calculating a Library Investment Index (previously named Expenditures-Focused Index) as an alternative to the historical index known as the ARL Membership Criteria Index. The Library Investment Index replaces the public availability of the ARL Membership Criteria Index. The Library Investment Index is highly correlated with the Membership Criteria Index and less affected by changes in the collections variables.[31]

Further, the index indicates that money spent on libraries reflects investments in capital (intellectual, scholarly, and community).

> Each year, ARL calculates an index for the university library members of ARL. The index is a summary measure of relative size among the university library members of the Association. The sole purpose of the index used to be a membership criterion for the Association of Research Libraries; it currently serves as one indicator of potential for membership. The ARL Membership Criteria Index comprises the five quantitative data elements in which ARL university libraries most resemble one another, and does not attempt to measure a library's services, quality of collections, or success in meeting the needs of users. The Membership Criteria Index allowed ARL to evaluate potential new members and track the maintenance of membership requirements.[32]

As chapter 4 discusses, the Public Library Data Service (PLDS) Statistical Report, a project of the Public Library Association, is published annually. As well, COUNTER (www.projectcounter.org) is an international initiative among librarians, publishers,

FIGURE 11.7

SAMPLE COMMUNITY ASSET MAP

This is a sample community asset map. Use the next page to document the assets of the local community surrounding your library.

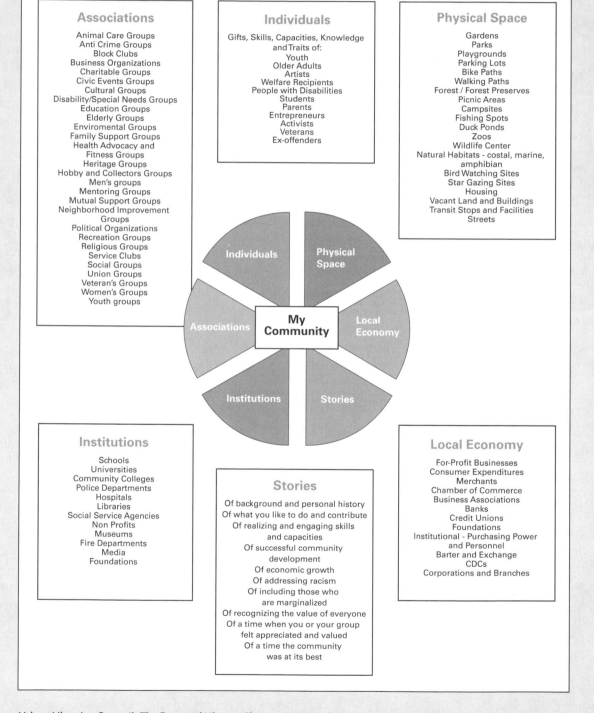

Associations

Animal Care Groups
Anti Crime Groups
Block Clubs
Business Organizations
Charitable Groups
Civic Events Groups
Cultural Groups
Disability/Special Needs Groups
Education Groups
Elderly Groups
Enviromental Groups
Family Support Groups
Health Advocacy and
Fitness Groups
Heritage Groups
Hobby and Collectors Groups
Men's groups
Mentoring Groups
Mutual Support Groups
Neighborhood Improvement
Groups
Political Organizations
Recreation Groups
Religious Groups
Service Clubs
Social Groups
Union Groups
Veteran's Groups
Women's Groups
Youth groups

Individuals

Gifts, Skills, Capacities, Knowledge
and Traits of:
Youth
Older Adults
Artists
Welfare Recipients
People with Disabilities
Students
Parents
Entrepreneurs
Activists
Veterans
Ex-offenders

Physical Space

Gardens
Parks
Playgrounds
Parking Lots
Bike Paths
Walking Paths
Forest / Forest Preserves
Picnic Areas
Campsites
Fishing Spots
Duck Ponds
Zoos
Wildlife Center
Natural Habitats - costal, marine,
amphibian
Bird Watching Sites
Star Gazing Sites
Housing
Vacant Land and Buildings
Transit Stops and Facilities
Streets

Institutions

Schools
Universities
Community Colleges
Police Departments
Hospitals
Libraries
Social Service Agencies
Non Profits
Museums
Fire Departments
Media
Foundations

Stories

Of background and personal history
Of what you like to do and contribute
Of realizing and engaging skills
and capacities
Of successful community
development
Of economic growth
Of addressing racism
Of including those who
are marginalized
Of recognizing the value of everyone
Of a time when you or your group
felt appreciated and valued
Of a time the community
was at its best

Local Economy

For-Profit Businesses
Consumer Expenditures
Merchants
Chamber of Commerce
Business Associations
Banks
Credit Unions
Foundations
Institutional - Purchasing Power
and Personnel
Barter and Exchange
CDCs
Corporations and Branches

Center diagram labels: Individuals, Physical Space, Associations, **My Community**, Local Economy, Institutions, Stories

Source: Urban Libraries Council, *The Engaged Library: Chicago Stories of Community Building* (Chicago: Urban Libraries Council, 2005), www.urbanlibraries.org/associations/9851/files/ULC_PFSC_Engaged_0206.pdf. Reprinted with permission.

FIGURE 11.8
THE ENGAGED LIBRARY

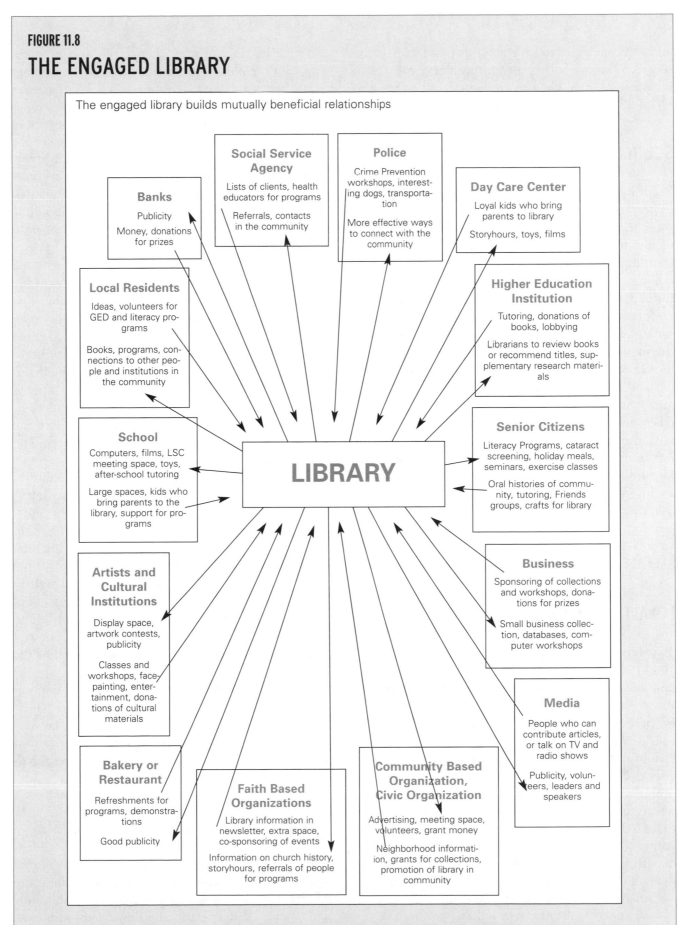

The engaged library builds mutually beneficial relationships

Banks

Publicity

Money, donations for prizes

Social Service Agency

Lists of clients, health educators for programs

Referrals, contacts in the community

Police

Crime Prevention workshops, interesting dogs, transportation

More effective ways to connect with the community

Day Care Center

Loyal kids who bring parents to library

Storyhours, toys, films

Local Residents

Ideas, volunteers for GED and literacy programs

Books, programs, connections to other people and institutions in the community

Higher Education Institution

Tutoring, donations of books, lobbying

Librarians to review books or recommend titles, supplementary research materials

School

Computers, films, LSC meeting space, toys, after-school tutoring

Large spaces, kids who bring parents to the library, support for programs

LIBRARY

Senior Citizens

Literacy Programs, cataract screening, holiday meals, seminars, exercise classes

Oral histories of community, tutoring, Friends groups, crafts for library

Artists and Cultural Institutions

Display space, artwork contests, publicity

Classes and workshops, face-painting, entertainment, donations of cultural materials

Business

Sponsoring of collections and workshops, donations for prizes

Small business collection, databases, computer workshops

Media

People who can contribute articles, or talk on TV and radio shows

Publicity, volunteers, leaders and speakers

Bakery or Restaurant

Refreshments for programs, demonstrations

Good publicity

Faith Based Organizations

Library information in newsletter, extra space, co-sponsoring of events

Information on church history, storyhours, referrals of people for programs

Community Based Organization, Civic Organization

Advertising, meeting space, volunteers, grant money

Neighborhood information, grants for collections, promotion of library in community

Source: Urban Libraries Council, *The Engaged Library: Chicago Stories of Community Building* (Chicago: Urban Libraries Council, 2005), www.urbanlibraries.org/associations/9851/files/ULC_PFSC_Engaged_0206.pdf. Reprinted with permission.

and intermediaries to set standards that facilitate the recording and reporting of online usage statistics in a consistent, credible and compatible way. (See also chapter 9.)

SOURCES OF RELEVANT METRICS

Published in 2009, *Viewing Library Metrics from Different Perspectives* offers numerous input, output, process, and outcome measures from the perspectives of libraries, customers, institutions of higher education, and assorted stakeholders.[33] Examples of internal customer measures include an employee culture index (rating of job satisfaction, recognition for job performance, satisfaction with salary, work environment, and communication with other employees in the organization) as well as customer perceptions of their assurance (knowledge and courtesy of employees and their ability to inspire trust and confidence) and empathy (caring, individualized attention to customers).[34] Turning to external customers, parents and students, for instance, want to know about return on investment (learning and services received for tuition dollars) and services offered (e.g., through an information or learning commons). Other useful usage statistics for customers relate to downloads, problems experienced in using collections and services, remote versus on-site use, and satisfaction with a service and the library.

LOYALTY AND INTENSITY

Two important questions are: who uses the library? and to what extent do they use it? Some public librarians are a bit uncomfortable with the oft-repeated statement that 20 percent of the patrons account for 80 percent of the circulation. Although this 80/20 rule is commonly found in many situations, perhaps it does not apply in some libraries.[35] The point is to check. Even if the rule holds, that in itself is not a problem. With the exception of garbage, water, and sewer, most taxpayers do not use government services to the same extent. Not everyone uses the public golf course, the library, or the services of the police or fire department. People without children do not utilize the school system, and people without automobiles use the roads less than car owners do.

Retention of customers, or holding power, is essential for any successful organization. Figure 9.4 indicates the length and strength of customers' relationship with the library. Librarians can analyze whether or not new borrowers continue as cardholders over time. If they do not, does the drop-off rate, particularly after the first year, represent a large proportion of new cardholders? Unless turnover among the service area population is extremely high, could some aspect within the library cause cardholders not to re-register? Can the library point with pride to long-term relationships with a significant proportion of its cardholders? How many of these customers are active, borrowing at least one item per year?

Libraries might compare the profile of the registered borrowers with the population of the service area. Are certain age groups not well represented among the cardholders? If so, would it be possible to target market to those groups? Do active borrowers tend to come from certain neighborhoods? Do they reflect certain age groupings? At what point does use by schoolchildren seem to decline? Can the library do anything to keep schoolchildren as active customers?

Academic libraries need information on both the status and the subject specialties of borrowers. The staff can look at both borrowers and virtual visitors by status. The campus identification number indicates status in most academic institutions and also serves as the borrower's identification. The numbers represented by each group are easily obtained from central administration. The staff might compare the total in each group with the number of borrowers in that group. It would not be unusual for general staff to be underrepresented as borrowers. Librarians might examine how many lower and upper division undergraduates were active borrowers. How many borrowed nothing? The same questions might be asked of the faculty.

It might be interesting to determine if the nonborrowing students are enrolled in departments whose faculty members are nonborrowers or slight borrowers. What do trends in borrowing indicate? Is borrowing declining as the number of electronic resources increases?

INTERPRETING CUSTOMER PREFERENCES

If the staff believes that the library collection should match the interests of most customers, then the relationship between holdings and circulation (or frequency of database use and downloads) is important. The collection can attract new customers and influence retention of existing ones. A new group of customers will be attracted to the public library when it acquires DVD movies and music. If these customers are valued and their continued patronage desired, then their interests must be satisfied. Some criticize this approach as being like a bookstore. Such criticism implies that bookstores pander to customers' unrefined taste. On the contrary, customers' taste in reading materials is quite diverse. Any library choosing the role of "popular materials center" or the new service response "current topics and titles" has, knowingly or not, opted to let customer preferences guide selection. Preferences are best determined by analyzing circulation patterns, or other indicators of borrowing and use, and adjusting buying accordingly.

Academic libraries have tended to amass quality collections but now find that their constituency prefers digital resources. Even a number of libraries whose institutions are members of the ARL find that library users, including those in the building, rely on digital resources much more than they do traditional services such as reference. They make infrequent use of backfiles of print journal collections and the book collection. In response, some libraries are downsizing the print collection and adding more digital resources. They are also purchasing and loaning equipment to read e-books, and are willing to convert microforms to a digital source and then e-mail them to the requester.

Cafés have been in public libraries for some time, but now academic libraries are adding them (perhaps generating revenue), increasing group study rooms, and engaging in other ventures that invite their constituent groups to visit. In its mission statement, the Sawyer Library, Suffolk University, reminds us that academic libraries provide "a[n inviting] place for students and faculty to read and study, to gather and deliberate, and to question, challenge and support one another."[36] Students may be unaware that the databases they use most often reside on library web pages and are purchased by the library, but they often appreciate an inviting space, especially if it is associated with an information or learning commons.

COMMUNICATING WITH STAKEHOLDERS

By choosing what data to report, librarians have created the standards by which they want to be measured. (No stakeholder ever initiated the category "new serials added per annum.") These self-defined categories emphasize growth, units of work processed, and the need to keep up with other libraries or with the publishing output. In essence, the categories have focused on resources. Some stakeholders now use those resources-based categories to question library efficiency and claims for more resources, because so much information on the Internet seems free. Stakeholders are also interested in the extent to which academic institutions achieve the aspirations expressed in their mission statement and what students actually learned through their program of study. For librarians a critical question is, how much of that learning can be attributed to the use of library space and collections? The answer requires the gathering and use of evidence that has implications for accountability and improved service.

As a society, we are conditioned to present information in two-dimensional form on paper. This format may not be the best way to get a point across, especially if the paper contains numbers. Consider how many librarians tend to skip over numbers in reports and articles and focus on the text. Making sense of a lot of numbers is difficult for most people, especially when they have little time or inclination to spend digesting their import because of the press of other business. For this reason, pictorial techniques such as dashboards may be appropriate.

It is not necessary that stakeholders know every number that the library has collected. With the exception of market penetration, we recommend that libraries selectively share the findings from the indicators presented in this book with decision makers. These indicators are intended to assess the roles specified in the mission statement and improve service quality. Information about activities needed for internal operations, such as cycle times and complaints, should stay internal to the organization. Information likely to create favorable public reaction (e.g., customer recognition programs) should be widely publicized. Compliments, testimonials, and other information about good customer service should be passed along to local officials.

Librarians might consider how to engage their communities and stakeholders in more assertive ways. Unless local officials personally come to the library, their impressions of what goes on are based on library experiences perhaps years out of date, or on a stereotype. Information about the business of the library and the people who use it is best communicated visually. However, getting local officials to schedule visits might be difficult. Videotaping the library during peak periods is an easy and effective way to communicate both vibrancy and activity. Videotaping also shows the diversity of the clientele—another factor important to local officials. Videotaping, however, should be done with caution. Some customers may resent the taping as an intrusion on their privacy and other rights. For example, videotaping individuals using the Internet might be taken as a form of censorship, as some people might alter their search patterns if they believe "Big Brother" is monitoring them.

Information about library activities should be presented in a form that the community and local officials can clearly understand. In addition to the techniques presented in this chapter, libraries might report the following:

- Every minute, twelve people come through the doors of the library.
- Every thirty seconds, an item is checked out.
- Every five minutes, someone asks a reference question.
- People from every neighborhood, every age group, etc., are library customers.
- Most customers have been cardholders for more than ten years.
- The annual per capita cost of library service is about the same as the cost of a movie for two with popcorn and drinks.
- The library provided reserve materials for 193 courses enrolling 2,477 students last academic year.
- Faculty requested 142 class presentations by librarians, last academic year, involving 963 students.
- Circulations to lower division students increased 12 percent over the past year.
- Faculty from thirty-nine of the forty-one departments on campus used the library last year by borrowing materials and by requesting reserve collections or presentations.

WHAT IS A LIBRARY?

It used to be easy to explain what a library is. The answer given in the past focused on the collection of books and periodicals, and the respondent might make reference to a warehouse or storage facility. Today it is harder to define a library; it is much more than print collections.[37] The academic library collab-

orates with others and might be the center of campus convergence and collaboration; and it might have a center for digital initiatives and increased emphasis on digital access and services.[38] Such a library might stress that it

> provides a comfortable, secure environment for individuals and groups to study and do research. A wireless network, as well as some standard ports, provides users with access to the Internet via personal laptop computers or those that can be checked out at the circulation desk. . . . [There are individual study rooms, the OPAC, a wide variety of databases, some of them are full-text, and general use computers.] Staff are available to answer questions and provide reference assistance.[39]

In 2008, an external review of the University of British Columbia library was conducted. The report presents an image of the twenty-first-century academic research library as a physical place but

> it will take on more of a trompe l'oeil character, with more of a commitment to learning space, social space, and collaborative space with maximum flexibility and adaptability. The library services must be increasingly untethered from the physical library, as the library professional works more routinely in the classroom, in the laboratory and at the bedside.

The academic research library, the report continues, will be defined by the following areas of strategic focus:

- distributed electronic access to content, tools, and services
- high-quality physical spaces
- high-quality virtual spaces
- special and distinctive collections
- global collections
- archiving of digital and analog content
- innovation applications of technology in support of learning and research
- high-quality technology infrastructure
- professional and support staff with deep and diverse expertise and a strong service ethic
- staff development and professional engagement
- leadership in information policy

- integration into the academic fabric of the university

- new knowledge driven by research and development

- innovative resource development capacity[40]

With the exception of the last three items on this list, public libraries have the same aspirations—to be a high-tech information agency with a staff highly committed to service. In addition, public libraries want to be seen as

- welcoming all people in the community

- being a focal point for information about the local community

- providing free space for community group meetings

- fostering a love for the discovery of learning in children so that they will continue to come to the library as adults

A FINAL WORD

No effort has been made to include every possible indicator that might be developed or to count every conceivable use or activity among the measures proposed in this book. Our focus has been on the customer and, to a lesser extent, on factors important to organizational administrators. Most customers do not care about how many *whatevers* the library owns or how many of such *whatevers* the library has processed.

Indicators of "How much?" are no substitute for those discussed in this book. Besides, no library can always increase the volume of business. When the volume reaches a plateau or declines (as it will), the library must increase its inputs—including the number of hours open—to reverse the trend. The challenge for libraries is to select from among the various suggestions in this book and to ensure that the mission, vision, goals, and objectives have a customer focus. It should not be assumed that, by addressing the expectations and preferences of customers, the quality of the collection will decline. At the same time, libraries must communicate with their broader community in understandable and meaningful terms.

Today, . . . the library is relinquishing its place as the top source of inquiry. The reason that the library is losing its supremacy in carrying out this fundamental role is due, of course, to the impact of digital technology.[41]

Notes

1. Brian Mathews, *Marketing Today's Academic Library: A Bold New Approach to Communicating with Students* (Chicago: American Library Association, 2009), 163.

2. Ellen Altman, "Reflections on Performance Measures Fifteen Years Later," in *Library Performance, Accountability, and Responsiveness: Essays in Honor of Ernest R. DeProspo* (Norwood, NJ: Ablex Press, 1990), 11, 12.

3. Terry G. Vavra, *Improving Your Measurement of Customer Satisfaction: A Guide to Creating, Conducting, Analyzing, and Reporting Customer Satisfaction Measurement Programs* (Milwaukee, WI: ASQ Quality Press, 1997), 267–268.

4. Because calculating factor analysis is complicated, it should only be attempted with a computer program (e.g., SPSS) that performs the calculations for you.

5. James Lynch, Robert Carver Jr., and John M. Virgo, "Quadrant Analysis as a Strategic Planning Technique in Curriculum Development and Program Marketing," *Journal of Marketing for Higher Education* 7, no. 2 (1996): 18.

6. Ibid.

7. Ibid., 19.

8. Ibid., 23.

9. Ibid., 25. "Only if the study includes groups that have different priorities (for example, students versus employers), is it likely that a significant number of the . . . [expectations] of high importance to one group will end up in the low importance quadrants for the group (and vice versa)" (p. 25).

10. Ibid.

11. Nicola Harwood and Jillene Bydder, "Student Expectations of, and Satisfaction with, the University Library," *Journal of Academic Librarianship* 24, no. 2 (March 1998): 161–171.

12. Texas Tech University, "Welcome Texas Tech University Planning and Assessment Reports 2008–2009" (Lubbock: Texas Tech University), http://techdata.irs .ttu.edu/stratreport/index.asp.

13. Robert S. Kaplan and David P. Norton, *The Strategy-Focused Organization: How Balanced Scorecard Companies Thrive in the New Business Environment* (Boston: Harvard Business School Press, 2001).

14. Paul R. Niven, *Balanced Scorecard Step-by-Step for Government and Nonprofit Agencies*, 2nd ed. (Hoboken, NJ: John Wiley and Sons, 2003), 166. See also Juha Kettunen, "A Conceptual Framework to Help Evaluate the Quality of Institutional Performance," *Quality Assurance in Education* 16, no. 4 (2008): 322–332.

15. Niven, *Balanced Scorecard Step-by-Step for Government and Nonprofit Agencies*, 169.

16. Ibid., 179.

17. Ibid., 181.

18. Martin Klubeck and Michael Langthorne, "Applying a Metrics Report Card," *EDUCAUSE Quarterly* 31, no. 2 (April–June 2008), www.educause.edu/ EDUCAUSE+Quarterly/EDUCAUSEQuarterly MagazineVolum/ApplyingaMetricsReportCard/162880.

19. Indiana State University, Cunningham Memorial Library, Report Card, http://panther.indstate.edu/cml/ reportcard.asp.

20. *The American Customer Satisfaction Index*, ACSI Scores and Commentary, www.theacsi.org/index .php?option=com_content&task=view&id=12&Item id=26.

21. Anne Martensen and Lars Grønholdt, "Improving Library Users' Perceived Quality, Satisfaction and Loyalty: An Integrated Measurement and Management System," *Journal of Academic Librarianship* 29, no. 3 (2003): 140.

22. See, for instance, Elizabeth Stephen, Daisy T. Cheng, and Lauren. M. Young, "A Usability Survey at the University of Mississippi Libraries for the Improvement of the Library Home Page," *Journal of Academic Librarianship* 32, no. 1 (2006): 35–51; "Website Usability: Research and Case Studies," *OCLC Systems & Services* 21, no. 3 (2005): 145–256; Maryellen Allen, "A Case Study of the Usability Testing of the University of South Florida's Virtual Library Interface Design," *Online Information Review* 26, no. 1 (2002): 40–53; Brenda Battleson, Austin Booth, and Jane Weintrop, "Usability Testing of an Academic Library Web Site: A Case Study," *Journal of Academic Librarianship* 27, no. 3 (2001): 188–198; Galina Letnikova, "Usability Testing of Academic Library Web Sites: A Selective Annotated Bibliography," *Internet Reference Services Quarterly* 8, no. 4 (2003): 53–68; John Kupersmith, "Library Terms Evaluated in Usability Testing and Other Studies," www.jkup.net/terms-studies.html.

23. Lisa M. Given and Gloria J. Leckie, "'Sweeping' the Library: Mapping the Social Activity Space of the Public Library," *Library & Information Science Research* 23, no. 4 (2003): 365. See also Gloria J. Leckie and Jeffrey Hopkins, "The Public Place of Central Libraries: Findings from Toronto and Vancouver," *Library Quarterly* 72, no. 3 (July 2002): 326–372.

24. Nancy Foster and Susan Gibbons, eds., *Studying Students: The Undergraduate Research Project at the University of Rochester* (Chicago: Association of College and Research Libraries, 2008).

25. There are some parallels between this approach and asking students to produce a sketch map from memory. That map might be of a particular floor of the library. See Mark Horan, "What Students See: Sketch Maps as Tools for Assessing Knowledge of Libraries," *Journal of Academic Librarianship* 25, no. 3 (1999): 187–201.

26. Joseph R. Matthews, "Customer Satisfaction: A New Perspective," *Public Libraries* 47, no. 6 (November/ December 2008), 52.

27. Urban Libraries Council, *The Engaged Library: Chicago Stories of Community Building*, www .urbanlibraries.org/associations/9851/files/ULC_ PFSC_Engaged_0206.pdf.

28. See, for instance, Bradley W. Bishop, "Use of Geographic Information Systems in Marketing and Facility Site Location: A Case Study of Douglas County (Colo.)," *Public Libraries* 47, no. 5 (September/ October 2008): 65–69.

29. Washington State Library, "News Release" (February 4, 2009), www.secstate.wa.gov/office/osos_news.aspx?i =7mGFpzDxwXmjyN4wEGiiVw%3D%3D.

30. Kristina Yates, "In Times of Recession, Libraries Flourish," *CNN Wire* (February 28, 2009), http://cnnwire.blogs.cnn.com/2009/02/28/in-times -of-recession-libraries-flourish.

31. Association of Research Libraries, Statistics and Measurement, *ARL Index*, www.arl.org/stats/index/ index.shtml.

32. Ibid.

33. Robert E. Dugan, Peter Hernon, and Danuta Nitecki, *Viewing Library Metrics from Different Perspectives* (Westport, CT: Libraries Unlimited, 2009).

34. Such measures might be placed within the context of "the employee promise continuum" that the Ritz-Carlton Hotel Company uses. It places "empowerment and innovation culture" within a much wider context. See Joseph A. Michelli, *The New Gold Standard: 5 Leadership Principles for Creating a Legendary Customer Experience Courtesy of The Ritz-Carlton Hotel Company* (New York: McGraw Hill, 2008), 100.

35. See Richard Trueswell, "Some Behavioral Patterns of Library Users: The 80/20 Rule," *Wilson Library Bulletin* 43 (January 1969): 458–461.

36. Suffolk University, Sawyer Library, *Long-Range Plan: Strategic Directions, July 1, 2005–June 30, 2010*, www.suffolk.edu/files/SawLib/2005-2010-strat-plan.pdf.

37. Pongracz Sennyey, Lyman Ross, and Caroline Mills, "Exploring the Future of Academic Libraries: A Definitional Approach," *Journal of Academic Librarianship* 35, no. 3 (May 2009): 252–259.

38. See Peter Hernon and Ronald R. Powell, ed., *Convergence and Collaboration of Campus Information Services* (Westport, CT: Libraries Unlimited, 2008).

39. Adapted from the University of Nebraska-Lincoln, "UNL Research Libraries: Nebraska's Comprehensive Research Library," www.unl.edu/libr/libs/love/.

40. The University of British Columbia, *Review of the University Library: Report of the Review Committee*, prepared by Karen Adams, Carole Moore, James Neal, and Lizabeth Wilson, www.library.ubc.ca/home/external_review_report_feb08.pdf.

41. Jerry D. Campbell, "Changing a Cultural Icon: The Academic Library as a Virtual Destination," *EDU-CAUSE Review* 41, no. 1 (January/February 2006), 16.

Embracing Change—Continuous Improvement

*It never ceases to amaze me that companies spend millions
to attract new customers (people they don't know) and spend
next to nothing to keep the ones they've got.*[1]

Academic, public, and other libraries are coping not only with extraordinary and complex changes—"financial, technological, political, social/demographic, and cultural—but also the accelerated pace of change."[2] At the same time, stakeholders are pressuring academic institutions for greater accountability in the form of student outcomes. Such outcomes can document graduation rates and the length of time that students spent in a program (entry to graduation). Student learning outcomes, on the other hand, document change in students' educational attainment throughout their program of study.

Figure 12.1, which was developed based on conversations with some state librarians and leaders in public libraries, suggests areas in which public librarians of today and tomorrow will need expertise as new challenges arise. Those areas help to define the library role in community building. Community building encompasses such matters as economic development, redevelopment and neighborhoods, workforce development, and civic engagement. Librarians must also be able to address funding models (e.g., revenue enhancement strategies, library referendums, friends and foundations, grants and partnerships). Figure 12.1 highlights critical issues confronting public and state libraries that library directors will be expected to deal with deftly. These critical issues serve as a reminder of the importance of leadership in organizational development and change management. Libraries need to develop leadership at all levels of the workforce. Careful thought and attention must be given to the recruitment and advancement of the workforce.

In reviewing this list of critical issues, Luis Herrera, city librarian of San Francisco, noted the importance of service development or reinventing service models. Reinventing service models includes defining reference services and roles, functions and processes, the library as a place, and virtual versus physical space. Accountability and assessment, he notes, should not exclude program evaluation and determining the value of library services. Technology and the Internet pose new challenges and opportunities as libraries engage in content creation and keep pace with new applications.[3]

FIGURE 12.1

CRITICAL ISSUES FACING PUBLIC AND STATE LIBRARIES

Issues	Components
Operating in the political environment	• Governing structures, governing bodies, and relationships • Politics • Statutory and legal issues
Fiscal/financial management and leadership	• Enterprise creation and management • Revenue enhancement • Resource allocation • Resource re-allocation (what to stop and start in tough times) • Collaborations for financial efficiency
Planning for leading	• Strategic planning • Tactical implementation • Demographics—who is served: aging, generations, ethnicity, and language
Accountability and assessment	• Outcomes and evidence-based research and decision-making • Performance standards and measures • Transparency as an organizational value
Ethical issues and values	• State and local ethics statutes/rules • Contracting issues
Interaction with stakeholders	• Building effective relationships • Education (primary school up) • Government agencies and officials • Small business • Other constituencies and collaborators • Library friends organizations • Library foundations and support organizations
Crisis management	• Media relations • Disaster management • Election/funding loss • Financial crisis • Intellectual freedom challenges • Library closings/hours reductions • Crime • Homelessness
Staff development	• Collective bargaining • Succession planning • Turnover and training
Service development	• Evaluating/embracing trends and fads • Marketing and public relations • Literacy (early childhood, adult, computer/technology)

Source: The contents of this figure comprise the topics covered in the course "Managerial Leadership in Public Settings," which is part of the curriculum for the Ph.D. Program in Managerial Leadership in the Information Professions, Simmons College, Graduate School of Library and Information Science, Boston.

Coping with the types of issues and challenges noted in figure 12.1 requires a workforce that is not confined to a particular area of the library and enjoys reaching out to the library's communities. Still, senior managers must guard against staff members who suffer "from mental and physical exhaustion, burnout, frustration, low morale, and other symptoms of stress. In some instances the library's structure adds to the distress by slowing response time, preventing cross-functional solutions to problems, and frustrating efforts to intervene."[4]

We might add that a number of libraries are experiencing reductions in operating budgets, which result in an inability to keep pace with inflation and having to take equipment purchases from the book and periodical acquisitions budget. Budget cuts also produce downsizing and staff reassignment; as a result, there is an increased workload for staff. Library staff has become more diverse; for instance, different generations have to learn to mesh their work ethos so that they can function smoothly together. Moreover, some libraries are consolidating services at the same time they are reconfiguring the physical plant. Complicating matters even more, a number of libraries are moving toward evidence-based decision making and a workforce committed to demonstrating accountability and improved services. All in all, these changes suggest an extremely challenging, but rewarding, time for libraries and their staffs.

EXPANDING THE MEASURES GATHERED AND USED

As the twenty-first century unfolds, there is greater dissatisfaction with the type of measures that libraries collect and report because these measures do not adequately reflect their contribution to their communities. Public libraries might report usage in terms of the number of

- new library card holders
- visitors to the library (and its branches)
- items checked out (and using self-checkout)
- reference questions asked
- uses of their public computers
- items downloaded
- hits to their home pages and databases
- presentations to community groups
- new partnerships with business and other communities

- attendance in early literacy programs, preschool story times, workshops, and so on

During the recession, they might highlight the above measures as well as such items as

- attendance at online job-hunting classes
- number of people requesting resume-writing assistance
- use of any dedicated workstations for current, active job listings
- use of any dedicated workstations for creating and posting resumes to a job-posting or employer website
- use of preformatted templates for preparation of resumes on computers with word-processing capability
- number of requests for resources on resume writing, cover letter writing, and interview skills
- number of additional titles purchased in response to the demand for resources on finding employment

With one exception (new titles purchased), these measures comprise outputs, but those highlighting library use during the recession have value to stakeholders. Still, none reflect customer-focused outputs (e.g., relating to service quality or satisfaction—see figure 12.2) and outcomes—the impact of programs and services. For instance, how many people using the resume or other job-related services found full-time employment? Do children increase their reading levels after attending summer reading programs? If yes, by how many grade levels?

For any of the above statistics, libraries could develop baseline data and make ongoing comparisons. It is important to remember that the Public Library Data Service (PLDS) survey focuses primarily on inputs but does include some outputs that reflect the volume of business conducted. Data depicting expenditures can be contrasted to outputs such as those reflecting circulation, library visits, and program attendance. "Expenditures are a primary concern of many libraries and often there is a need to validate that an expenditure has yielded a desired result."[5] Still, without consistency in data collection among the participating libraries in the PLDS survey as well as collecting data that address outcomes and outputs that portray stakeholder perspectives, librarians should be cautious in making interpretations such as, "for each $1,000 of library expenditures, public libraries on average generated 154 library visits. . . ."[6]

Any organization must balance the needs of the library with those of other units, recognizing that budgeting occurs within a political context (competition with academic and other units, and with other government agencies), while addressing issues of "How well?" "How satisfied?" "How productive?" and so forth. (See chapter 4.) As a result, organizations change how they do business and how they ensure quality. In fact, the measurement of quality is changing. As a result, the types of measures that libraries use merit revisiting.[7] In so doing they should settle on the qualitative and qualitative benefits that the library provides to its community.[8] Those benefits should not

be cast solely from the library perspective and focus exclusively on outputs.

LIBRARY WEBSITES

In addition to providing content, a library's website has a marketing function, and gives customers the opportunity to ask questions and to vent about service. If libraries fail to provide such an opportunity, they are not taking advantage of one of most popular ways to find out what their customers are thinking about the library's services and online applications. Libraries might set up listening platforms on such popular websites as Facebook, MySpace, YouTube, and, to a lesser extent, Twitter.

FIGURE 12.2

SAMPLE CUSTOMER-RELATED MEASURES (BY ATTRIBUTE)

AVAILABILITY

Staff availability—at service points and to receive telephone calls[a]

Availability of seating or equipment

SPEED

Speed with which items are reshelved (e.g., within a certain time limit):

   Reference material

   Current periodicals

   Backfiles of periodicals

   Microforms

   Course reserve material

Number of reference queries received on the home page for which a response is given within a specified time frame

Average speed in providing answers to questions

CONNECTIVITY (PHONE SERVICE)

Encountering busy signal when calling the library

Abandoned call rate

Service level (total calls minus busy signals and abandoned calls)

First call resolution

QUEUING

Length of time that customers must wait at service desks to have their information needs met

SATISFACTION

Willingness to return to the same library, same service, and same staff member

OPERATIONAL

Working order of equipment:

   Photocopiers

   Computer printers

   Microform readers and printers

   The OPAC

COMPLIMENTS AND COMPLAINTS

Promptness with which complaints are handled

Number of signed suggestions responded to within a specified time frame (e.g., two working days)

[a]Includes occupancy rate (number of staff answering calls) and agent availability (time answering customer calls and cost per call).

These social networking sites are extensions of blogs, and many of them are now being used to facilitate customer-to-provider conversations and customer-to-customer vents. In fact, a customer dissatisfied when his Dell computer purchase did not meet his expectations became one of the first bloggers to vent. Unable to get satisfaction from Dell, he decided to take his case to the Internet. His approach caught on and now thousands of customers both dissatisfied and satisfied are using the Internet to opine about products and services.

According to a marketing expert who closely monitors what is being written about major brands for Nielson Online and who coined the term "consumer-generated media," the Internet has given customers "not only a collective voice but also a platform and a forum for those voices."[9] He also calls it a "real-time accountability scorecard."[10]

Library customers, including students, have not yet caught on to blogging about library service. However, the library should aggressively encourage such feedback and respond appropriately. How is it possible to monitor what bloggers are writing among the millions of Internet sites out there? Well, there are amazing devices called content-mining engines. Many of these are commercial services that few libraries can afford. However, there are some free ones that cover millions of blogs, social networking pages, and videos. These include

- Technorati Blog Search
- Nielson Blog Pulse
- Google Blog Search
- Ice Rocket, which searches not only blogs but also MySpace, YouTube, and Google Video Search, which make the content of their databases available

Content mining engines tell

- how many comments are made about a particular item
- how widely these comments are viewed by others
- the distribution between favorable and unfavorable comments
- how customers feel about an organization
- the extent of dispersion of the comment as it spreads
- the authors and where they are located

Consumer-generated media will grow in volume and importance. Libraries should take advantage of this valuable way to understand the needs of their customers.

WHAT IS QUALITY?

Chapter 1 presented quality in terms of service quality and satisfaction. A different view of quality includes five dimensions (conformance, expectations, market perception, strategic quality, and excellence), which are interrelated. Conformance quality focuses on reducing errors or mistakes, such as the number of incorrect referrals, and on service delivery time. In filling interlibrary loan requests, what is an acceptable delay or length of time in meeting the request? Furthermore, how can the library initiate practices to ensure that it meets the time limit? The temptation is to say that time boundaries are outside the control of the library initiating the request and, thus, to avoid any time commitment. Alternatively, there might be concern that, by meeting or exceeding expectations, the number of requests will dramatically increase, thereby placing additional pressures on the library to meet these expectations on a recurring basis, without any promise of increased resources to meet the demand. Managers, therefore, link conformance quality with budget priorities.

Quality, when defined in terms of expectations, evaluates performance in terms of customer expectations and serves as the foundation to this book. It is not sufficient merely to know expectations; that knowledge must be translated into improved service performance and delivery.

Market perceived quality compares performance between or among libraries: how well does one library rank in comparison to its competitors? Of course, there must be a meaningful basis on which to make valid comparisons.

Strategic quality focuses on an organization's strategic position, relative to competitors, expressed in terms of quality and price.

Excellence is an important but elusive dimension of quality. The temptation is to equate excellence with the amount of expenditure, the volume of business, or the meeting of state or national standards. Excellence is intertwined with local, regional, national, and international recognition, but requires new ways of examination and measurement. Nevertheless, a number of academic disciplines still reward the *production* of scholarship more than the *quality* of scholarship. In other words, they focus on the quantity of output, rather than on how the quality is assessed, by whom, and what this indicates.

It is important to validate that we are, indeed, focusing on excellence itself and not on the production of excellence. Toward this end, excellence might be defined in terms of the placement of graduating students in the workforce or graduate programs, student achievement, student retention, meeting enrollment quotas while admitting students with certain qualities (e.g., scores on achievement tests), and the extent of discounting (offering financial aid to attract more students). An important but poorly addressed question is: How can the library provide the institution or local government with performance indicators— meaningful ones—reflecting a contribution to these larger issues of quality? Thus, the intent is to show the library as an integral part of the community and not a support service or mere appendage.

GOING BEYOND "HOW MUCH?"

Libraries, when they report measures, most often list those relating to budget allocation (input measures), turnstile counts or volume of business (output measures). Although such countables are easily gathered (e.g., a hash mark for each reference question fielded or title processed), they fail to indicate more than "How much?" and to address the questions raised in chapter 4. The answers to these questions cannot be inferred from "How much?" in part because countables may not deal with what is important to customers or convey organizational effectiveness. Furthermore, they do not address academic success or reflect the outcome of a visit to the library.

Arnold Hirshon issues an important reminder:

Staff may claim that "we know what the customer wants." Staff also may overgeneralize customer behavior based on only those customers they serve. For example, all customers of reference services are customers of the library, but many library customers are not customers of reference services at all.[11]

Hirshon also remarks that "we project on the customer changes that we ourselves do not like"[12] and offers suggestions for change: "changing where we work" and "the way we work."[13] Clearly, the meeting or exceeding of customer expectations has a direct impact on organizational effectiveness, the creation and maintenance of customer loyalty, and customer satisfaction.

Pat L. Weaver-Meyers and Wilbur A. Stolt address a significant question: Why do academic (or public) libraries need loyalty when their services are free?

Such might be the first question posed by academic librarians, who usually run the only library on campus. However, it is an inadequate answer for university administrators looking at options to fund library collection development or purchase document delivery vendor contracts. Without customer loyalty, libraries may see customers defect when vendors become viable alternatives.[14]

Whatever measures libraries develop must reflect what is important to the institution, and there must be a cohesiveness among the measures adopted. One measure or customer-related indicator does not tell the complete story. How many are needed? Which ones? Libraries have choices about what they might assess and report; they should concentrate on those indicators most meaningful to the organization in order to ensure that it maintains and, it is hoped, enhances its strengths, overcomes its weaknesses, and meets the challenges of the future.

Libraries need indicators reflecting the management of the library and how the library serves the broader organization or institution. Those indicators reflecting management should, in part, be customer-focused and lead to improved service performance and delivery, including the promotion of customer self-sufficiency. (See figure 12.2 for examples.) Regarding the broader organization, a typical college would be interested in attracting students (preferably without discounting the cost of tuition); retaining them through graduation and, if appropriate, through graduate study; and assisting them in job placement. A typical university would share the same interest and concerns as a college, but it would also expect the faculty to be active in attracting grants—sizable ones— and sustaining research and scholarship. More than likely, the college and university would be interested in measuring learning, other than subjectively, and faculty productivity, however defined. A number of faculty members and others view good teaching, like good coffee, as subjective, and dismiss the validity of these assessments. Nonetheless, subjectivity may produce useful insights.

Higher education is, to some extent, also sensitive to the cost of education and the desire of those paying to receive value for their money. Thus, there is a need for indicators reflecting more than the quantity of teaching (e.g., number of students enrolled in a program or class) and the number of publications produced. Furthermore, the intensity of the competition for students has an impact on programs, departments, and schools. Which ones will be continued, consolidated, or discontinued? Thus, faculty members who ignore numbers and resist continuous improvement risk losing competitive advantage to other institutions (e.g., corporate universities) and corporate (and professional association) training programs. As well, university systems may be forced to eliminate some specialties, departmental programs, or entire departments to reduce duplication at each campus.

Figure 12.3 identifies typical areas that the academic institution undoubtedly would appreciate assistance from the library in addressing.

For public libraries, one of the principal factors in the well-being of any community is economic development. Attracting and retaining successful businesses ensure the continued well-being of the community, not only through the taxes paid by businesses, but also through the taxes paid by their workers and by the other local jobs generated by the workers' spending. Libraries have been cited as one factor in assessing community attractiveness for businesses contemplating relocation. More recently, the hottest issue between local government and its public library is the library's contribution to the economic life of the community. Research is currently under way seeking to establish how to calculate that contribution in terms of actual dollars spent on and recouped as a result of library service.

Another contribution that local government expects from its library is assistance in preparing an educated workforce. The enhancement of literacy, the improvement of children's reading ability, and help for adults who need to improve their reading or English-language skills are important contributions in achieving a well-educated workforce. The issue of equity deals with the combination of opportunities to improve reading and general access to information and educational materials, regardless of circumstance, race, income, and so forth. Local government, through the library, assumes responsibility for ensuring equal access, regardless of ability to pay.

Academic and public libraries should not limit the measures that they report to ones demonstrating their uniqueness within the broader organization (inputs and outputs). Rather, they should address their role, for instance, in attracting and retaining faculty, students, or businesses; advancing learning; educating a workforce to gain local jobs; providing an educational

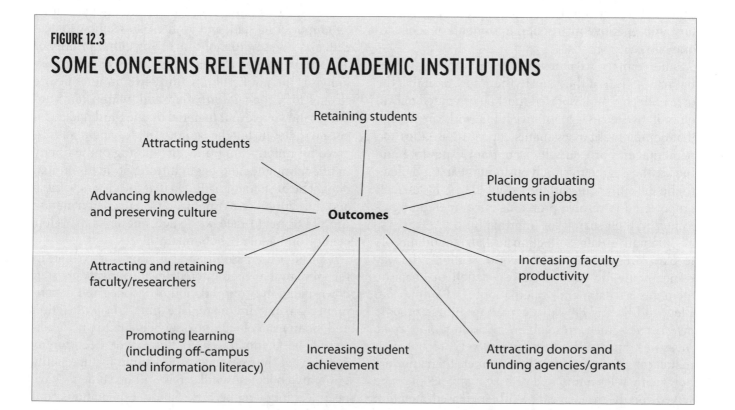

FIGURE 12.3

SOME CONCERNS RELEVANT TO ACADEMIC INSTITUTIONS

Retaining students

Attracting students

Placing graduating students in jobs

Advancing knowledge and preserving culture

Outcomes

Attracting and retaining faculty/researchers

Increasing faculty productivity

Promoting learning (including off-campus and information literacy)

Increasing student achievement

Attracting donors and funding agencies/grants

or a cultural facility; and assisting the job placement process. A library should be a partner with central administration, with the faculty, and with other community groups in providing services that customers need and expect.

For example, more academic institutions now expect incoming freshmen to have a certain level of computer literacy, and even to have their own computers. Together with the faculty, the library, before the start of the fall term (perhaps during orientation week), might offer a program to provide freshmen with a level of technological literacy (e.g., with a particular browser, search engine, or portal). That literacy might also expose students to evidence-based practice (skepticism concerning the quality of the information publicly available and, thus, a need to validate that information before relying on it) and critical thinking. Of course, meeting such broad goals would require a lot of contact hours with students. At any rate, whatever is done could be converted into such measures as

$$\frac{\text{Number of students who mastered specific competencies}}{\text{Number of students taking the technological literacy program}} \times 100 = \underline{\hspace{1cm}} \%$$

Such measures can provide useful information for the faculty while, it is hoped, lessening the amount of time that library staff has to spend providing elementary and repetitive instruction to students on a one-to-one basis.

The primary weakness of the examples given in figure 12.2 is that they create the impression that the data collected and reported must be presented only in quantitative terms. Qualitative frameworks are needed that complement assessments expressed as ratios and percentages. For example, important issues to examine are the degree to which customers can (and prefer to) be self-sufficient and the extent to which staff feels empowered to resolve problems encountered by customers in their search for information.

Qualitative data collection has an important role to play in representing "subjective reality," "the way things really are rather than . . . such mechanistic elements as data and calculations."[15] Connie Van Fleet and Danny P. Wallace, perhaps in jest, propose *defectiveness* measures, *offput* measures, *how come* measures, and *futility* measures;[16] yet, are not such matters of greater concern to customers than knowing how many titles circulated or how many people were served for the fiscal year? With increased attention

being given to assessment within government, business, and industry, "new generations of measurement philosophies and techniques" will emerge.[17] This is not bad; the key is to select those measures and assessment techniques that have real value to the library and to institutional planning and decision making, taking into account the expectations and satisfaction of library customers with the services provided or planned. After all, the demand for continuous improvement, and for evidence-based decision making and planning, will only increase.

STAFF DEVELOPMENT AND TRAINING

Staff training and development programs (STDPs) maximize the potential and effectiveness of employees to cope with the types of issues depicted in figure 12.1 and to become effective leaders, either at the team level or beyond. Improved service delivery and performance are key elements for STDPs. A library must decide which expectations it wants to and is able to meet, and it must learn to look at the organization from the perspective of the customers.

STDPs provide a means to assist staff members in coping with customers—not just so-called problem customers—and their expectations (i.e., with those expectations the library regards as its highest priority to meet). STDPs also afford an excellent opportunity for empowering staff, and for them to see how to deal with and defuse situations involving either priority or nonpriority service expectations. For instance, a person visits the public library thirty-five minutes before closing to request information and, within ten minutes, is shown relevant material on the third floor. The person settles in, but the janitorial staff—members of a powerful union—announce the closing of the library in fifteen minutes and begin turning off lights on that floor. The customer is irritated that the closing is early and she cannot see to photocopy the needed material. An STDP might deal with such questions as, "How would you handle the complaint?"

Consider the case of an academic library that, in recent years, has encountered drastic budget cuts, staff downsizing, the consolidation of services and departments, an inability to replace librarians who retire, and the transfer of technical service staff to public services. The faculty has, to a large extent, been forgiving of what they perceive as a decline in the quality of library collections and services. The students have been less forgiving because faculty expectations concerning course assignments have not declined—in some cases, they have noticeably increased. Thus, some customers might apologize for being critical of the library, whereas others would not. The faculty, especially in the humanities and social sciences, are also concerned about a perceived lack of balance in the collection. They believe that the library stresses access over ownership and favors use of databases over the availability of physical objects in the collection. As libraries such as this one persist in providing a full array of services, during times of hardship—including the assignment of more responsibilities to a diminishing number of staff—they can only provide a lesser quality of service. Faculty may complain about items not reshelved for a week or more, items misshelved, and students using the library as a study hall and not for research and other purposes. Students complain that they have to wait long periods of time for access to the Internet and that the library staff does not have a good command of new databases. Again, how are the complaints handled? Moreover, complaining customers are offering the library an opportunity to keep them as customers—ones delighted with the service provided. (See figure 12.4.)

Figure 12.5 offers other examples for exploration in focus group interviews, role-playing sessions, and so forth, which bring together staff from different units, along with members of the senior management team and the frontline staff.

SERVICE

Service *drives* the library, not vice versa. For this reason, it is important to develop a service vision that stakes out "an innovative competitive position"[18] that addresses future expectations related to customer service quality and satisfaction. Such a vision should be brief, clear, challenging, stable, abstract, future-oriented, and desirable or have the ability to inspire.[19]

James G. Neal argues that "a series of radical changes" in twelve areas shape "the organization and delivery of services" in academic libraries. The first area of change or revolution is service quality and accepting users as customers. The other areas include reengineering, or "rethinking of processes and structures in the face of economic trends and expanding, market competition"; demographics (dramatic shifts "in the diversity of the populations and sectors served"); personal computing or expanded "power to access, analyze, and control information individu-

ally"; electronics "producing vast amounts of digital information . . . and software . . . to enable effective search and retrieval"; networks; the multimedia presentation of information, fueled by the social interactive networks such as Facebook; values such as the "growing political schisms in society and the increasing threats to intellectual freedom, privacy, and the open flow of information"; accountability; higher education; partnerships; and the knowledge worker.[20] These revolutions often intertwine and introduce new problems and challenges.

More libraries and other organizations are being held accountable, and accountability may be rigorously defined. Accountability requires the adoption of a multiple-stakeholder framework and recognition that librarians are managers of complex service organizations.

Improving Service

From reading the professional literature and numerous reports available on library websites, it is often not possible to determine if libraries merely collect evidence or if they actually apply it to service improvement. Further, when they engage in benchmarking, do they try to improve on the data-gathering process? Such changes, however, complicate the extent to which comparisons across years are possible. Among the general targets of the University of Edinburgh Library for 2007–2008, we find, for instance: "The overall user satisfaction rating for the Library will be at least 85% (i.e. excellent/good ratings)." Among the accompanying comments, it is noted that

> an . . . online survey during the year asked staff and students "How satisfied were you with the Library service overall?" For staff the score was 77% (up from 73% in 2006/7) for "very satisfied" or "satisfied," while for students the score was 78% (as in 2006/7). The response rate was low.[21]

The library's annual report indicates that the staff is engaged in evidence gathering and seems to apply it to ensure that the library delivers "value for money"[22] (www.clc.hss.ed.ac.uk/docs/open/Paper_0919_Annex_B.pdf).

Exemplary Service

Attention should shift from the provision of service, or from continuing to be all things to all people, to what libraries can do well or outstandingly. An effort should be made to identify, recognize, encourage, and reward exemplary service. What library has recognized and rewarded (not necessarily financially) the staff member who just served her ten thousandth customer, and has maintained a steady commitment to the provision of outstanding service? Librarians should not assume that the service they provide is exemplary, or that they automatically answer more than 55 percent of the reference questions correctly.[23] They should also not assume that they automatically know or can anticipate the expectations of their customers. They should set priorities, goals, and objectives; benchmark performance over time; and commit the resources necessary to maintain levels of exemplary service—that is, service that customers regard as exemplary.

Collections and goals, such as educating students to be intelligent and evaluative consumers of information in libraries and available through the information superhighway, cannot exist outside a service environment and without meeting customer expectations. John M. Budd maintains that, "libraries have a history of concern regarding use and users and have tried to structure services, collections, and access to

meet user needs."[24] He perpetuates the myth that, because a library exists, customers (in large numbers) will come, be satisfied, be loyal, and be supportive—willing to vote in favor of local propositions providing financial support to the public library. What matters the most to customers, and how can the knowledge gained be applied to improve service delivery? These are the real challenges, and they present an excellent opportunity for libraries to serve their customers better. Service quality, satisfaction, and customer service are not the only issues, but they are fundamental to dealing with other issues and to improving the quality of library services.

Libraries should take the quality journey, meet changing expectations of customers, delight current customers, and seek out new customers. They should learn from their successes and mistakes and believe that everything can be improved. A belief that service is *good enough* does not inspire an organization to improve and to challenge itself. The mission and vision statements become hollow and staff is not empowered and challenged. Continuous improvement is a worthy goal and measures of *how many* or

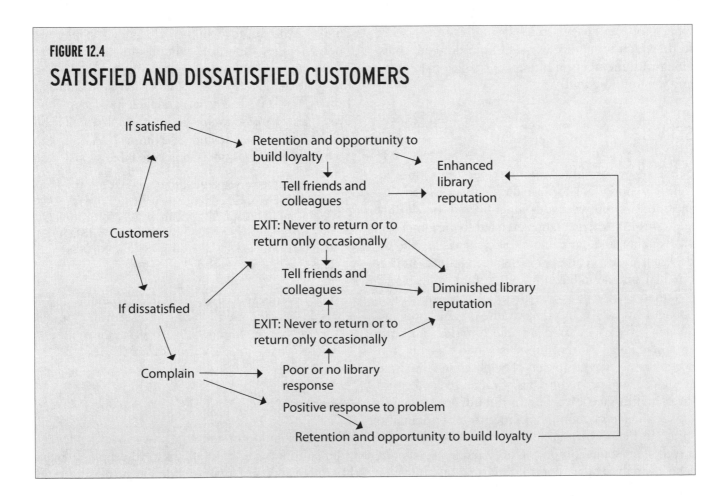

FIGURE 12.4
SATISFIED AND DISSATISFIED CUSTOMERS

FIGURE 12.5

EXAMPLES OF DISCUSSION TOPICS FOR AN STDP

1. A person visits the library late Friday afternoon. A stop has been placed on her borrowing because she owes a sizable amount of money in overdues. She offers to give you cash to cover the costs and clear her record. She desperately needs the materials for a paper due on Monday. You cannot accept the money; the cashier is closed. How do you handle the situation?*

2. A customer asks to check out reserve materials but forgot to bring any identification. He does not have time to walk or drive home and return before the library closes. How do you handle the situation?*

3. A community customer has a borrowing card for which she pays $50 per year and has done so for the past four years. While visiting the library, she discovers a policy change—the need to show photo identification to use a library service. She has, however, neglected to bring such identification and does not understand why she was not informed about the policy change (even through a form letter). The staff members that she first consults will not waive the policy. How would you handle the situation?

4. The library generates a recall notice before a holiday, but the staff neglects to mail the notice to the individual until after the holiday. The person is visiting the library and wants to borrow some books, but the computer says that the overdue material was not returned and the staff wants to assess a late fee and to have the item returned before lending new material. How would you handle the situation?

5. Toward the end of the workday, a customer informs the reference staff that the keyboard for the OPAC is very dirty and that there are fingerprints on the screen, making the image difficult to read. In fact, the same condition applies to each terminal and screen. The customer asks if someone can clean the screen and keyboard now. How do you handle the situation?

6. Toward the end of the semester, a faculty member complains that he cannot find the desired book on the shelf and notes that the OPAC lists it as available. Furthermore, he comments that, for days, a number of books have been on tables and carts waiting reshelving. How do you handle the situation? (Would your answer differ if that person were a dean? An undergraduate student? A graduate student?)

7. One library, every Sunday, employs only the security guard. The OPAC is turned off on the grounds that someone might need help in using it, thus shutting it off to those who already know how to use it. Even though the library acquired a self-issue machine, it allows no circulation on Sunday. The machine is turned off. What might the library do?

8. The façade of the new public library is very pleasing and matches other city buildings in the area. There is a main entrance to the ground floor and an alternate entrance, which leads to the mezzanine level. If someone enters on the mezzanine level, located between floors one and two, he or she must go downstairs before being able to go back up. Once inside the library, customers confront stairways leading in different directions, ramps running up and down, and lots of glass and metal decorative features. No shelves of books are in sight.

   The stairways, which have railings and glass siding, are clean and attractive. The marble surface is slippery. To prevent accidents, the marble has nonskid strips affixed to it. When looking out (from the stairway), there is an appearance of open space. Walking up and down the stairway poses an awkward sensation for those afraid of heights.

   A customer searching for large print books would find no mention of them on the library map. Now, let's say that an elderly customer could not find a staff member on the first floor who knew the location of these books. The staff on the other floors were unwilling to leave their desks to provide directions, and the customer became confused by their conflicting suggestions. Nevertheless, the person persists and wanders throughout the library. She finally finds the books located next to works for teenagers. Titles on the shelves are arranged alphabetically by author with fiction and nonfiction interfiled. This makes it difficult to locate a biography unless she knows the author's name.

   If she had known where the books were located, she would still have had to circumnavigate at least two stairways or use an elevator.

   Assuming the customer complains to you about receiving the "runaround," about the difficulty of finding the large print books, and about the layout of an "unfriendly environment," how would you handle the complaint?

*Taken from Association of Research Libraries, Office of Management Services, *Staff Training and Development,* compiled by Kosas Messas, SPEC Kit 224 (Washington, DC: ARL, 1997), 141. Additional incidents appear on pages 137, 141, 146–147.

how much do not deal with issues central to any service organization at a time of intense competition.

THE LIBRARY AS A LEARNING ENTERPRISE

Higher education theorist Peggy L. Maki, who specializes in the area of assessment, defines learning as encompassing "not only knowledge leading to understanding but also abilities, habits of mind, ways of knowing, attitudes, values, and other dispositions that an institution and its programs and services assert they develop."[25] Academic libraries contribute to student learning and the advancement of knowledge and scholarship. For this reason, they need to move from course assessment to program assessment and assist faculty in measuring student progress throughout a program of study. As public libraries adopt an assessment perspective they might measure the impact of their contribution to the service responses that they consider as highest priority.[26]

While Brian Quinn would probably agree with Maki's definition of learning, he decries what he views as the "McDonaldization" of society and academic libraries. He is concerned about measuring quality in terms of quantity and seems not to have a high regard for customer service and components such as self-sufficiency.[27] The purpose of customer service, Quinn argues, is to deter students from taking their business to a competing institution.[28] His views are evidently not shared by many of his colleagues in other ARL libraries. In a report published seven years after his 2000 article, the ARL Research Committee reviewed the literature and talked with many librarians about the future of academic libraries and developed a list of assumptions about the future. They assumed that higher education would increasingly model itself as a business and that students would increasingly view themselves as customers.[29] (See chapter 5 for a complete list and discussion of the assumptions.)

COMPETITIVE ENVIRONMENT

Contrary to the assumption of some librarians, libraries do face competition, and the number and diversity of those competitors will increase in an age of electronic information delivery. Depending on which question the customer asks, different competitors already exist. For instance, there are

- bookstores, including super-bookstores and secondhand bookstores (see, read, or own it)
- social networks (see, hear, understand, play with, adapt, and interact with it, as well as look it up)
- course packets (see, read, understand, and own it, as well as look it up)
- journal (service) vendors (see, read, and own it, as well as look it up)
- photocopy services (see, read, own, and interact with it, as well as look it up)
- term paper services (see, adapt, and own it)
- video stores and departments as well as Netflix (see, hear, understand, play with, and interact with it)
- virtual courses and universities (see, hear, interact with, and understand it)
- Internet (see, hear, understand, play with, adapt, and interact with it as well as look it up)
- other libraries (see, read, hear, and understand it)

In such a competitive environment, addressing the issues raised in figure 12.1 should encourage librarians to listen to the voice of customers, relating to them on a one-to-one basis, and answering such questions as

- Do you create a learning relationship with your customers?
- Do you keep your customers?
- Do you organize around customers?[30]
- Do you attract new customers and build loyalty among all (or at least a majority of) customers?

A FINAL WORD—TIME FOR ACTION, NOT EXCUSES

"A lack of resources" is the common response to suggestions that libraries offer new services, change some aspect of the organization, or adopt new indicators, such as those proposed in this book. A lack of resources is also the explanation that academic and government managers frequently give to requests for increased library funding. The actual reason is either an unwillingness to change or the library is not as high a priority as fire, public safety, and education.

In surveying the landscape of performance measurement over the past twenty-five years and looking at its actual adoption among libraries, Rowena Cullen concluded that, "as a profession, we have not embraced performance measurement in the decisive way that we have adopted technology."[31] She characterized the adoption of technology as reactive, originated by vendors, while the failure to adopt performance measures is due to lack of incentives and imprecise outcomes/impacts from the present measures. She also proposed a new and innovative model of organizational effectiveness whose dimensions are represented by three separate axes: focus/value/purpose.[32] (See figure 12.6.)

Focus is a continuum ranging from highly internal (emphasizing staff issues) to highly external (emphasizing customers). *Value* reflects the organization's emphasis on inputs (size, budget, and resources) as compared to its emphasis on outputs (the services provided). *Purpose* refers to "that aspect of organization culture which reflects organizational unity, a sense of common purpose and movement towards that purpose."[33]

Lack of incentives, no pressure to show profit, no shareholders to satisfy, and no need to prove value and worth combine to allow (indeed, to foster) an inward focus. By the same token, traditional measures of library performance—ARL rankings, most Public Library Data Service data categories, and those of the National Center for Education Statistics (NCES), based on state library agency reports—focus heavily on inputs and processes and minimally on outcomes. After all, it is traditional to do so! All these factors combine to lessen any resolve to adopt performance measurement. As a result, most libraries determining their standing on focus/value/purpose would find themselves in the upper left quadrant of figure 12.6.

The *lack of resources* explanation may be more accurate these days, as both government and education are more financially constrained. Opportunities for either to generate any significant increase in revenue appear limited. Libraries are making significant and continuing investments in information technology and digital resources, and are making cutbacks in other areas, such as print and microform collections.

FIGURE 12.6

CRITICAL FACTORS INFLUENCING THE POSITIVE OUTCOME OF PERFORMANCE MEASURES: FOCUS/VALUES/PURPOSE MATRIX

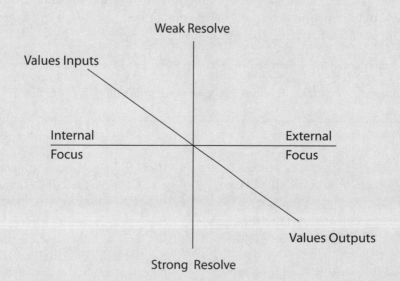

Source: Rowena J. Cullen, "Does Performance Measurement Improve Organisational Effectiveness? A Post-modern Analysis." In *Proceedings of the 2nd Northumbria International Conference on Performance Measurement in Libraries and Information Services,* 3–20. Newcastle upon Tyne, England: Department of Information and Library Management, University of Northumbria at Newcastle, 1998, 11. Reproduced with permission of the author.

The NCES reported that budgets for academic libraries had declined in the twenty-year period from the 1970s to the 1990s, from 4.065 to 3.082 percent and that expenditures for public libraries remained at less than one percent of all local government expenditures.[34] According to more recent data, the situation for public libraries in 2007 is relatively unchanged. They received 0.8 percent of government expenditures, whereas the budget decline has gotten worse for academic libraries. Their share of educational spending for higher education in 1990 was 3.082 percent; by 2006 it had fallen to 1.6 percent. In all the libraries spent $6,234,191,836, whereas their parent institutions spent $373 billion.[35]

Even though budgets are static or declining, library managers try to provide what most people want most of the time, and it is important for them to know

- the demographic characteristics of customers and the intensity of their relationship to the library
- customers' preferences for materials, based on their information-gathering behavior—what they actually use
- customers' views of library performance on such factors as timeliness, helpfulness, courtesy, reliability, and responsiveness

With information about customers—their characteristics and preferences—libraries can apply target marketing strategies to such constituencies as students, senior citizens, or parents. Knowing the types of materials actually borrowed allows for more precise selection of items of interest and the avoidance of likely shelf-sitters. The old explanation of "perhaps someday, someone might want . . ." is not acceptable when funds for materials are limited. Customers' evaluations help libraries respond so that they can cultivate loyal customers who will rally support for bond issues or actively oppose threatened budget cuts. For a library, the payoff of learning about its customers and their requirements is heavy use of materials and services and an enhancement of the library's service and resource reputation.

Cullen points out that where an organization sits on any of the axes depicted in figure 12.6 is "as much a matter of choice as a function of its history and organizational culture."[36] Each library must choose its position on an axis as it reviews the methods discussed in this book, learns about its customers, and translates that knowledge into an action plan. Sponsoring organizations also have choices about which units will be funded and to what extent.

Present and potential customers make choices. Ease of use and likelihood of obtaining what is desired, among other factors, drive these choices. The library's value, impact, and benefit can only be experienced and judged by customers. Is it worth the time, money, and staff to find out who they are, what they want in terms of materials and services, and how satisfied they are with those materials and services? We think it is. Now is the time for action: improved customer service linked to the type of framework discussed in this book.

Today . . . the library is relinquishing its place as the top source of inquiry.[37]

Notes

1. Jeffrey Gitomer, *Customer Satisfaction Is Worthless, Customer Loyalty Is Priceless* (Austin, TX: Bard Press, 1998), 54.

2. Thomas W. Shaughnessy, "Lessons from Restructuring the Library," *Journal of Academic Librarianship* 22, no. 4 (July 1996): 252.

3. Luis Herrera, "Public Library Issues," unpublished presentation for the public library cohort, Ph.D. Program in Managerial Leadership in the Information Professions (Boston: Simmons College, April 25, 2009).

4. Shaughnessy, "Lessons from Restructuring the Library," 252.

5. Virgil E. Varvel Jr. and Xinrong Lei, "Characteristics and Trends in the Public Library Data Service 2008 Report," *Public Libraries* 48, no. 2 (March/April 2009): 12.

6. Ibid.

7. See Robert E. Dugan, Peter Hernon, and Danuta A. Nitecki, *Viewing Library Metrics from Different Perspectives* (Westport, CT: Libraries Unlimited, 2009).

8. See San Francisco Public Library, *Providing for Knowledge, Growth, and Prosperity: A Benefit Study of the San Francisco Public Library*, http://sfpl.lib.ca.us/news/berkstudy.htm. The study shows that "for every

dollar spent supporting SFPL, the citizens of San Francisco see a return in the range of $1.40 to $3.34."

9. Pete Blackshaw, *Satisfied Customers Tell Three Friends, Angry Customers Tell 3,000* (New York: Doubleday, 2008), 9, 4.

10. Ibid, 10.

11. Arnold Hirshon, "Running with the Red Queen: Breaking New Habits to Survive in the Virtual World," in *Advances in Librarianship*, vol. 20, ed. Irene Godden (San Diego: Academic Press, 1996), 9.

12. Ibid.

13. Ibid., 10–13.

14. Pat L. Weaver-Meyers and Wilbur A. Stolt, "Delivery, Speed, Timeliness and Satisfaction: Patrons' Perceptions about ILL Service," *Journal of Library Administration* 23, no. 1–2 (1996): 39.

15. Connie Van Fleet and Danny P. Wallace, "Fourth-Generation Measures of Library Products and Services," *RQ* 36, no. 3 (Spring 1997): 377.

16. Ibid.

17. Ibid., 376.

18. Sooksan Kantabutra and Gayle C. Avery, "Visions Effects in Customer and Staff Satisfaction: An Empirical Investigation," *Leadership & Organization Development Journal* 28, no. 3 (2007): 211.

19. Ibid., 209.

20. James G. Neal, "Academic Libraries: 2000 and Beyond," *Library Journal* 121, no. 12 (July 1996): 76.

21. University of Edinburgh, University Library Committee, "Service Targets: Report on the 2007/2008 Session," www.lib.ed.ac.uk/about/policy/targets report2007-8.pdf.

22. University of Edinburgh, Academic Policy Committee, *Annual Report 2005–2006*. www.lib.ed.ac.uk/about/documents/annrep06.pdf.

23. See Peter Hernon and Charles R. McClure, "Unobtrusive Reference Testing: The 55 Percent Rule," *Library Journal* 111, no. 7 (April 15, 1986): 37–41.

24. John M. Budd, "A Critique of Customer and Commodity," *College & Research Libraries* 58, no. 4 (July 1997): 310–321.

25. Peggy L. Maki, *Assessing for Learning: Building a Sustainable Commitment across the Institution* (Sterling, VA: Stylus Publishing, 2004), 3.

26. Charles R. McClure and Paul T. Jaeger, *Public Libraries and Internet Service Roles: Measuring and Maximizing Internet Services* (Chicago: American Library Association, 2009).

27. Brian Quinn, "The McDonaldization of Academic Libraries?" *College & Research Libraries* 61, no. 3 (May 2000): 248–261.

28. Ibid., 259.

29. James L. Mullins, Frank R. Allen, and Jon R. Hufford, "Top Ten Assumptions for the Future of Academic Libraries and Librarians: A Report from the ACRL Research Committee," *College & Research Libraries News* 68, no. 4 (April 2007): 240–241, 246.

30. The first three questions come from "How You Can Help Them," *Fast Company* 11 (October–November 1997): 128.

31. Rowena J. Cullen, "Does Performance Measurement Improve Organisational Effectiveness? A Post-Modern Analysis," in *Proceedings of the 2nd Northumbria International Conference on Performance Measurement in Libraries and Information Services* (Newcastle on Tyne, England: Information North, 1998), 12. See also Rowena Cullen, "Operationalising the Focus/Values/Purpose Matrix: A Tool for Libraries to Measure Their Ability to Deliver Service Quality," *Performance Measurement and Metrics* 7, no. 2 (2006): 83–99.

32. Cullen, "Does Performance Measurement Improve Organisational Effectiveness?" 11.

33. Ibid., 14.

34. Department of Education, National Center for Education Statistics, *The Status of Academic Libraries in the United States: Results from the 1990 and 1992 Academic Library Surveys*, NCES 97-413 (Washington, DC: Government Printing Office, 1997), 17–22.

35. Department of Education, National Center for Education Statistics, *Academic Libraries: 2006, First Look*, http://nces.ed.gov/pubs2008/2008337.pdf.

36. Cullen, "Does Performance Measurement Improve Organisational Effectiveness?" 14.

37. Jerry D. Campbell, "Changing a Cultural Icon: The Academic Library as a Virtual Destination," *EDUCAUSE Review* 41, no. 1 (January/February 2006): 16.

Bibliography

ARTICLES

Allen, Maryellen. "A Case Study of the Usability Testing of the University of South Florida's Virtual Library Interface Design." *Online Information Review* 26, no. 1 (2002): 40–53.

"Alternative System Rates Public Libraries." *American Libraries* (April 2009): 21.

Applegate, Rachel. "Models of User Satisfaction: Understanding False Positives." *RQ* 32, no. 4 (Summer 1993): 525–539.

Atkins, Stephen. "Mining Automated Systems for Collection Management," *Library Administration & Management* 10, no. 1 (Winter 1996): 16–19.

Baruch, Yehuda. "Response Rate in Academic Studies: A Comparative Analysis." *Human Relations* 52, no. 4 (April 1999): 421–438.

Baruch, Yehuda, and Brooks C. Holtom. "Survey Response Rate Levels and Trends in Organizational Research." *Human Relations* 61, no. 8 (August 2008): 1139–1160.

Battleson, Brenda, Austin Booth, and Jane Weintrop. "Usability Testing of an Academic Library Web Site: A Case Study." *Journal of Academic Librarianship* 27, no. 3 (2001): 188–198.

Bishop, Bradley W. "Use of Geographic Information Systems in Marketing and Facility Site Location: A Case Study of Douglas County (Colo.)." *Public Libraries* 47, no. 5 (September/October 2008): 65–69.

Bitner, Mary Jo, Bernard H. Booms, and Mary Stanfield Tetreault. "The Service Encounter: Diagnosing Favorable and Unfavorable Incidents." *Journal of Marketing* 52, no. 1 (January 1990): 71–84.

Buczynski, James A. "Libraries Begin to Engage Their Menacing Mobile Phone Hordes without Shhhhh!" *Internet Reference Services Quarterly* 13, no. 2–3 (2008): 261–269.

Budd, John M. "A Critique of Customer and Commodity." *College & Research Libraries* 58, no. 4 (July 1997): 310–321.

Calvert, Philip, and Peter Hernon. "Surveying Service Quality within University Libraries." *Journal of Academic Librarianship* 23, no, 5 (1997): 408–415.

Campbell, Jerry D. "Changing a Cultural Icon: The Academic Library as a Virtual Destination." *EDUCAUSE Review* 41, no. 1 (January/February 2006): 16–30.

Chase, Lynne, and Jaquelina Alvarez. "Internet Research: The Role of the Focus Group." *Library & Information Science Research* 22, no. 4 (Winter 2000): 357–369.

Connell, Ruth S. "Academic Libraries, Facebook and MySpace, and Student Outreach: A Survey of Student Opinion." *portal: Libraries and the Academy* 9, no. 1 (January 2009): 25–36.

Converse, Patrick D., Edward W. Wolfe, Xiaoting Huang, and Frederick L. Oswald. "Response Rates for Mixed-Mode Surveys Using Mail and E-mail/Web." *American Journal of Evaluation* 29, no. 1 (March 2008): 99–107.

Cullen, Rowena. "Operationalising the Focus/Values/Purpose Matrix: A Tool for Libraries to Measure Their Ability to Deliver Service Quality." *Performance Measurement and Metrics* 7, no. 2 (2006): 83–99.

Curry, Ann. "Managing the Problem Patron." *Public Libraries* 35, no. 3 (May/June 1996): 181–188.

Denscombe, Martyn. "The Length of Responses to Open-Ended Questions: A Comparison of Online and Paper Questionnaires in Terms of a Mode Effect." *Social Science Computer Review* 26, no. 3 (Fall 2008): 359–368.

Dewdney, Patricia, and Catherine S. Ross. "Flying a Light Aircraft: Reference Service Evaluation from a User's Viewpoint." *RQ* 34, no. 2 (Winter 1994): 217–229.

Duffy, Jocelyn S., Damon E. Jaggars, and Shanna E. Smith. "Getting Our Priorities in Order: Are Our Service Values in Line with the Communities We Serve?" *Performance Measurement and Metrics* 9, no. 3 (2008): 171–191.

Dugan, Robert E., and Peter Hernon. "Outcomes Assessment: Not Synonymous with Inputs and Outputs." *Journal of Academic Librarianship* 28, no. 6 (November 2002): 376–380.

Flanagan, John C. "The Critical Incident Technique," *Psychological Bulletin* 51, no. 4 (July 1954): 327–358.

Galbi, Douglas A. "Book Circulation per U.S. Public Library User since 1856." *Public Library Quarterly* 27, no. 4 (2008): 351–371.

Given, Lisa M., and Gloria J. Leckie. "'Sweeping' the Library: Mapping the Social Activity Space of the Public Library." *Library & Information Science Research* 23, no. 4 (2003): 365–385.

Harwood, Nicola, and Jillene Bydder. "Student Expectations of, and Satisfaction with, the University Library." *Journal of Academic Librarianship* 24, no. 2 (March 1998): 161–171.

Healey, Benjamin. "Drop Downs and Scroll Mice: The Effect of Response Option Format and Input Mechanism Employed on Data Quality in Web Surveys." *Social Science Computer Review* 25, no. 1 (Spring 2007): 111–128.

Hébert, Françoise. "Service Quality: An Unobtrusive Investigation of Interlibrary Loan in Large Public Libraries in Canada." *Library & Information Science Research* 16, no. 1 (1994): 3–21.

Heerwegh, Dirk, and Geert Loosveldt. "Personalizing E-Mail Contacts: Its Influence on Web Survey Response Rate and Social Desirability Response Bias." *International Journal of Public Opinion Research* 19, no. 2 (Summer 2007): 258–268.

Hennen Jr., Thomas J. "HALPR vs. LJ Index." *Library Journal* (April 1, 2009): 10.

Hernon, Peter, and Philip Calvert. "E-service Quality in Libraries: Exploring Its Features and Dimensions." *Library & Information Science Research* 27, no. 3 (2005): 377–404.

———. "Methods for Measuring Service Quality in University Libraries in New Zealand." *Journal of Academic Librarianship* 22, no. 5 (1996): 387–391.

Hernon, Peter, and Robert E. Dugan. "Assessment and Evaluation: What Do the Terms Really Mean?" *College & Research Libraries News* 70, no. 3 (March 2009): 146–149.

Hernon, Peter, and Charles R. McClure. "Unobtrusive Reference Testing: The 55 Percent Rule." *Library Journal* 111, no. 7 (April 15, 1986): 37–41.

Holt, Glen E. "What Makes a Great Library?" *Public Library Quarterly* 24, no. 2 (2005): 83–89.

Horan, Mark. "What Students See: Sketch Maps as Tools for Assessing Knowledge of Libraries." *Journal of Academic Librarianship* 25, no. 3 (1999): 187–201.

Jiao, Qun G. "Library Anxiety: Characteristics of 'At-risk' College Students." *Library & Information Science Research* 18, no. 2 (1996): 151–163.

Jordan, Mary W. "What Is Your Library's Friendliness Factor?" *Public Library Quarterly* 24, no. 4 (2005): 81–99.

Kantabutra, Sooksan, and Gayle C. Avery. "Visions Effects in Customer and Staff Satisfaction: An Empirical Investigation." *Leadership & Organization Development Journal* 28, no. 3 (2007): 209–229.

Kaplan, Robert S., and David P. Norton. "The Balanced Scorecard—Measures That Drive Performance." *Harvard Business Review* 70, no. 1 (January/February 1992): 71–79.

Kettunen, Juha. "A Conceptual Framework to Help Evaluate the Quality of Institutional Performance." *Quality Assurance in Education* 16, no. 4 (2008): 322–332.

Kroon, George E. "Improving Quality in Service Marketing." *Journal of Customer Service in Marketing and Management* 1, no. 2 (1995): 13–28.

Kuchi, Triveni. "Communicating Mission: An Analysis of Academic Library Web Sites." *Journal of Academic Librarianship* 32, no. 2 (March 2006): 148–152.

Kuh, George D., and Robert M. Gonyea. "The Role of the Academic Library in Promoting Student Engagement in Learning." *College & Research Libraries* 64, no. 4 (July 2003): 256–282.

Larsen, Patricia M. "Mining Your Automated System for Better Management." *Library Administration & Management* 10, no. 1 (Winter 1996): 10.

Leckie, Gloria J., and Jeffrey Hopkins. "The Public Place of Central Libraries: Findings from Toronto and Vancouver." *Library Quarterly* 72, no. 3 (July 2002): 326–372.

Lenzer, Robert, and Stephen S. Johnson. "Seeing Things as They Really Are: An Interview with Peter Drucker," *Forbes* 159 (March 10, 1997): 122–128.

Letnikova, Galina. "Usability Testing of Academic Library Web Sites: A Selective Annotated Bibliography." *Internet Reference Services Quarterly* 8, no. 4 (2003): 53–68.

Line, Maurice B. "Line's Five Laws of Librarianship . . . and One All-Embracing Law." *Library Association Record* 98, no. 3 (March 1996): 144.

———. "Use of Library Materials" [book review], *College & Research Libraries* 40, no. 6 (November 1979): 557–558.

———. "What Do People Need of Libraries, and How Can We Find Out?" *Australian Academic & Research Libraries* 27, no. 2 (June 1996): 77–86.

Lloyd, Stratton. "Building Library Success Using the Balanced Scorecard." *Library Quarterly* 76, no. 3 (July 2006): 352–361.

Lynch, James, Robert Carver Jr., and John M. Virgo. "Quadrant Analysis as a Strategic Planning Technique in Curriculum Development and Program Marketing" *Journal of Marketing for Higher Education* 7, no. 2 (1996): 17–32.

"Making Them Work Like Roman Orchard Slaves: A Dilbert's-eye View of the Modern Office," *Newsweek* 129, no. 19 (May 6, 1996): 50.

Marco, Guy A. "The Terminology of Planning: Part 1." *Library Management* 17, no. 2 (1996): 17–23.

———. "The Terminology of Planning: Part 2," *Library Management* 17, no. 7 (1996): 17–24.

Martensen, Anne, and Lars Grønholdt. "Improving Library Users' Perceived Quality, Satisfaction and Loyalty: An Integrated Measurement and Management System." *Journal of Academic Librarianship* 29, no. 3 (2003): 140–147.

Matthews, Joseph R. "Customer Satisfaction: A New Perspective." *Public Libraries* 47, no. 6 (November/December 2008): 52–55.

Mullins, James L., Frank R. Allen, and Jon R. Hufford. "Top Ten Assumptions for the Future of Academic Libraries and Librarians: A Report from the ACRL Research Committee." *College & Research Libraries News* 68, no. 4 (April 2007): 240–241, 246.

Neal, James G. "Academic Libraries: 2000 and Beyond." *Library Journal* 121, no. 12 (July 1996): 74–76.

Nitecki, Danuta A., and Peter Hernon. "Measuring Service Quality at Yale University Libraries," *Journal of Academic Librarianship* 26, no. 4 (2000): 257–273.

Parasuraman, A., Leonard L. Berry, and Valarie A. Zeithaml. "Refinement and Reassessment of the SERVQUAL Scale." *Journal of Retailing* 67, no. 4 (1991): 201–230.

Poll, Roswitha. "Benchmarking with Quality Indicators: National Projects." *Performance Measurement and Metrics* 8, no. 1 (2007): 41–53.

———. "Performance, Processes, and Costs: Managing Service Quality with the Balanced Scorecard." *Library Trends* 49, no. 4 (Spring 2001): 709–717.

Quinn, Brian. "The McDonaldization of Academic Libraries?" *College & Research Libraries* 61, no. 3 (May 2000): 248–261.

Radford, Marie L., and Gary P. Radford. "Power, Knowledge, and Fear: Feminism, Foucault, and the Stereotype of the Female Librarian." *Library Quarterly* 67, no. 3 (July 1997): 250–266.

Ross, Catherine S., and Patricia Dewdney. "Best Practices: An Analysis of the Best (and Worst) in Fifty-Two Public Library Reference Transactions." *Public Libraries* 33, no. 5 (September/October 1994): 261–266.

Rubin, Howard A. "In Search of the Business Value of Information Technology," *Application Development Trends* 1, no. 12 (November 1994): 23–27.

Sampson, Scott E. "Ramifications of Monitoring Service Quality through Passively Solicited Customer Feedback." *Decision Sciences* 27, no. 4 (Fall 1996): 601–621.

Saracevic, Tefko, and Paul B. Kantor. "Studying the Value of Library and Information Services. Part II. Methodology and Taxonomy." *Journal of the American Society for Information Science* 48, no. 6 (1997): 543–563.

Saunders, E. Stewart. "Meeting Academic Needs for Information: A Customer Service Approach." *portal: Libraries and the Academy* 8, no. 4 (October 2008): 357–371.

Sennyey, Pongracz, Lyman Ross, and Caroline Mills. "Exploring the Future of Academic Libraries: A Definitional Approach." *Journal of Academic Librarianship* 35, no. 3 (May 2009): 252–259.

Shaughnessy, Thomas W. "Lessons from Restructuring the Library." *Journal of Academic Librarianship* 22, no. 4 (July 1996): 251–256.

Shih, Tse-Hua, and Xita Fan. "Comparing Response Rates from Web and Mail Surveys: A Meta-Analysis." *Field Methods* 20, no. 3 (August 2008): 249–271.

Stephen, Elizabeth, Daisy T. Cheng, and Lauren. M. Young. "A Usability Survey at the University of Mississippi Libraries for the Improvement of the Library Home Page." *Journal of Academic Librarianship* 32, no. 1 (2006): 35–51.

Stoffle, Carla J., Barbara Allen, David Morden, and Krisellen Maloney. "Continuing to Build the Future: Academic Libraries and Their Challenges," *portal: Libraries and the Academy* 3, no. 3 (July 2003): 363–380.

Thompson, Bruce, Martha Kyrillidou, and Colleen Cook. "Item Sampling in Service Quality Assessment Surveys to Improve Response Rates and Reduce Respondent Burden." *Performance Measurement and Metrics* 10, no. 1 (2009): 6–16.

Trueswell, Richard. "Some Behavioral Patterns of Library Users: The 80/20 Rule." *Wilson Library Bulletin* 43 (January 1969): 458–461.

Van Fleet, Connie, and Danny P. Wallace. "Fourth-Generation Measures of Library Products and Services." *RQ* 36, no. 3 (Spring 1997): 376–380.

Varvel Jr., Virgil E., and Xinrong Lei. "Characteristics and Trends in the Public Library Data Service 2008 Report." *Public Libraries* 48, no. 2 (March/April 2009): 6–12.

Weaver-Meyers, Pat L., and Wilbur A. Stolt. "Delivery, Speed, Timeliness and Satisfaction: Patrons' Perceptions about ILL Service." *Journal of Library Administration* 23, no. 1–2 (1996): 23–42.

Webber, Alan M., and Heath Row. "How You Can Help Them." *Fast Company* 11 (October–November 1997): 128–136.

"Website Usability: Research and Case Studies," *OCLC Systems & Services* 21, no. 3 (2005): 145–256.

Wehmeyer, Susan, Dorothy Auchter, and Arnold Hirshon. "Saying What We Will Do, and Doing What We Say: Implementing a Customer Service Plan." *Journal of Academic Librarianship* 22, no. 3 (May 1996): 173–180.

Weiler, Angela. "Information-seeking Behavior in Generation Y Students: Motivation, Critical Thinking, and Learning Theory." *Journal of Academic Librarianship* 31, no. 1 (January 2005): 46–53.

Weiner, Sharon. "The Contribution of the Library to the Reputation of a University." *Journal of Academic Librarianship* 35, no. 1 (2009): 3–13.

Weiner, Sharon A. "Library Quality and Impact: Is There a Relationship between New Measures and Traditional Measures?" *Journal of Academic Librarianship* 31, no. 5 (September 2005): 432–437.

Willis, Alfred. "Using the Balanced Scorecard at the University of Virginia Library: An Interview with Jim Self and Lynda White." *Library Administration & Management* 18, no. 2 (Spring 2004): 64–67.

Zammuto, Raymond F., Susan M. Keaveney, and Edward J. O'Connor. "Rethinking Student Services: Assessing and Improving Service Quality." *Journal of Marketing for Higher Education* 7, no. 1 (1996): 45–70.

BOOKS

Anthony, William P. *Practical Strategic Planning.* Westport, CT: Quorum Books, 1985.

Association of Research Libraries. *Measures for Electronic Resources (E-metrics),* 3 parts. Washington, DC: ARL, 2002.

Baltimore County Public Library's Blue Ribbon Committee. *Give 'Em What They Want! Managing the Public's Library.* Chicago: American Library Association, 1992.

Barlow, Janelle, and Claus Møller. *A Complaint Is a Gift: Recovering Customer Loyalty When Things Go Wrong.* San Francisco: Berrett-Koehler Publishers, 2008.

Bhote, Keki R. *Beyond Customer Satisfaction to Customer Loyalty.* New York: American Management Association, 1996.

Blackshaw, Pete. *Satisfied Customers Tell Three Friends, Angry Customers Tell 3,000.* New York: Doubleday, 2008.

Carr, Clay. *Front-Line Customer Service: 15 Keys to Customer Satisfaction.* New York: Wiley, 1990.

Childers, Thomas A., and Nancy Van House. *What's Good? Describing Your Public Library's Effectiveness.* Chicago: American Library Association, 1993.

Disend, Jeffrey E. *How to Provide Excellent Service in Any Organization: A Blueprint for Making All the Theories Work.* Radnor, PA: Chilton Book Company, 1991.

Drucker, Peter F. *The Essential Drucker: Selections from the Management Works of Peter F. Drucker.* New York: HarperCollins, 2001.

———. *Managing the Nonprofit Organization: Principles and Practices.* New York: HarperCollins, 1990.

Dugan, Robert E., Peter Hernon, and Danuta A. Nitecki. *Viewing Library Metrics from Different Perspectives.* Westport, CT: Libraries Unlimited, 2009.

Evans, G. Edward, and Sandra M. Heft. *Introduction to Technical Services,* 6th ed. Littleton, CO: Libraries Unlimited, 1995.

Foster, Nancy, and Susan Gibbons, eds. *Studying Students: The Undergraduate Research Project at the University of Rochester.* Chicago: Association of College and Research Libraries, 2008.

Fragasso, Phil. *Marketing for Rainmakers: 52 Rules of Engagement to Attract and Retain Customers for Life.* New York: Wiley and Sons, 2008.

Freed, Jann E., and Marie R. Klugman. *Quality Principles and Practices in Higher Education: Different Questions for Different Times.* Phoenix, AZ: Oryx Press, 1997.

Garcia, June, and Sandra Nelson. *2007 Public Library Service Responses.* Chicago: Public Library Association, 2007 (e-book).

Gitomer, Jeffrey. *Customer Satisfaction Is Worthless, Customer Loyalty Is Priceless.* Austin, TX: Bard Press, 1998.

Hawken, Paul. *Growing a Business.* New York: Simon and Schuster, 1987.

Hernon, Peter, and Philip Calvert, ed. *Improving the Quality of Library Services for Students with Disabilities.* Westport, CT: Libraries Unlimited, 2006.

Hernon, Peter, and Robert E. Dugan, ed. *Outcomes Assessment in Higher Education: Views and Perspectives.* Westport, CT: Libraries Unlimited, 2004.

Hernon, Peter, Robert E. Dugan, and Candy Schwartz, ed. *Revisiting Outcomes Assessment in Higher Education.* Westport, CT: Libraries Unlimited, 2006.

Hernon, Peter, and Charles R. McClure. *Evaluation and Library Decision Making.* Norwood, NJ: Ablex, 1990.

Hernon, Peter, and Ronald R. Powell, ed. *Convergence and Collaboration of Campus Information Services.* Westport, CT: Libraries Unlimited, 2008.

Hernon, Peter, and John R. Whitman. *Delivering Satisfaction and Service Quality: A Customer-Based Approach for Libraries.* Chicago: American Library Association, 2001.

Hope, Tony, and Jeremy Hope. *Transforming the Bottom Line: Managing Performance with the Real Numbers.* Boston: Harvard Business School Press, 1996.

Hughes, Arthur M. *The Customer Loyalty Solution: What Works (and What Doesn't) in Customer Loyalty Programs.* New York: McGraw-Hill, 2003.

Hyken, Shep. *The Cult of the Customer: Create an Amazing Customer Experience That Turns Satisfied Customers into Customer Evangelists.* New York: Wiley and Sons, 2009.

Jarvis, Jeff. *What Would Google Do?* New York: Collins Business, 2009.

Johnston, Catharine G. *Beyond Customer Satisfaction to Loyalty.* Ottawa: The Conference Board of Canada, 1996.

Kaplan, Robert S., and David P. Norton. *The Strategy-Focused Organization: How Balanced Scorecard Companies Thrive in the New Business Environment.* Boston: Harvard Business School Press, 2001.

Kazanjian, Kirk. *Exceeding Customer Expectations: What Enterprise, America's #1 Car Rental Company, Can Teach You about Creating Lifetime Customers.* New York: Doubleday, 2007.

Krames, Jeffrey A. *Inside Drucker's Brain.* New York: Portfolio, 2008.

Krueger, Richard A. *Focus Groups: A Practical Guide for Applied Research.* London: Sage, 1988.

Liswood, Laura A. *Serving Them Right: Innovation and Powerful Customer Retention Strategies.* New York: Harper Business, 1990.

Lynch, Richard L., and Kelvin F. Cross. *Measure Up! Yardsticks for Continuous Improvement.* Cambridge, MA: Blackwell, 1991.

Maki, Peggy L. *Assessing for Learning: Building a Sustainable Commitment across the Institution.* Sterling, VA: Stylus Publishing, 2004.

Malvasi, Martina, Catherine Rudowsky, and Jesus M. Valencia. *Library Rx: Measuring and Treating Library Anxiety.* Chicago: American Library Association, 2009.

Mathews, Brian. *Marketing Today's Academic Library: A Bold New Approach to Communicating with Students.* Chicago: American Library Association, 2009.

Matthews, Joseph R. *The Evaluation and Measurement of Library Services.* Westport, CT: Libraries Unlimited, 2007.

———. *Scorecards for Results: A Guide to Developing a Library Balanced Scorecard.* Westport, CT: Libraries Unlimited, 2008.

McClure, Charles R., and Paul T. Jaeger. *Public Libraries and Internet Service Roles: Measuring and Maximizing Internet Services.* Chicago: American Library Association, 2009.

McClure, Charles R., Amy Owen, Douglas L. Zweizig, Mary J. Lynch, and Nancy A. Van House. *Planning and Role Setting for Public Libraries: A Manual of Options and Procedures,* 2nd ed. Chicago: American Library Association, 1987.

Michelli, Joseph A. *The New Gold Standard: 5 Leadership Principles for Creating a Legendary Customer Experience Courtesy of The Ritz-Carlton Hotel Company.* New York: McGraw Hill, 2008.

Miller, Glenn. *Customer Service and Innovation in Libraries.* Fort Atkinson, WI: Highsmith Press, 1996.

Nelson, Sandra. *The New Planning for Results: A Streamlined Approach.* Chicago: American Library Association, 2001.

———. *Strategic Planning for Results.* Chicago: American Library Association, 2008.

Niven, Paul R. *Balanced Scorecard Step-by-Step for Government and Nonprofit Agencies,* 2nd ed. Hoboken, NJ: John Wiley and Sons, 2003.

Performance Research Associates. *Delivering Knock Your Socks Off Service,* 3rd ed. Revisions by Ron Zemke. New York: AMACOM, 2003.

Poll, Roswitha, and Peter te Boekhorst. *Measuring Quality: Performance Measurement in Libraries,* 2nd rev. ed. Munich, Germany: Saur, 2007.

Price, Bill, and David Jaffe. *The Best Service Is No Service: How to Liberate Your Customer from Customer Service, Keep Them Happy, and Control Costs.* San Francisco: Jossey Bass, 2008.

Rosenbaum, Ed. *A Taste of My Own Medicine.* New York: Ballantine Books, 1991.

Rossi, Peter H., and Howard E. Freeman. *Evaluation: A Systematic Approach,* 4th ed. Newbury Park, CA: Sage, 1989.

———. *Evaluation: A Systematic Approach,* 5th ed. Newbury Park, CA: Sage, 1993.

Rubin, Rhea Joyce. *Demonstrating Results: Using Outcome Measurement in Your Library.* Chicago: American Library Association, 2006.

Rust, Roland T., and Richard L. Oliver. *Service Quality: New Directions in Theory and Practice.* Thousand Oaks, CA: Sage, 1994.

Sanders, Betsy. *Fabled Service: Ordinary Acts, Extraordinary Outcomes.* San Diego, CA: Pfeiffer, 1995.

Schneider, Benjamin, and David E. Bowen. *Winning the Service Game.* Boston: Harvard Business School Press, 1995.

Solove, Daniel J. *The Future of Reputation: Gossip, Rumor, and Privacy on the Internet.* New Haven, CT: Yale University Press, 2007.

Spector, Robert. *The Nordstrom Way: The Inside Story of America's #1 Customer Service Company.* New York: Wiley, 1995.

Underhill, Paco. *Why We Buy: The Science of Shopping.* New York: Simon and Schuster, 2000.

Utts, Jessica M. *Seeing through Statistics,* 3rd ed. Belmont, CA: Thompson Brooks/Cole, 2005.

Van House, Nancy A., Beth T. Weil, and Charles R. McClure. *Measuring Academic Library Performance: A Practical Approach.* Chicago: American Library Association, 1990.

Vavra, Terry G. *Improving Your Measurement of Customer Satisfaction: A Guide to Creating, Conducting, Analyzing, and Reporting Customer Satisfaction Measurement Programs.* Milwaukee, WI: ASQ Quality Press, 1997.

Weingand, Darlene E. *Customer Service Excellence: A Guide for Librarians.* Chicago: American Library Association, 1997.

Weiss, Carol H. *Evaluation: Methods for Studying Programs and Policies.* Upper Saddle Road, NJ: Prentice Hall, 1998.

Wood, Elizabeth J., Rush Miller, and Amy Knapp. *Beyond Survival: Managing Academic Libraries in Transition.* Westport, CT: Libraries Unlimited, 2007.

Woodward, Jeannette. *Creating the Customer-Driven Academic Library.* Chicago: American Library Association, 2009.

Yellin, Emily. *Your Call Is (Not That) Important to Us: Customer Service and What It Reveals about Our World and Our Lives.* New York: Free Press, 2009.

Zeithaml, Valarie A., A. Parasuraman, and Leonard L. Berry. *Delivering Quality Service: Balancing Customer Perceptions and Expectations.* New York: The Free Press, 1990.

CHAPTERS (BOOKS)

Altman, Ellen. "Reflections on Performance Measures Fifteen Years Later." In *Library Performance, Accountability, and Responsiveness: Essays in Honor of Ernest R. DeProspo,* 9–16. Norwood, NJ: Ablex Press, 1990.

Collier, David A. "Measuring and Managing Service Quality." In *Service Management Effectiveness,* edited by David E. Bowen, Richard B. Chase, Thomas G. Cummings, and Associates, 234–265. San Francisco: Jossey-Bass, 1990.

Connaway, Lynn Silipigni, Marie L. Radford, and Jocelyn DeAngelis Williams. "Engaging Net Gen Students in Virtual Reference: Reinventing Services to Meet Their Information Behaviors and Communication Preferences." In *Pushing the Edge: Explore, Engage, Extend; Proceedings of the Fourteenth National Conference of the Association of College and Research Libraries,* edited by Dawn M. Mueller, 10–27. Chicago: Association of College and Research Libraries, 2009.

Cullen, Rowena J. "Does Performance Measurement Improve Organisational Effectiveness? A Post-Modern Analysis." In *Proceedings of the 2nd Northumbria International Conference on Performance Measurement in Libraries and Information Services,* 3–20. Newcastle on Tyne, UK: Information North, 1998.

Fornell, Claes. "A National Customer Satisfaction Barometer: The Swedish Experience." In *Performance Measurement and Evaluation,* edited by Jacky Holloway, Jenny Lewis, and Geoff Mallory, 95–123. London: Sage, 1995.

Hackman, J. Richard, and Richard E. Walton. "Leading Groups in Organizations." In *Developing Effective Work Groups,* edited by Paul S. Goodman and Associations, 72–119. San Francisco: Jossey-Bass, 1986.

Hernon, Peter. "Traces of Academic Library Leadership." In *Academic Librarians as Emotionally Intelligent Leaders,* edited by Peter Hernon, Joan Giesecke, and Camila A. Alire, 57–73. Westport, CT: Libraries Unlimited, 2008.

Hirshon, Arnold. "Running with the Red Queen: Breaking New Habits to Survive in the Virtual World." In *Advances in Librarianship,* vol. 20, edited by Irene Godden, 1–26. San Diego, CA: Academic Press, 1996.

Nitecki, Danuta A. "Assessment of Service Quality in Academic Libraries: Focus on the Applicability of the SERVQUAL." In *Proceedings of the 2nd Northumbria International Conference on Performance Measurement in Libraries and Information Services,* 193–196. Newcastle upon Tyne, UK: Department of Information and Library Management, University of Northumbria at Newcastle, 1998.

Norman, Ralph. "The Scholarly Journal and the Intellectual Sensorium." In *The Politics and Processes of Scholarship,* edited by Joseph M. Moxley and Lagretta T. Lenker, 77–87. Westport, CT: Greenwood Press, 1995.

Oliver, R. L. "A Conceptual Model of Service Quality and Service Satisfaction: Compatible Goals, Different Concepts." In *Advances in Services Marketing and Management: Research and Practice*, vol. 2, edited by T. A. Swartz, D. E. Bowen, and S. W. Brown, 65–85. Greenwich, CT: JAI Press, 1993.

Stein, Joan. "Feedback from a Captive Audience: Reflections on the Results of a SERVQUAL Survey of Interlibrary Loan Services at Carnegie Mellon University Libraries." In *Proceedings of the 2nd Northumbria International Conference on Performance Measurement in Libraries and Information Services*, 217–222. Newcastle upon Tyne, UK: Department of Information and Library Management, University of Northumbria at Newcastle, 1998.

Webster, Duane E. "Foreword." In *Beyond Survival: Managing Academic Libraries in Transition*, by Elizabeth J. Wood, Rush Miller, and Amy Knapp. Westport, CT: Libraries Unlimited, 2007.

DISSERTATIONS AND THESES

Griffin, Darryl A. "A Manual for Turning Customer Complaints into Opportunities to Improve Customer Service and Satisfaction in the Service Industry." Master's thesis, California State University, Dominquez Hills, 2009, AAT 1461578. Available from *Dissertations and Theses Full Text*.

Nitecki, Danuta A. "An Assessment of the Applicability of SERVQUAL Dimensions as Customer-based Criteria for Evaluating Quality of Services in an Academic Library," Ph.D. dissertation, University of Maryland, 1995.

GOVERNMENT PUBLICATIONS (PRINT)

Department of Commerce, Office of Consumer Affairs, *Managing Consumer Complaints: Responsive Business Approaches to Consumer Needs*. Washington, DC: Government Printing Office, 1992.

Department of Education, National Center for Education Statistics. *The Status of Academic Libraries in the United States: Results from the 1990 and 1992 Academic Library Surveys*, NCES 97-413. Washington, DC: Government Printing Office, 1997.

General Accounting Office. *The Government Performance and Results Act: 1997 Governmentwide Implementation Will Be Uneven*, GAO/GGD-97-109. Washington, DC: GAO, 1997.

General Accounting Office, Program Evaluation and Methodology Division. *Case Study Evaluations*, Transfer Paper 9. Washington, DC: GAO, 1990.

Minnesota Office of the Legislative Auditor. *State Agency Use of Customer Satisfaction Surveys: A Program Evaluation Report*. St. Paul, MN: The Office, 1995.

National Performance Review. *Serving the American Public: Best Practices in Customer-Driven Strategic Planning*. Washington, DC: Government Printing Office, 1997.

National Performance Review. *Serving the American Public: Best Practices in Resolving Customer Complaints*. Washington, DC: Government Printing Office, 1996.

GOVERNMENT PUBLICATIONS (WEB-BASED)

Department of Commerce, Bureau of the Census. www.census.gov; explanation of racial categories in 2010 census, https://ask.census.gov/cgi-bin/askcensus.cfg/php/enduser/std_adp.php?p_faqid=7375&p_created=1219235812&p_sid=IoTrCuvj&p_accessibility=&p_lva=&p_sp=cF9zcmNoPSZwX3NvcnRfYnk9JnBfZ3JpZHNvcnQ9JnBfcm93X2NudD0mcF9wcm9kcz0mcF9jYXRzPSZwX3B2PSZwX2N2PSZwX3BhZ2U9MQ**&p_li=&p_topview=1&p_search_text=race%20defined%202010%20census.

Department of Commerce, National Institute of Standards and Technology, The *2009–2010 Criteria for Performance Excellence* [Baldrige National Quality Program]. Gaithersburg, MD: NIST, 2009. www.quality.nist.gov/PDF_files/2009_2010_Business_Nonprofit_Criteria.pdf.

Department of Education, National Center for Education Statistics. *Academic Libraries: 2006, First Look*. Washington: DC: Government Printing Office, 2008. http://nces.ed.gov/pubs2008/2008337.pdf.

Department of Education, National Center for Education Statistics. The Integrated Postsecondary Education Data System. Washington, DC: NCES, 2009. http://nces.ed.gov/IPEDS/.

Department of Labor, Bureau of Labor Statistics. *Occupational Classification System Manual*. Washington, DC: Bureau of Labor Statistics, 2009. www.bls.gov/ncs/ocs/ocsm/commain.htm.

General Accounting Office. *Best Practices Methodology: A New Approach for Improving Government Operations*, GAO/NSIAD-95-154. Washington, DC: GAO, 1995. www.gao.gov/archive/1995/ns95154.pdf.

Institute of Museum and Library Services. "Grant Applications: Outcome Based Evaluation." www.imls.gov/applicants/faqs.shtm.

Institute of Museum and Library Services. "Library Statistics." http://harvester.census.gov/imls/pub_questdefs.asp.

Office of Management and Budget, Office of Information and Regulatory Affairs. *Revisions to the Standards for the Classification of Federal Data on Race and Ethnicity*. Washington, DC: OMB, 1997. www.whitehouse.gov/omb/fedreg/1997standards.html.

REPORTS

Association of Research Libraries, Office of Management Services. *Staff Training and Development*, SPEC Kit 224. Washington, DC: ARL, 1997.

Borrett, Rochelle M., and Danielle P. Milam. *Welcome Stranger: Public Libraries Build the Global Village* (Tool Kit), 2 vols., plus CD-ROM. Chicago: Urban Libraries Council, 2008.

Pew Internet in American Life Project, the University of Illinois, and Princeton Research Associates. *Information Searches That Solve Problems*. Champaign, IL: University of Illinois, 2007.

WEB RESOURCES

Abram, Stephen, *Stephen's Lighthouse*. http://scanblog.blogspot
.com/2009/02/library-roi-brief-webliography.html.

American Library Association. "Articles and Studies Related to
Library Value (Return on Investment)." www.ala.org/ala/
research/librarystats/roi/index.cfm.

American Library Association, Association of College and
Research Libraries. "Information Literacy Competency
Standards for Higher Education." www.acrl.org/ala/mgrps/
divs/acrl/standards/informationliteracycompetency.cfm.

American Library Association, Reference and User Services
Association. "Guidelines for Behavioral Performance of
Reference and Information Service Providers." Chicago:
American Library Association, 2004. www.ala.org/ala/
mgrps/divs/rusa/resources/guidelines/guidelinesbehavioral
.cfm.

Association of Research Libraries. "ARL Statistics." www.arl.org/
stats/annualsurveys/arlstats/.

Association of Research Libraries. "LibQUAL+." www.libqual
.org.

Association of Research Libraries. "Measures for Electronic
Resources (E-Metrics), 5 parts." www.arl.org/resources/
pubs/monographs/index.shtml.

Association of Research Libraries. "News: ARL to Pilot
LibQUAL Lite." www.arl.org/news/enews/enews-jan08
.shtml#16.

Association of Research Libraries. "StatsQUAL." www.digiqual
.org.

Association of Research Libraries, Office of Management Services. *Staff Training and Development*, compiled by Kosas
Messas, SPEC Kit 224. www.arl.org/bm~doc/spec-224-flyer
.pdf

Association of Research Libraries, Statistics and Measurement.
"ARL Index." www.arl.org/stats/index/index.shtml.

Association of Southeastern Research Libraries. "Shaping the
Future: ASERL's Competencies for Research Librarians."
www.aserl.org/statements/competencies/competencies.htm.

Council for the Aid to Education. "Voluntary Support of
Education Survey." www.cae.org/content/pro_data_trends
.htm.

COUNTER. "About Counter." www.projectcounter.org/about.
html.

COUNTER. COUNTER Codes of Practice, "The COUNTER
Code of Practice, Journals and Databases, Release 3."
www.projectcounter.org/r3/Release3D9.pdf.

Francoeur, Stephen. "Why Don't Our Students Ask for Help?"
Digital Reference (May 2, 2008). www.teachinglibrarian
.org/weblog/2008/05/why-dont-our-students-ask-for-help
.html.

George, Steve. "Baldrige.com." www.baldrige.com.

Hennen's American Public Library Ratings. "Rating Methods."
www.haplr-index.com/rating_methods.htm.

Indiana State University, Cunningham Memorial Library.
"Reference Live! Chat Online with Your Reference
Question." http://lib.indstate.edu/tools/reflive.html.

Indiana State University, Cunningham Memorial Library.
Report Card. http://panther.indstate.edu/cml/reportcard.asp.

Indiana University Bloomington. College Student Experiences
Questionnaire Assessment Program. http://cseq.iub.edu.

International Archive of Education Data. "Welcome." www
.icpsr.umich.edu/IAED/welcome.html.

Jacksonville Public Library. "Customer Satisfaction Survey."
http://jpl.countingopinions.com.

Klubeck, Martin, and Michael Langthorne. "Applying a Metrics
Report Card," *EDUCAUSE Quarterly* 31, no. 2 (April-
June 2008). www.educause.edu/EDUCAUSE+Quarterly/
EDUCAUSEQuarterlyMagazineVolum/
ApplyingaMetricsReportCard/162880.

Kupersmith, John. "Library Terms Evaluated in Usability Testing
and Other Studies." www.jkup.net/terms-studies.html.

"LibQUAL+ Services and Fees." www.libqual.org/About/
FeeSchedule/index.cfm.

"LibQUAL+ Survey 2007: Timeline and Action Plan."
http://library.queensu.ca/webir/libqual/timeline.htm.

"Library Success: A Best Practices Wiki," www.libsuccess.org.

"Library Use Value Calculator: Calculate the Value of YOUR
Library Use." www.chelmsfordlibrary.org/library_info/
calculator.html.

Lincoln Trail Libraries System. "Bibliography of Return on
Investment (ROI) Resources." www.ltls.org/features/2009
-10roibib.html.

New England Association of Schools and Colleges, Commission
on Institutions of Higher Education, "Standards for
Accreditation: Standard Seven: Libraries and Other
Information Resources." http://cihe.neasc.org/standards_
policies/standards/standard_seven/.

"New Signage Directs Hillman Library Patrons," *University
Times* [University of Pittsburgh] 41, no. 8 (December 4,
2008). http://mac10.umc.pitt.edu/u/FMPro?-db=ustory
&-lay=a&-format=d.html&storyid=8442&-Find.

Online Computer Library Center. "College Students'
Perceptions of Libraries and Information Resources."
www.oclc.org/reports/perceptionscollege.htm.

Orange County Library System. "Customer Satisfaction Survey."
http://ocls.countingopinions.com.

Orange County Library System. "Performance Scorecard
for Annual 2007/2008." www.ocls.info/about/
balancedscorecard/default.asp?bhcp=1.

Persch, Oliver. "Project COUNTER and SUSHI: An Overview."
Philadelphia, PA: NFAIS Forum: Online Usage Statistics:
Current Status and Future Directions, 2006. www.niso.org/
workrooms/sushi/info/NFAIS-COUNTER-SUSHI.ppt.

Public Library Association. "ALA/PLA Awards and Grants."
http://pla.org/ala/mgrps/divs/pla/plaawards/index.cfm.

Public Library Association. "Polaris Innovation in Technology
John Iliff Award." www.ala.org/ala//pla/plaawards/John_Iliff_
Award.cfm.

Rabiee, Fatemeh. "Focus-group Interview and Data Analysis,"
Proceedings of the Nutrition Society 63 (2004), 655.
http://journals.cambridge.org/action/displayFulltext?type=6
&fid=902304&jid=&volumeId=&issueId=&aid=902300.

San Francisco Public Library. *Providing for Knowledge, Growth,
and Prosperity: A Benefit Study of the San Francisco Public
Library*. http://sfpl.lib.ca.us/news/berkstudy.htm.

San Jose Public Library. "Message from the Dean."
www.sjlibrary.org/about/sjsu/.

San Jose Public Library. "Mission, Vision, Values."
www.sjlibrary.org/about/sjpl/vision.htm.

Seattle Public Library. "Mission." www.spl.org/default
.asp?pageID=about_mission.

SJLibrary.org. "Our Vision." www.sjlibrary.org/about/vision/
index.htm.

Suffolk University, Sawyer Library. *Long-Range Plan: Strategic Directions, July 1, 2005–June 30, 2010.* www.suffolk.edu/files/SawLib/2005-2010-strat-plan.pdf.

Suffolk University, Sawyer Library. "Suggestion Box." http://fs3.formsite.com/sawyerlibrary/form409839305/index.html.

SurveyMethods. "Is Your Business *Really* Customer-Focused?" www.surveymethods.com/glossary/article_business_seg_1.aspx.

Texas State Library. "Outcome Measures." www.tsl.state.tx.us/outcomes/.

Texas Tech University. "Welcome Texas Tech University Planning and Assessment Reports 2008–2009." http://techdata.irs.ttu.edu/stratreport/index.asp.

University of British Columbia. *Review of the University Library: Report of the Review Committee,* prepared by Karen Adams, Carole Moore, James Neal, and Lizabeth Wilson. www.library.ubc.ca/home/external_review_report_feb08.pdf.

University of Edinburgh, Academic Policy Committee. *Annual Report 2005–2006.* www.lib.ed.ac.uk/about/documents/annrep06.pdf.

University of Edinburgh, University Library Committee. *Service Targets: Report on the 2007/2008 Session.* www.lib.ed.ac.uk/about/policy/targetsreport2007-8.pdf.

University of Michigan, School of Business. The American Customer Satisfaction Index™: "ACSI Scores and Commentary." www.theacsi.org/index.php?option=com_content&task=view&id=12&Item id=26.

University of Nebraska-Lincoln. "UNL Research Libraries: Nebraska's Comprehensive Research Library." www.unl.edu/libr/libs/love/.

University of Pittsburgh, University Library System. "Ask-a-Librarian." www.library.pitt.edu/reference/.

University of Virginia Library. "Balanced Scorecard: 2007–08 Balanced Scorecard Metrics." www2.lib.virginia.edu/bsc/metrics/all0708.html.

Urban Libraries Council. *The Engaged Library: Chicago Stories of Community Building.* www.urbanlibraries.org/associations/9851/files/ULC_PFSC_Engaged_0206.pdf.

Washington State Library. "News Release" (February 4, 2009). www.secstate.wa.gov/office/osos_news.aspx?i=7mGFpzDxwXmjyN4wEGiiVw%3D%3D.

Wilson, Anne, and Leeanne Pitman. *Best Practice Handbook for Australian University Libraries.* Canberra Department of Education, Training and Youth Affairs, Evaluations and Investigations Programme, Higher Education Division, 2000. www.dest.gov.au/archive/highered/eippubs/eip00_10/00_10.pdf.

WilsonWeb. "Enhanced Usage Statistics." www.hwwilson.com/Documentation/WilsonWeb/usagestats.htm.

Yates, Kristina. "In Times of Recession, Libraries Flourish," *CNN Wire* (February 28, 2009). http://cnnwire.blogs.cnn.com/2009/02/28/in-times-of-recession-libraries-flourish.

UNPUBLISHED MATERIAL

Herrera, Luis. "Public Library Issues," unpublished presentation for the public library cohort, Ph.D. Program in Managerial Leadership in the Information Professions. Boston: Simmons College, April 25, 2009.

Index

Note: Page numbers followed by *f* indicate figures.